The Team Coaching Casebook

The Team Coaching Casebook

edited by

David Clutterbuck, Tammy Turner, and Colm Murphy

 Open University Press

Open University Press
McGraw Hill
8th Floor, 338 Euston Road
London
England
NW1 3BH

email: enquiries@openup.co.uk
world wide web: www.openup.co.uk

First edition published 2022

Copyright © Open International Publishing Limited, 2022

All rights reserved. Except for the quotation of short passages for the purposes of criticism and review, no part of this publication may be reproduced, stored in a retrieval system, or transmitted, in any form or by any means, electronic, mechanical, photocopying, recording or otherwise, without the prior written permission of the publisher or a licence from the Copyright Licensing Agency Limited. Details of such licences (for reprographic reproduction) may be obtained from the Copyright Licensing Agency Ltd of Saffron House, 6–10 Kirby Street, London EC1N 8TS.

A catalogue record of this book is available from the British Library

ISBN-13: 9780335249350
ISBN-10: 0335249353
eISBN: 9780335249367

Library of Congress Cataloging-in-Publication Data
CIP data applied for

Typeset by Transforma Pvt. Ltd., Chennai, India

Fictitious names of companies, products, people, characters and/or data that may be used herein (in case studies or in examples) are not intended to represent any real individual, company, product or event.

Praise page

"The Team Coaching Casebook is a brilliant asset in the field of team coaching. This compendium brings together a diverse array of team coaching techniques, theories, and inspiring case examples that will serve beginning and experienced practitioners alike. This book is like having 27 mentoring conversations and coaching explorations. Readers will take away a tangible sense of current team coaching practice and frameworks and feel more capable, knowledgeable, and confident working with teams."
  Dr. Catherine Carr, Team Coach, Supervisor and Systemic Team Coaching Instructor, Co-Author of High Performance Team Coaching

"The Team Coaching Casebook offers a nuanced and realistic portrayal of the journeys that teams and their coaches go through together. The case authors put their stories in context, but still offer general practical knowledge about the kinds of tripwires and triumphs we encounter in the complex work of developing teams. If you're just getting into the field of developing teams, or want to deepen your team coaching practice, this casebook offers inspiration and wisdom from an impressive array of experienced practitioners."
  Ruth Wageman, PhD., Author of Senior Leadership Teams: What it Takes to Make them Great, Founder of 6 Team Conditions

"An outstanding group of editors have drawn together an experienced set of contributors to offer an insightful input to the literature of team coaching. This new book provides a practice-focused contribution, helping connect the blue sky thinking of models and theories about team coaching with the brown earth practice of real team coaches, working with genuine clients on the challenges facing organisational team's today".
  Prof Jonathan Passmore, Director Henley Centre for Coaching & Senior VP CoachHub

"Anyone new to team coaching - and also anyone steeped in a single approach to team coaching - will find the 23 (!) different cases of team coaching in this casebook eye-opening and highly informative. An important characteristic of the book is the critical commentary offered by the introduction to each section. Team coaches will profit from reflecting on both the cases and the commentaries."
  William R. Torbert, Boston College Leadership Professor Emeritus, Co-Founder, Global Leadership Associates and Amara Collaboration, Author of Numbskull in the Theatre of Inquiry: Transforming Self, Friends, Organizations, and Social Science *(2021)*

This book presents action research at its best. With its diverse array of settings, the book conveys practical wisdom related to the challenges and opportunities of team coaching. Its many chapters, written by a set of thoughtful scholars and practitioners, share an emphasis on systems thinking as a way to approach coaching work in a changing and complex world.

> Amy C. Edmondson, Professor at Harvard Business School, Author of The Fearless Organization: Creating Psychological Safety in the Workplace for Learning, Innovation, and Growth

"This is a welcome addition to the rapidly growing lexicon on Team Coaching. The focus on case studies by practicing team coaches from a wide range of methodologies, models, industry sectors and countries, provides valuable insights into the complexities of actually delivering team coaching. There are lots of ideas, tools and approaches to learn from and all illustrated on how they have been implemented in practice."

> John Leary-Joyce, Chair of AoEC, Co-founder of Systemic Team Coaching programmes

Contents

List of contributors	x
Setting the stage	xv

CONTEXT   1

FOREWORD: CONTEXT REGARDING TEAM SITUATIONS   3
    Nick Smith

WHAT IF WE KNEW THEN WHAT WE KNOW NOW – A COACHING STORY   7
    Lucy Bleasdale, David Buggie, and Malcolm Tulloch

WHOSE BIAS IS IT? MOVING THE DIAL FROM 'ME' TO 'WE': A SYSTEMIC CHALLENGE FOR TEAM COACHING   15
    Elizabeth Hughes and Tammy Turner

FOUNDATIONS TO SUSTAINABILITY: A LEADERSHIP TEAM COACHING CASE STUDY   23
    Melissa J. Sayer and Colm Murphy

SYSTEMIC TEAM COACHING ESSENTIALS: GLOBAL LEADERSHIP COMMUNITY CASE STUDY   30
    Michael Shell

TEAM COACHING IN A PROFESSIONAL SERVICES FIRM: A CASE STUDY OF INTERNAL AND EXTERNAL TEAM COACHING IN A COMPLEX ADAPTIVE SYSTEM   37
    Angela Wright and Sarah Tennyson

UNFOLDING TEAM POWER AND INCREASING PSYCHOLOGICAL SAFETY BY EFFECTIVELY ADDRESSING A TABOO SUBJECT   45
    Robert Wegener

THE GOOD, THE BAD, AND THE UNEXPECTED IMPACT OF INTERNAL COACH ON A HIGH-PERFORMING TEAM DEVELOPMENT JOURNEY   53
    Helen Zink

MODELS & TOOLS   63

FOREWORD: MAPS, MODELS, AND MUDDLES!   65
    Peter Hawkins

NAVIGATING CRISIS WITH INTEGRATIVE SYSTEMIC TEAM COACHING (ISTC)   69
  Radvan Bahbouh and Pauline Willis

TEAM COACHING FOR COMMUNICATION CONTINUITY   79
  Michelle Chambers

TEAM INTELLIGENCE (TQ™) ASSESSMENT THAT INFORMED EFFECTIVE TEAM COACHING APPROACHES AND GENERATED IMPROVEMENTS IN FINANCIAL PERFORMANCE   87
  Solange Charas

INSPIRING COLLECTIVE LEADERSHIP AT AN AUSTRALIAN PUBLIC SECTOR ORGANISATION   97
  Pauline Lee and Sarah Cornally

THE HR PARTNER TEAM AT THE SWEDISH MIGRATION AGENCY   107
  Peter Englén and Anders Troedsson

A CASE STUDY ON TEAM COACHING USING AN APPRECIATIVE INQUIRY APPROACH IN AN EDUCATIONAL INSTITUTION   114
  Paul S.H. Lim

TEAM COACHING FOR CULTURE CHANGE   122
  Jacqueline Peters

INTO THE VOID: BUILDING LEADERSHIP THROUGH TEAM COACHING IN THE EXECUTIVE TEAM OF A GOVERNMENT AGENCY   131
  Declan Woods and Georgina Woudstra

PHILOSOPHIES   139

FOREWORD: PHILOSOPHIES SECTION   141
  Paul Lawrence

ETHICALCOACH ETHIOPIA PROJECT: A CASE STUDY OF PRO BONO TEAM COACHING THROUGH THE LENS OF TEAM COACHING COMPETENCIES   146
  Jane Cooke-Lauder and Sebastian Fox

WHAT COACHING IS APPROPRIATE FOR DEVELOPING LEADERSHIP WITHIN A TEAM CONTEXT?   154
  Sue Fontannaz

ON PAIRING FOR TEAM COACHING   163
  Lynn Keenaghan and Beatrice Sigrist

TEAM COACHING IN AGILE SOFTWARE DEVELOPMENT CASE STUDY   172
  Stanly Lau

A STRENGTH-BASED APPROACH TO DEVELOPING TEAM LEADERSHIP AND EFFECTIVENESS *Doug MacKie*	181
TOWARDS AN UBUNTU TEAM COACHING PERSPECTIVE *Dumisani Magadlela*	192
A DO OR DIE SITUATION *Michel Moral*	200
SHARING THE DRIVING SEAT: A TICKET FOR THE GAME *Asher Rickayzen*	210
SO, WHAT DID WE LEARN? FINAL REFLECTIONS BY THE EDITORS *David Clutterbuck, Tammy Turner, and Colm Murphy*	217
Index	220

List of contributors

Radvan Bahbouh is an Associate Professor and Head of the Department of Psychology at Charles University (Prague, Czech Republic) and Director of the QED Group. He developed sociomapping, a research-based method for monitoring team communication and cooperation, which is used as a team coaching tool in different companies and institutions.

Lucy Bleasdale works in an organisational development role within a large global engineering company. She works with teams and individuals by enabling more humanity, connected networks, and a learning mindset. She has a degree in Social Science, a diploma in Executive Coaching, and ultimately believes in bringing out the best in people.

David Buggie is an independent team coach following a management career in a large global engineering company. David holds a degree in Engineering and an MBA and diplomas in Executive and Team Coaching. He works with senior leaders to develop highly effective teams and is motivated by the potential for successful organisations to have a positive impact in the world.

Michelle Chambers is the Chief People, Culture & Strategy Officer of Teams Matter & Chambers & Associates, a small boutique OD consulting and team coaching services firm. She is a senior faculty member for Team Coaching International and lead faculty for the Masters Certificate in Organization Development at Schulich Executive Education Centre, York University.

Solange Charas, PhD is CEO and founder of HCMoneyball, Adjunct Professor (masters level) at Columbia, USC, and NYU, and Distinguished Principal Research Fellow at The Conference Board. She served as the CHRO for three large organisations, as a public-company board director, and held senior-level positions at E&Y and Arthur Andersen. She is a certified team coach.

David Clutterbuck is one of the earliest pioneers of coaching and mentoring. Co-founder of the European Mentoring and Coaching Council, he is visiting professor at Henley Business School and three other universities. David is author or co-author of more than 70 books, including Coaching the Team at Work. He is a distinguished fellow of The Conference Board, Practice Lead of Coaching & Mentoring International and Co-Dean of the Global Team Coaching institute.

Jane Cooke-Lauder was the Vice Chair of EthicalCoach from 2018 to 2020. She lives in Canada currently where she works with leaders across the healthcare system nationally and internationally to design, test, and scale innovation. Her areas of expertise include effective decision-making, inter-organisational and intersectoral collaboration, and women and physician leadership development.

Sarah Cornally is a systemic leadership advisor with deep experience in consulting to organisations focused on evolving their leaders and transforming their organisations to respond to dynamic and emerging conditions. She is a partner in Acumen Global Partners and Executive Associate with The Leadership Circle and Full Circle Group and faculty member of The Leadership Circle.

Peter Englén is a senior team and executive coach at BestTeam Sweden, Director of Coaching Research & Science, International Coaching Federation, Swedish Chapter, and Chairman of the Association of Swedish Team Coaches.

Sue Fontannaz is the founder of Oxford Team Leadership Coaching, which focuses on balancing team wellbeing, growth, and performance. She is also a researching professional, completing her doctorate in coaching at Oxford Brookes University and is currently a Transformational Leadership Fellow at Oxford University.

Sebastian Fox has been with EthicalCoach since 2017 and is the Team Lead for the implementation of the Ethiopia pilot project. He is a qualified team and executive coach, working with teams to help them achieve their full potential and performance through developing the relationships and connectedness within the team and with the wider organisation. He also coaches individuals, particularly in the area of business development.

Peter Hawkins, PhD is a global thought leader in systemic coaching, systemic team coaching, and coaching supervision. He is author of *Leadership Team Coaching in Practice* (Kogan Page, 2nd edition 2018) and *Leadership Team Coaching* (Kogan Page, 3rd edition 2017). He runs masters level training programmes and supervises systemic team coaches in over 50 countries through www.renewalassociates.co.uk and www.aoec.com. He is Professor of Leadership at Henley Business School and co-founder of the Global Team Coaching Institute.

Elizabeth Hughes is an entrepreneurial business leader, leadership consultant, and coach. She is dedicated to working alongside executives, managers, and their teams who want to deliver commercial performance through contributing positively to society and the environment. In 2015, Elizabeth founded The Mindful Executive and engages in all things mindful and learning voraciously about the rapidly changing world we live in.

Lynn Keenaghan brings 20 years of senior leadership experience across the NHS, public sector, and third sector, working with multidisciplinary and multiagency teams. As an executive and team coach she specialises in supporting leaders through transitions and developing their teams through pioneering systemic and relational team coaching. She is co-founder of Thriving-teams.

Stanly Lau is an experienced software development coach and trainer at Odd-e. He helps organisations become more agile by adopting better development and people practices through experiments and congruent actions. He is also one of the early leaders of the Agile Singapore community.

Paul Lawrence has a PhD in Psychology, conducts research on a regular basis, and has published more than a dozen academic articles, book chapters, and four books. Paul teaches coaching at the Sydney Business School, University of Wollongong, is an Honorary Research Associate at Oxford Brookes University, and represents the Association for Coaching and Association of Coaching Supervisors in Australia.

Pauline Lee is an Organisational Psychologist, certified Immunity to Change Coach, and a practising team coach. She has practised extensively in the Australian Federal Government sector over the past 15 years. She is a published author on teams, and a former lecturer at the University of Melbourne and University City Dublin, and a faculty member of The Leadership Circle.

Paul Lim is a leadership consultant, executive, and team coach based in Singapore. With a background in both private and public sectors, he operates mainly within Asia-Pacific.

Doug MacKie is a business psychologist, executive coach, and independent academic with over 30 years' experience in the assessment and development of executive, leadership, and team capability across organisations in the UK, Asia, and Australia. He is a recognised expert in positive leadership and strength-based approaches to capability development and has recently founded the Centre for Climate Change Leadership in Organisations. He can be contacted on doug@csaconsulting.biz.

Dumisani Magadlela is an international executive coach and coach trainer; a faculty member at The Integral Africa Coaching Centre and the Global Team Coaching Institute (GTCI); and part-time faculty at University of Stellenbosch Business School. Dumi is a trustee on the international board of the International Coaching Federation (ICF) Foundation. He works with Ubuntu coaching and Ubuntu intelligence.

Michel Moral spent most of his career in an international environment as a manager and executive in Europe, the Middle East, and Africa. In 2003, he created a coaching and supervision practice. He currently supervises coaches (EMCC ESIA) and coaches executives, executive teams, and organisations (teams of teams). He also trains supervisors (EMCC ESQA).

Colm Murphy is a team coach and Managing Director of Dynamic Leadership Development. He is also the head of Coaching Programmes for University College Dublin's Executive Development. Colm is completing his doctorate on 'How does team coaching contribute to team effectiveness?' at Portsmouth Business School. He lives in Dublin, Ireland.

Jacqueline Peters has supported clients to achieve better results through executive, team, and leadership coaching and development work for over 20 years. She has authored and/or co-authored three books and numerous articles, presentations, and webinars on high-performance teams and relationships, including an award-winning doctoral dissertation on team coaching.

Asher Rickayzen is an executive coach working with individuals and teams. He held executive positions for more than 20 years before establishing his own coaching business. He has a degree in Civil Engineering and a masters in Organisational Change. He is an EMCC Accredited Coach at Senior Practitioner level.

Melissa J. Sayer is a team coach and the Managing Partner of Performance HUB. She is Adjunct Assistant Professor in Leadership at Trinity Business School, Trinity College Dublin and a faculty member of 6 Team Conditions. Melissa is completing her doctorate on 'How does team coaching contribute to organisational learning?'

Michael Shell has been supporting leaders, teams, and organisations since 1999. As the founder of Global Leadership Partners Asia and the Global Leadership Community he successfully created a leadership coaching eco-system across Asia. He has over 2,000 hours of experience coaching teams and team leaders.

Beatrice Sigrist, PhD, PCC created a venture capital business in China, founded Sigrist Coaching in Zurich, and is co-founder of Thriving-teams. She is a former Big 4 consultant. Beatrice specialises in coaching executives and teams underpinned by somatic experiencing. She serves on the board of ICF Switzerland.

Nick Smith has been an organisational change consultant, executive coach, and supervisor for over 20 years. He works across global business organisations, the UK Civil Service, and the Third Sector, in the US, Europe, Middle East, and Asia. He is co-author (with Peter Hawkins) of *Coaching, Mentoring and Organizational Consultancy: Supervision and Development* (Open University Press, 2nd edition 2013) and (also with Peter Hawkins) of the chapter 'Transformational coaching', in *The Complete Handbook of Coaching* (Sage, 3rd edition 2018).

Sarah Tennyson is a partner in CEC Global, a team coach, an executive coach, and a coach supervisor who works with organisations worldwide on leadership development and team performance. Sarah has delivered coaching and development programmes to over 20,000 individuals in more than 20 countries.

Anders Troedsson is a senior team and executive coach at BestTeam AB, Sweden. Andy has, together with Peter Englén, written a book on team coaching, *Att leda TEAM* (Vulkan, 2018). He is also a co-founder and Director of the Association of Swedish Team Coaches.

Malcolm Tulloch has spent a large part of his career in the field of organisation change and learning, holding a number of senior roles in private and public sector organisations. He gravitates to the world of engineering and now works as an independent change practitioner, coach, and advisor. His practice is grounded in action research.

Tammy Turner, ICF MCC, EMCC, EISA Master EIA & ITCA is CEO of Turner International and Core Faculty and Head of Supervision, Global Coach Training Institute (GTCI). Since 2001 Tammy has coached teams and groups, chief executives and their decision-making teams, and individuals, enhancing their impact to the wider organisation. She has been a contributing author to numerous articles and textbooks.

Robert Wegener, PhD has many years of experience in coaching education. Furthermore, Robert is an experienced business coach and organiser of the International Conference 'Coaching Meets Research' at the University of Northwestern Switzerland. In his practical and academic work, Robert is fascinated by the co-creation of meaningful moments in coaching.

Pauline Willis is a director of Lauriate Ltd and practitioner of Integrative Systemic Team Coaching (ISTC) solutions for leaders and organisations across a range of industries and sectors internationally. She also supervises team coaches and is expert in embedding sociomapping and the Team Diagnostic Survey with a range of complementary psychodiagnostics in coaching programmes.

Declan Woods is a top team coach, boardroom psychologist and founder of teamGenie® – a specialist team coaching company. He created the teamSalient® diagnostic tool to measure team effectiveness (HYPERLINK "http://www.teamsalient.com" www.teamsalient.com). Declan is the Association for Coaching's Global Head of Team Coaching Standards and Accreditation, and co-programme director with Team Coaching Studio. HYPERLINK "http://www.teamgenie.com" www.teamgenie.com

Georgina Woudstra specialises in coaching CEOs and top teams. She is also the founder and principal of the Team Coaching Studio, an organisation founded to develop the practice of team coaching in order to foster greater collaboration in the world (www.teamcoachingstudio.com).

Angela Wright is a partner in CEC Global, a specialist coaching and leadership firm. She practises as coach, team coach, and coach supervisor globally. Her PhD is focused on coach education and how coaches remain relevant and fit for purpose. In 2018, she received the EMCC coaching supervision award.

Helen Zink is a leadership development coach, team development coach, and consultant, with significant hands on business and leadership experience at a senior level. Helen has a passion for growing leaders and teams to be the best they can be and is the Director of Grow to be Limited (HYPERLINK "http://www.growtobe.co.nz" www.growtobe.co.nz) specialising in this area. She also has a passion for growing herself and holds many qualifications and certifications, including: ACC (ICF), MSc (Coaching Psychology), MBA, BMS(hons), CA.

Setting the stage

As the dust begins to settle on identifying and defining what team coaching is, it has become clear that there are multiple perceptions about how to approach such a complex task. In this book and in our own work with teams, we've observed that just as teams are all different, there is no 'one-size-fits-all' form of team coaching methodology. We see this diversity not as a problem, but as a strength. Our objective in this book is to illustrate a range of approaches through the lens of case studies that bring these diverse approaches to life. As the demand and supply of team coaching increases, and the field begins to mature through standards and emergent research, we believe it is crucial that we step into the room with the team coach and the teams to highlight the practices and the learnings of a global cohort of practitioners.

Where is the team coaching industry currently?

Team coaching has grown in relevance and importance with the conjunction of several trends. One key trend is the recognition within organisations that the traditional focus on heroic leaders and on individual recognition and reward is hindering organisational agility. Instead, employers around the world are increasingly reliant on teams to respond to rapid change. In a survey conducted by the Global Team Coaching Institute (GTCI), corporate respondents overwhelmingly said that the shift of emphasis needed to move towards team recognition and development is towards distributed, collective leadership.

Another key trend is that coaches are finding that traditional one-to-one coaching is coming under threat, partly because so many organisations are creating internal coaching functions, but also because of a growing recognition that coaching an individual without addressing the systems around them is often ineffective. If a client is to achieve significant personal change, they typically need the support of the systems around them – and the two most important systems in this respect are those between the leader and their boss, and between the leader and their team.

At the same time, the literature on team coaching in the workplace has grown significantly in less than two decades. Team coaching is now a regular theme at coaching conferences and is an increasing area of focus for masters and doctoral research. The year 2020 also marks the point at which the major coaching professional bodies have turned their attention to setting standards and differentiating team coaching from other disciplines, such as team facilitation or team-building.

What do we mean by team coaching?

Because team coaching (outside of sport) is a relatively new kid on the block, it is subject to the same uncertainties of any new discipline – as indeed was the case in the first 20 years of individual coaching (where the dust has yet to settle, even now!). The development of theory and practice go hand in hand. Practitioners experiment based on the particular mix of previous practice from other contexts which have shaped their approach. Theorists search the existing literature for parallels and then look for evidence in the diversity of practice.

Our role as editors has been to help accelerate the evolution of practice and theory by bringing together as eclectic a mixture of case studies as possible, within a general consensus of what team coaching involves. From our dialogue with practitioners and academics across the world, we can assert, with a high degree of confidence, that it is now generally accepted that a team coach:

- works with an entire team, rather than its individual members (although the team coaching engagement may also include individual coaching);
- employs coaching principles of questioning, reflection, and honest conversation to raise the individual and collective levels of reflectivity and responsibility within the team so that it can make better collective decisions;
- aims to improve how the team works together, now and in the future, by improving its awareness of its internal and external worlds;
- challenges the team to develop its own sustainable solutions and practices;
- builds the relationships between the team members, their internal and external stakeholders, and across the organisation; and
- fosters continual learning.

Definitions of team coaching vary, and, in this book, we have attempted not to impose a partisan perspective. We can, however, point to an underpinning mechanism of all team coaching, which we believe is:

> *Team coaching helps a team become more aware of the systems that affect its function, relationships, and/or performance. These systems may be internal, external, and/or boundary-crossing; and are constantly evolving. With understanding comes the ability to make better decisions that sustain the team and make it future-fit.*

By its nature, therefore, team coaching is systemic. Each of our contributors describes an approach to team coaching in their own way and from their own perspective, but each addresses the team as a system or as a system of systems; and some as a complex, adaptive system nested within other complex, adaptive systems.

Setting the stage **xvii**

What do we mean by a systemic approach?

As the case contributors take a variety of approaches to work within systems, we thought it would be useful to provide a framework of potential approaches (the following descriptions are adapted from the blog *Beyond systems thinking in coaching and team coaching*, published by David Clutterbuck, 24 August 2020):

Linear approaches aim to solve a team issue in a narrow context without the benefit of engaging the entire system. Characteristics of linear thinking include:

- Fixing the problem, rather than understanding the context
- Maintaining control, rather than enabling and empowering
- Finding discrete solutions, rather than interconnected solutions
- Predicted or predictable outcomes, rather than emergent and evolving outcomes
- Static processes and procedures, rather than an evolving process
- Hierarchical communication, rather than unbounded communication
- Seeking certainty, rather than living with uncertainty.

Simple (closed) systems work with a small number of feedback loops. They map the relationship between key components in a bounded system and seek to modify these to create optimum outcomes.

Systemic approaches work with the client's or team's connections with different stakeholders. In particular, they address the question: 'What do our stakeholders require of us?' In theory, they should also address 'What do we expect of our stakeholders?', but this reciprocity is not always present. When we look at what many coaches and team coaches, who describe themselves as working systemically, actually do, they primarily address a series of simple systems perspectives with multiple stakeholders. A great value of systemic team coaching is that it brings into the picture a much wider range of stakeholders than a team would normally consider. Indeed, identifying the hitherto ignored stakeholder is a key contribution of systemic team coaching. The best-known systemic model of team coaching is Hawkins' 5Cs (2017), which features on pages 17–18.

Complex, adaptive systems work with the interconnectedness *between* systems and between elements of systems. Among the key principles here are that:

- The team is a complex, adaptive system connected to multiple other complex, adaptive systems.

- No problem can be satisfactorily resolved (beyond short-term fixes) without understanding the complexity of factors influencing it; nor can it be fully solved by addressing the needs of stakeholder (groups) in isolation. Indeed, seeking a *solution* may be a mirage, when what is needed is a percipient *process* for continuous adaptation.
- Understanding how the team is influenced by its own and other systems creates more effective responses to challenges, by engaging the *system of systems* in supporting desirable change.

The PERILL model (Clutterbuck, 2019, described on pages 97–99) can be used in a complex adaptive systems approach to enhance or undermine performance.

These four systems thinking approaches are illustrated by the cases in this book. By purposely including the perspectives of relevant stakeholders, influencers, team members, and leaders, as well as the team coaches, we have insight into the interdependencies of the relevant systems so that we can learn how they experienced team coaching.

Why a casebook?

In our role as team coaching educators, we've been increasingly asked to illustrate what team coaching is, how it works in the room, and what impact it might have. The reason we haven't written another 'how to' book is to showcase the complexity and messy nature of the work. Team coaching cannot be done using formulaic approaches.

Instead, we wanted a casebook that represented a great variety of approaches, methodologies, industries, and types of teams to show the breadth and depth of team coaching as a specific intervention. Going 'off script' for the team to make sense of its particular circumstances and to find new insights and directions is the essence of effective team coaching.

What's distinctive about this book?

We had four key objectives for this case book since its inception:

1 Ensure the cases and contributors represent the global nature of our world and of our clients systems
2 Seek contributors both new and experienced in being published
3 Each case to clearly set out the learning for other team coaches
4 Each case to include the voice of the wider system through stakeholders such as team leaders, team members, team stakeholders, etc.

How is the book structured?

Categorising the case studies has been one of the most difficult tasks for us as editors. The three categories we have chosen (*Context, Models & Tools,* and *Philosophies*) are not exclusive – many of the cases illustrate two or more perspectives. We find ourselves in a similar situation to the team coach, trying to understand the complex dynamics of a team in its environment. Everything is messy and volatile. The patterns that we have chosen to attend to are a select few of many. We encourage you to look for other patterns as you compare and contrast cases.

We have invited three luminaries within the world of team coaching to address the themes of the three sections – Peter Hawkins, Paul Lawrence, and Nick Smith – in line with our desire to present diverse perspectives. In each foreword they challenge us to think about our ongoing team coaching practice and extending what we're doing in the room for wider societal impact.

And finally …

There is no such thing as best practice – only evolving good practice. When we come to revise this book in a few years' time, we expect to see even greater diversity of approach, much stronger theoretical underpinning to practice, and more substantial evidence of how team coaching works.

References

Clutterbuck, D. (2019) Towards a pragmatic model of team function and dysfunction, in D. Clutterbuck, J. Gannon, S. Hayes, I. Iordanou, K. Lowe, and D. MacKie (eds.) *The Practitioner's Handbook of Team Coaching* (pp. 150–160). London: Routledge.

Hawkins, P. (2017) *Leadership Team Coaching: Developing Collective Transformational Leadership*, 3rd edition. London: Kogan Page.

Context

Foreword: Context regarding team situations

Nick Smith

This book is a testament to the fast-evolving nature of team coaching. In the last 10 years it has developed stronger methodologies for working with complex teams and has responded to the increasing complexity of the sectors in which team coaching takes place. It has made its practitioners more aware of the systemic nature of team and organisational life. But, more recently, it has also alerted us to the fact that, as practitioners, there are still bigger challenges that we need to grapple with. I have been working from a systemic perspective for over 40 years, as social worker, family therapist, organisational consultant, and executive coach. In all that time, I have been constantly surprised by the wisdom systems bring to our activity if we listen to their messages.

In writing this foreword, I am reminded not only of the great strides team coaching is making but also the gaps in our awareness and practice that need to be addressed as we go forward. One of the changes we are noticing, among businesses and social organisations, is that they are starting to become aware that they not only need to deliver the goals for which they were set up, but also to actively participate in addressing the systemic imbalances currently causing so much disruption in our world (such as extreme weather events, failures of food security, mass migration, and regional political and social instability, to name a few).

Where team coaching is strong is in exploring ways of getting clarity of purpose and practice for its teams, so that they clearly fit in to their immediate environment and its needs. The following seven case studies show the richness of this practice. We can see the use of single or multiple coaches for the team; the different dynamics that internal and/or external team coaches bring; working with nested teams;[1] the varied use of structured (model driven) and emergent responses; the balance between intra-team, inter-team, and systemic purpose; the varied use of supervision; and the varying focus between operational, cultural, and strategic change. But what the cases also highlight is the development work that still needs to be done. What is not talked about points to potential blind spots in our current practice.

In reading these cases, I'm aware of the important role coaches can play and I believe one of the core issues for us as team coaches is that we must play our part in widening society's awareness of how things are connected to each other.

This requires us to understand our current dualistic mindset and why this mindset is making it hard for humanity at present to make the changes it will need to make if we are to progress. Humanity has over-relied on it, since it has been responsible for many great advancements in the way we live our lives. As Gregory Bateson (1972: 279 ff.) and others have pointed out though, our reflective learning is currently based upon intellect, rather than direct experience. When we reflect on, say, what our customers want next season, we are constructing a mental process in which the relevant data and our thinking about it become independent of each other. Dualistic thinking creates a perceptual distance that separates someone from their direct experience, because it constantly sets up two contrary points of reference rather than the one point of direct experience.

Such dualistic thinking is the hallmark of what Bateson called Level Two learning, the mindset responsible both for great technical or medical advances, as well as creating the detached mindset that has seriously compromised the more-than-human world in which we live. We cannot allow ourselves to fall into the belief that dualistic language is 'wrong', it is just not the answer to every situation. As we know from many systemic thinkers, it is impossible to fundamentally shift a situation caused by dualistic thinking, by using the same method. Bateson said that the way one can shift Level Two thinking (which causes the disassociation between us and the world we live in) is through Level Three learning. Level Three learning is predicated on direct experience, not rational thinking about things. It is the disassociation, which accompanies Level Two thinking, that is costing us so dearly at the moment.

Up to now team coaches have worked within the nested systems of the individual, the team, the organisation, and its immediate environment and, in so doing, have contributed positively to their clients' business activity. What we are noticing now is that working within this group of systems, without holding awareness of the broader systems (like global business dynamics or global environmental patterns), has meant that business has not positively impacted on the global issues that are challenging our health, whether physical, psychological, or economic. If we do not embrace the wider systemic challenges when coaching teams, we are in danger of metaphorically rearranging the deckchairs on the *Titanic*, as it heads for that huge iceberg. Although we still need to attend to how things are working inside and outside the organisation, we now also need to mirror what the more-than-human world is needing from us, in order to create the safer ecological niche that we all need for ourselves and our grandchildren's grandchildren!

In these professionally challenging times, we may find some of the teams and organisations we work with are already grappling with the twin tensions of creating a strong business, while making an equally strong contribution to tackling major environmental issues. But we may find other teams responding to uncertainty by becoming more focused on their own internal processes and behaviours, and not believing it is their responsibility to engage in these wider discussions. When exploring with the client team, as a practitioner I may find that they are ahead of me in their thinking or that they are finding it hard to embrace new challenges, but, either way, I need to hold an ability to deeply listen to what they and the wider system are saying.

What is clear from each of the following case studies is that it is hard to bring all the possible aspects of a team coaching approach to bear on a problem. It may not even be helpful. But it highlights an existential issue coaches are now facing more sharply than ever before. When we are dealing with challenges within the realms of the known, our methodologies are strong, and we know how to move forward. But when we are supporting teams around what they should do to help with the global, intractable problems, it is safe to say, we do not know what to do with any certainty. Perhaps all we can say is that to work in this area will require very different working practices. Competition, for example, has been the backbone of business up to now. To address these global problems may require, instead, a change to a practice of deep collaboration with 'competitors' in some areas, while competing with them in others. Coaches will need to bring compassionate inquiry to the fore, rather than using problem-solving skills, in order not to let assumptions and biases distort the need being expressed.

When the team or organisation is focused on their immediate needs, how does the coach stay aware of the broader needs at play and bring them into awareness in the room, without minimising or disregarding the client's expressed need? I have frequently heard the criticism that coaches should not drag these concerns into the coaching room if it is our agenda rather than theirs. When issues are not in our awareness though, it doesn't mean that they do not exist in that context or are not relevant. All the global issues humanity faces are with us the whole time. It is not about dragging them in from 'outside', it is about giving a voice to what is being ignored that is already in the room. We are holding up a mirror. A mirror does not have an agenda. It can, however, make us challenge our assumptions, some deeply held, about who we are and what is happening to us that we are not addressing if we stop our chatter and listen.

This major shift in consciousness has been described as 'listening to the future', a little-used art in Western business thinking currently. I want to point to examples of this new way of approaching our current challenges. They discuss how we work with the known, while responding creatively and skilfully together to the unknown. For example, Otto Scharmer's Theory U (Scharmer, 2009) proposes a radical new way of creating change and responding to the complexity of need out there in the environment. It calls for a shift in consciousness. Scharmer's challenge to us is: 'we need to go beyond the concept of leadership. We must discover a more profound and practical integration of the head, heart and hand – the intelligences of the open mind, open heart, and open will – at both an individual and a collective level' (2009: 20). This seems to me to capture the biggest shift in the coaching mindset that we are faced with at the present moment. It is a question of how we deeply listen, not just to our clients and their immediate ecological niche, but also listen without judgement to the future of our planet and what it needs.

When we don't know the answers, then we must use approaches that take account of that. As we said earlier, we need to move from tell to listen. As we read the following seven case studies, it may be useful for the reader to practise seeing each case in a wider systemic context. After you have read each one, you could ask yourself a series of systemic questions to start exercising these systemic muscles and thereby develop this very necessary capability.

- What are the wider systemic issues here, and how could I raise them in this context?
- How would I encourage this team not to rush into solution, but rather stay with listening and not knowing for a while?
- How could I become more comfortable standing out for doing things differently?
- How can I coach this team, when no one, including me, has the answers?

We do not have to make a decision here between two ways of approaching a problem. This is not an either/or choice. We are being asked to hold different consciousness at the same time. To stand any chance of making changes that will bring forth new opportunities and new resolutions to our current challenges, the teams we work with will have to be prepared not only to sharpen their delivery skills, but more importantly to be able to set aside current assumptions and deeply listen without bias. To do this they will need the support of team coaches who are also prepared to go along with this process and play their part in co-creating a necessary new reality. To do this we need to support ourselves and our clients in stepping beyond what is currently known. Such spaces can generate a deep fear of the unknown, and therefore we need to give ourselves the capacity to approach them with an open heart.

Note

1 This term is used to describe the systemic phenomenon illustrated by the concept of Russian dolls, with a small doll inside increasingly larger dolls. An example would be a team within a function, within a division, within an organisation. These would be 'nested teams'.

References

Bateson, G. (1972) *Steps to an Ecology of Mind*. New York: Ballantine Books.
Scharmer, O. (2009) *Theory U: Leading from the Future as it Emerges*. San Francisco, CA: Berrett-Koehler.

What if we knew then what we know now – a coaching story

Lucy Bleasdale, David Buggie, and Malcolm Tulloch

Introduction

Why is it that some teams respond so positively to team coaching and others – to be kind to them and us – are less enthusiastic?

Our intention here is to illustrate our experience, as a team of three coaches – one external and two internal coaches – using team coaching to bring about organisational, systemic change.

The journey was complex, often frustrating, but also a lot of fun. In recalling and reflecting, we have experienced different perspectives and insights – well, what's new? With this in mind, we decided to write as a triad as well as giving individual accounts, believing that this gives a truer sense of how our story unfolded.

The writing is illustrative rather than comprehensive. We have focused on our experience of getting teams together, willingness to engage, reflect and learn, and readiness to commit to action.

There are a number of characters who appear: the MD, the members of the leadership team, an operations director, and a site manager and his team. Throughout the text, we use 'we' to mean the three of us.

The timeline below gives a sense of our engagement:

Getting started

We began our work with Harry, the MD, who wanted to engage his senior leadership team (SLT) to develop a more cohesive strategy and to enable change across different business units. Markets were changing rapidly and the future was uncertain, and it was clear the SLT and wider division needed to respond and cooperate in different ways.

8 The Team Coaching Casebook

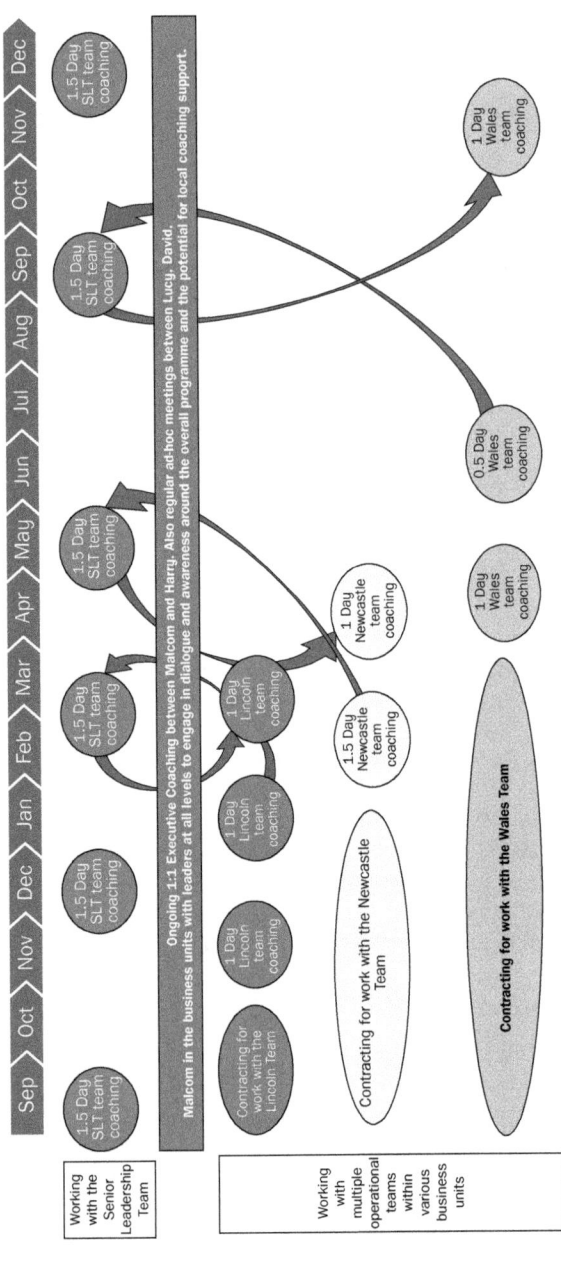

Figure 1 Connecting the work: Working with the senior leadership team and local operational teams

> *Harry*: 'I'm used to having full ownership – and ability to make things happen, but I know this will need something else, from what I've seen and what you've said'.

We advocated a coaching approach to change, with a basis of inquiry and dialogue skills. We also wanted to gain support for coaching teams at different levels; to cycle back to the leadership team with those involved; to raise the issues that emerged; and to seek action that would lead to more synergistic working. Getting this up and running would require Harry to engage in some personal coaching with us.

> *Harry*: 'I find I really value the time to stand back and reflect once we're engaged – but it's hard with so many daily demands. This is going to mean me leading in a very different way and I value the help I'm getting'.

The senior leadership team

Malcolm: The three of us arrived at a rather run-down city centre hotel in Manchester for a workshop with Harry's leadership team. The workshop was to consist of an evening session, followed by dinner, then the whole of the next day. We were anxious. Harry had called the meeting, which was more of a demand than an invitation.

He was keen to get things moving – to create a shared strategy for the future and commit to a programme of change – but we asked for some caution. In advance, we had asked him several questions: 'Is this a team? Do they want a shared strategy? Do they see value in meeting to explore a shared set of goals – looking for more synergy and collective ownership?'

To date, the directors had worked largely independently, with reporting lines to global business divisions. Harry's direct control was limited, but he was accountable if the various business units didn't perform. The group comprised about 20 people.

We set the room out with a circle of chairs.

As people trickled in and took their seats, we picked up on the now familiar quips: 'I'm an alcoholic' and 'where can I put my computer?'.

Harry arrived and gave a preamble, without saying much about what we were doing there and what to expect. This went on a bit … we wanted him to show some authority, but none seemed forthcoming. We introduced the agenda and the idea of a 'check-in' so that all voices could be heard at the outset. We also said a little about the importance of voicing, respect, and inquiry.

Someone postured about the importance of their own business and 'where the company is going'. Harry became agitated. We tried to catch his eye. At a later event we would probably have said something openly about him letting people speak, but we were also 'new' participants – a bit nervous, a bit unsure, and worried about the risk of being dismissed. It happens to the best of us.

Something finally set Harry off. He dramatically fell off his chair and started banging the carpet with his fist. Some laughed, some were dismayed. Others simply sat expressionless. Was it funny? Was it an attempt to break the mood? It certainly changed things. The openness and honesty that we thought we were beginning to establish started to fade. The conversation returned to something more superficial and jokey.

We had a hard stop at 8pm for drinks and dinner – which was a relief. You could feel it as the clock moved to that point.

The three of us took some time to reflect on the evening. We noticed how unpredictable people were in voicing their diversity in thought; and there was a marked variation in levels of engagement or presence. Our challenge was holding the space, with some structure, yet being fluid and allowing people their own space. We had given everyone their own minute to check in – some had taken ten seconds, others three minutes. At least this group were together and talking.

Already we sensed tension in the team. Most people felt connected to their global business organisations. Being on Harry's leadership team was a consequence of geography. We got the impression that for some this meeting was an inconvenience. For others there was real enthusiasm. We checked in with Harry and caught one or two others at the bar. Here are some snippets:

> *Harry*: 'I can see how a packed agenda kills the conversation we need'.
>
> 'I also see that I might be part of the problem – I keep on wanting to jump in with a solution'.
>
> 'I suspect it's a bit frustrating for some – either me jumping in – or, for one or two, not having the usual business updates'.
>
> *Others*: 'This is the first time in a long time I think we are having an honest conversation'.
>
> 'This is our chance to make a difference'.
>
> 'This is so important – we're not a team and need to be'.
>
> 'I am not really interested in conversations, I want to see results; why are people not taking responsibility – less talking, more action!'

David: As mentioned, the leadership team meeting started with an evening session. It was Harry's meeting, but he had handed over the design and coaching largely to us.

This was our chance to engage them in coaching and for Harry to get their agreement to a wider programme of change. Harry was going out on a limb for us.

The prevailing thinking of the SLT was planning, measuring, project managing, and continuous improvement. Expertise and experience were highly valued. We were careful not to diminish these ways of managing, but for what Harry wanted we felt something else was needed; more reflection and inquiry – and an openness to coaching.

Harry made the case that the SLT needed to adapt to external changes, and not to do so would ultimately end in failure. The more Harry pushed them, the more hesitant they became and the conditions for coaching and inquiry diminished.

He eventually said, 'either we agree to do it, or we abandon this work'.

It felt like an ultimatum and most people looked uncertain. Slowly a few heads started nodding, then a few more, until everyone in the room was nodding together. Harry decided to call it a night. We shuffled down to the restaurant for dinner, with a sense of relief that the evening meeting was over and we had got an agreement, of sorts, to proceed.

Malcolm: In many ways, we colluded with Harry in his push to gain a level of acceptance for the work. David calls it 'the night of the nodding heads'. Were they really engaged? Was the meeting pragmatic enough for them? How bold were we? During the next day though we had a few minor breakthroughs. A simple short exercise on 'generous listening' prompted one participant to say, 'I had no idea what a difference this makes'.

Contracting for team coaching with Tom's team

Lucy: The second day had been up and down. Discussions, a bit of confusion, and some breakthroughs. We had an agreement to contract with teams within Harry's division for local coaching. A few weeks later, David and I took a trip to spend some time with the leader of a large business with distributed teams across the UK. He was part of Harry's SLT, but hadn't spent much time with us yet to explore what we were offering.

Getting time in people's diaries through formal processes was challenging. In practical terms, we were learning about the value of just showing up and hanging out – catching people as they walked past, rather than booking time in their diaries. We would ask people how they were and what was going on. It both seemed to deepen our relationship with people and find out the 'inside scoop'.

Hanging out doesn't sound very professional, but there was something in the spontaneity and informality that made people open up. We weren't telling or trying to convince them about anything. Instead, we were asking deeper questions, listening, and creating understanding through dialogue.

David: In the months after Harry's first leadership meeting, we wanted to get local team coaching under way, but it wasn't always straightforward. Most people told us how busy they were and getting diary time took weeks. We agreed to coach a team in Wales, led by Tom. However, there were layers of management between the SLT and the operational teams. One example was Mike, the operations director, who was not in the SLT but sat a few levels above Tom. We felt it was important to have Mike's support to do the work. I was keen to get working with Tom's team, but Mike kept asking me to hold off.

In an effort to break the deadlock, we decided to sit in the HQ for a few days and we 'bumped into' Tom. Hanging out was becoming more part of our practice. We sensed an opportunity to break the deadlock with Mike. 'Dropping by' Mike's office we asked if he had some free time. Within a few minutes we managed to get Mike, Tom, and the three of us talking about how we might get started.

After months of formal scheduled calls and emails with Mike, the breakthrough came from an unplanned five-minute conversation.

Starting team coaching with Tom's operational team

David: We were in North Wales for a full day with Tom and his team. We started with some framing and Tom shared the process and context; then a check-in. There were about 15 sitting in the circle, mostly men, mostly technicians; the guys who head out to machines every day to carry out advanced maintenance.

Within the first hour it became clear that they were up for some coaching. Our approach was to provide skills and structure to conversations, to improve quality listening, reflection, and inquiry. We encouraged them to work together in more generative and creative ways.

As a team they were curious, connected, fun, openly vulnerable, and committed to their mission: to safely care for the equipment and deliver the best performance for their customer. They also had some clear views on how the wider organisation was helping or hindering progress. This felt completely different to the leadership team meeting months earlier.

Anyone who questions if 'tough operational types' value coaching, wouldn't do so if they were with us on those first few days with Tom's team. I remember plenty of laughs and some emotional moments. The team had an appetite for ownership and new ways of working. Everyone in the room was participating. There was a sense that by working together they could achieve real improvements.

Connecting Tom's team with the senior leadership team

David: Our intention with Harry was to stimulate positive change across the whole division, including hundreds of operational teams. Our goal was to connect learning from the operational teams to the leadership team who held the formal authority to influence system-wide change.

A few months later, we involved Tom in one of the SLT sessions. We invited him to share his experience of development and change with the SLT. Our intention was to 'hold the space' for the senior leaders to listen, reflect, and make sense of Tom's experience in the context of wider systemic issues.

We held the following questions:

- Based on the progress Tom and his team have made, what could they learn about how change happens at an operational level?
- What does this mean for their individual leadership practice?
- Reflecting on the learning, how can they use their formal authority to create the conditions for systemic change?

I'm not sure they really listened and engaged as much as we'd hoped. Informal meetings after this revealed some frustration and dissent from one or two people:

> 'This is really simple. It is about defining where we want to go and communicating that to everyone'.
>
> 'If I get asked again "What question am I holding?", I might hit someone'.

Lucy: We needed to feed back our observations, which was easier said than done. The structure and engineering culture of Harry's division was largely about compliance and control. Formal authority was not always helpful and enabling. Quite often it was inhibiting creativity. Yes, we got results, but was the organisation preparing itself for an unpredictable future?

We asked ourselves if we would be capable of changing our organisation as a result of hearing how local leaders were transforming.

I think there is a definite role for leaders to bring about change, using their power in a way that is enabling, inquiring, and encouraging. We were beginning to realise we had to balance our relationship with leaders, to support both their real (or sometimes perceived) agendas to help them to be open to real change.

Learning and conclusions

Malcolm: We found ourselves in the midst of group dynamics, hidden agendas, alliances, power plays, and unspoken criticism. Some we spotted, others we didn't. Working together meant we had the space and ability to reflect on our experience and observations – either during sessions when groups were working together, or over a much needed beer.

Our practice, espoused method, and approach was always about seeking shared commitment and authority to do work that would change organisational dynamics, culture, and ways of working in a changing world. Our premise was that the local work would highlight wider systemic issues.

Lucy: I have heard some people say that what we do is 'wizardry'. I have also heard some people proclaim that we come in with no plan or no agenda, or that real change cannot come from 'just a conversation'. It makes me laugh sometimes. We may hold a plan lightly and adapt it as the situation or conversation changes, but we most definitely have a plan. We have battled between the plan's helpfulness – or not – and showing the plan or 'model' before starting, as often requested by teams. We've found that if we overly drive the agenda, the team sits back; instead, we're hoping to support participant-led work.

On one occasion in Harry's team people said, 'If only you had shown us this model in the first place'. We said, 'that is interesting, let's explore how we have used this up to now ...' – but inside we were thinking 'WE DID'. Perhaps we avoided saying it quite so abruptly, through fear of being viewed as critical. Sometimes it was easy to forget that others may not have the time to explore and work with the models enough to remember them.

Malcolm used to say, 'meet people where they are'. I tried, yet it would often feel frustrating, even now. But I have also seen people step beyond their constraints to transform their own leadership.

I still have the same internal role and other coaches have stepped in to join me and continue the work. Harry was promoted. As the dust settles on the latest reorganisation, new businesses in the division have started to work together and requests for team coaching have re-emerged. We are busier than ever in responding to that demand.

David: It has been some time since the work with Tom and his team. I have left the organisation to develop my own team coaching practice. The team coaching with Tom's team, at an operational level, was very effective, but took time to get started. Harry's team started quickly because it was 'driven' by Harry, but the use of formal power was met with some resistance. We have learned a lot from this experience about how to partner with leaders and create the conditions for team coaching to enable the best outcomes.

It feels like our work was much more systemic than it felt at the time. Coaching has become part of the DNA of the division and that it is now seen as integral to achieving its purpose. Changing the culture and embedding a coaching mindset, making the conditions more supportive for teaming is the lasting change.

Malcolm: As the 'external', I experienced a huge development in confidence, knowledge, and skill in our little group. Our commitment to learning, practice, and looking at different ways of thinking about teams, coaching, and the nature of organisations was essential. We learned to be less critical and more accepting of different agendas. We held regular calls and met formally, but a lot was achieved when we were travelling and 'hanging out' – from some tricky moments together, to being highly collaborative. We've become good friends, and though I've moved on, we still look after each other.

The difference between the SLT, which consisted of people working in complex matrix environments, and the local operational teams was stark. Operational people are working to clearly defined shared goals; so the outputs of coaching are often very tangible. This begs the question, 'when do people need to work as a team and to what end?'

Many teams would often rather work with internal coaches. Perhaps the external coach is more useful in the leadership work, where the stakes are high for internal coaches. Externals are more dispensable and can be put off more easily. I believe that an internal/external partnership is very powerful.

The legacy of our early work continues – and continues to grow.

Whose bias is it? Moving the dial from 'me' to 'we': a systemic challenge for team coaching

Elizabeth Hughes and Tammy Turner

Introduction

Poised for organisational expansion either through merger or acquisition, this multinational resources organisation, with operations in Canada and Australia, had the opportunity to fulfil the client's articulated hope of becoming a key player in its sector. To support momentum around this identified need, a staggered pilot team coaching programme was introduced to a range of key Australian stakeholders and the global head of human resources.

Under the guidance of the global head of HR and Australian operations leader, yet without clear CEO buy-in, two team coaches, Elizabeth Hughes and Tammy Turner, were engaged to design and deliver this aspirational pilot programme. It initially comprised two senior leadership site teams, and a few months later was to include the formative Australian operations team.

The intent of the pilot was multifaceted: to bridge the gap between the current individual 'heroic leadership' approach and catalyse 'inclusive leadership'; and to drive organisational performance and anticipated growth. One site leader echoed the programme intent as, 'to learn how to engage more effectively while achieving the operational purpose'.

With strong domestic organisational support, a solid academic programme, and the teams' ongoing commitment, collective leadership through the pilot was gaining momentum. Team leaders were beginning to use the team coaching approach with their own team for greater levels of inclusion.

Why, then, did the pilot team coaching programme experience an untimely 'pause'? And what impact did this 'pause' have on the programme, in terms of moving the dial beyond individual heroic to inclusive leadership at a team level and organisationally? And what role did bias play in the engagement choice points?

This case will look at systemic bias – 'any trend or deviation from the truth in data collection, data analysis, interpretation and publication which can cause false conclusions' (Šimundić, 2013: 12) – specifically focusing on design, collaboration, gender, and cognitive diversity biases that forged the 'us, to we, to them' systemic bias and shaped the unconscious team coaching agreement.

Context

Like many in its industry, the leaders of International Mining Company (IMC) were more accustomed to a 'command and control' (heroic) style of leadership than an inclusive one. Enhancing cross-functional capability and inclusive leadership across the Australian business would be advantageous. IMC was comprised of one long-term residential site, another more 'junior' start-up site, and an Australian operations team, which had yet to be either fully staffed or have country-wide executive functions.

The Canadian headquarters oversaw the Australian operations, focusing on driving the gross production profile to create shareholder value. For the Australian operations to be well positioned for future acquisitions, to take full advantage of their physical ore bodies, as well as to have a healthy balance sheet and culture, their leaders required further development. It was hypothesised, by IMC's global head of human resources (the programme sponsor) and the Australian operations executive, that more efficient domestic solutions could be found by developing senior level people in Australia. These factors informed the initial individual coaching pilot, headed by Elizabeth Hughes.

It was an aspirational time for the organisation, its leaders, and the project lead, Hughes. To ready the leaders for these larger team responsibilities, IMC embarked upon a 12-month, 20-person pilot individual coaching programme. To bridge the 'heroic' to 'inclusive' leadership paradigm, Hughes held a two-hour team session with each Australian site to explore their individual talent dynamics (TD) profile (Hamilton, 2014) to better understand themselves, their team members' strengths and corresponding dynamics, and the Australian business as a whole. A survey conducted after the first three months revealed: greater effort to work collaboratively with the coachees' line manager and peers; greater understanding and acceptance of themselves and others; improved communication; and a greater focus on leading their teams. The data were shared with the client sponsor and the global CEO at a quarterly business review meeting.

Although this was a step in the right direction, Hughes realised that individual coaching alone would not be sufficient to meet the aspirational organisational imperative. She wanted to bridge the gap between the 'heroic leadership' that she saw in the individual coaching and 'inclusive leadership' to better prepare the leaders for the upcoming rapid organisational growth. She floated the idea of team coaching to the client sponsor, who agreed to extend the pilot into a multisite team coaching engagement. To ensure 'best practices' of team coaching, Hughes engaged Tammy Turner to work with her as the lead team coach on this Australian-wide project. They began designing an organisational change approach from 'me' to 'we' that included individual and systemic team coaching, as well as input from the leaders' peers, direct reports, and that of their internal and external stakeholders. As colleagues who had not previously worked together, our learning unfolded in parallel with that of the clients.

Design bias

Our early assumption was that the client wanted a collective teaming approach to leadership that included integrated leadership development and team coaching to foster a 'we' culture. Consequently, team coaching commenced with an introduction to the five conditions (5Cs) model (Hawkins, 2011) at a quarterly meeting with each team. Hughes hoped through individual coaching, a TD profile, and a leadership development plan that leaders would get an insight into what would be required to work collectively. She observed several leaders were looking at ways to enhance the performance of their own teams, yet struggling to make time to coach their direct reports. She thought the team coaching would fill that gap.

Each leadership team underwent a team orientation session using the 5Cs model before attending a two-day off-site team-building workshop. During the workshop they identified their teams' commission and focus areas, learned essential leadership skills such as listening, powerful questioning, giving and receiving feedback, and examined the results of their TEAM Connect 360 assessment. Team members commented, 'Talent dynamics was important, and the TEAM Connect 360 process was excellent', psychological safety and the "in and out of flow" activity was great'.

Monthly individual coaching sessions with Hughes continued. In between team coaching sessions, Hughes and Turner met fortnightly to integrate their insight and themes from the individual coaching into the bespoke design. The team coaches agreed the design without specific client sign-off before delivery. Team members discussed their identified focus areas and small experiments during monthly face-to-face two-hour hybrid facilitation/team coaching sessions with Hughes and Turner using a bespoke team coaching process (Dresdner, 2019). We suggested they practise the team coaching process in their leadership team meetings immediately after the first team coaching session, which was a mistake. The feedback from one team member was: 'the team coaching process needed to demonstrate the value of the process before people committed to it; therefore, some struggled with the following sessions. However, after a few team coaching sessions, the team began to take a risk with both their peers and direct reports using this process.

Figure 2 The 3 Factor RAA model: Responsibility, Accountability, and Authority
© 2020 Turner International and Tammy Turner. All rights reserved.

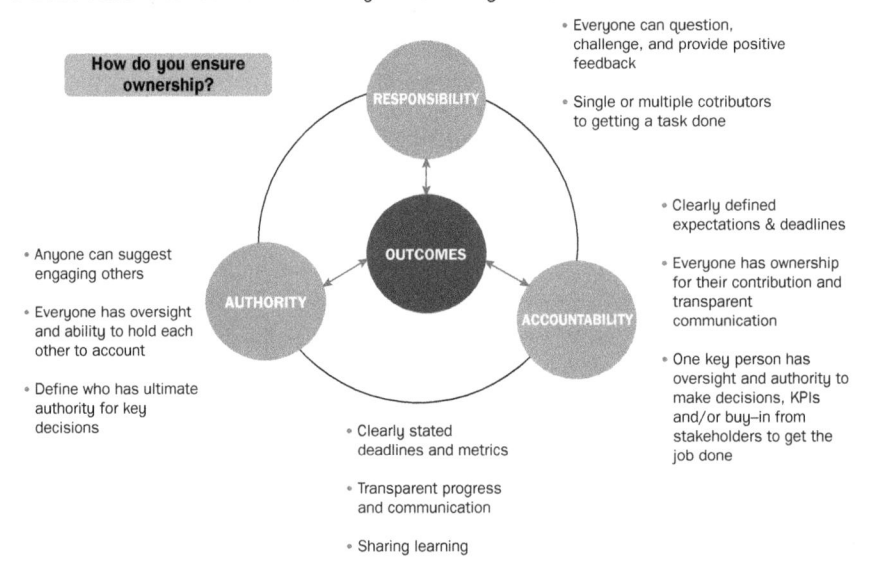

How do you ensure ownership?

RESPONSIBILITY
- Everyone can question, challenge, and provide positive feedback
- Single or multiple cotributors to getting a task done

ACCOUNTABILITY
- Clearly defined expectations & deadlines
- Everyone has ownership for their contribution and transparent communication
- One key person has oversight and authority to make decisions, KPIs and/or buy-in from stakeholders to get the job done

OUTCOMES
- Clearly stated deadlines and metrics
- Transparent progress and communication
- Sharing learning

AUTHORITY
- Anyone can suggest engaging others
- Everyone has oversight and ability to hold each other to account
- Define who has ultimate authority for key decisions

The teams found it difficult to navigate the 5Cs model. Stuck in between a Canadian headquarters and Australian operations team, middle management leaders did not have a true commission. Additionally, co-learning and connecting to their stakeholders were not commonplace, and very little individual or team development had been done previously. Team coaching became increasingly more blended learning: training, facilitation, as team coaching. To support their learning, a number of models and concepts were introduced, including psychological safety (Edmondson, 2012), 3 Factor RAA model: Responsibility, Accountability, and Authority (Turner, 2018), and API: Authority, Presence, and Impact (Hawkins, 2017).

Learning on design bias: As the brief was for team coaching, Turner was biased towards a 'pure team coaching approach' in the early design. A more integrated approach to teaming was adopted later, though programme review data indicated that some team leaders expressed there was an opportunity for greater structure and clarity around the purpose of the two-hour team coaching sessions. In exit feedback, one leader observed, "There wasn't enough follow-up in the sessions. We should have always gone back to the previous session, reviewed it, and talked about why it was never resolved". The group did start to use the process of putting bigger issues aside to be reviewed weekly as a management team, but this only lasted a week due to the mine closure. "The subgroups were great, but again, they did not follow through. The group needed to be held accountable with meeting minutes. They needed to be more focused around consensus versus commitment to make things stick".

Collaboration: Heroic vs. inclusive leadership bias

Individual coaching revealed that 'hub and spoke' heroic leadership prevailed on both sites and struggled with how to be a collaborative leader. This was underscored by the global sponsor's feedback that he saw leaders operating in their 'silos of direct accountability'. Site leaders and stakeholders said, 'problems are being caused by frontline leaders not "stepping up" to what they were being asked to do', resulting in trust being impacted.

We naively assumed the leaders' stated objective 'to have a clear purpose to be the best leaders and communicators while leading IMC the best we could' was a desire for collective leadership. In fact, they translated 'coaching leadership' as individual 'heroic leadership' to be used with their direct reports. They were concerned with "How can I maintain control, engage my team's strengths, and become a better leader of my direct reports?" We interpreted it as 'inclusive leadership' both across their leadership team and downward with their own teams to create 'one IMC'. As previously mentioned, our design and how we worked in the room upheld this bias.

Capitalising on the 'heroic leadership' paradigm, early team coaching sessions engaged the site leader on specific challenges related to site objectives agreed in the offsite workshops around operational success and engaging stakeholders to provide opportunities to experience 'inclusive leadership'. One team spent an entire session focusing on invoicing protocols; identifying accountable and responsible parties, training required, uniformity of systems, and formation of a working party. Other sessions focused on safety contacts, rostering issues, mixing up team meetings to discuss strategic vs. project/business-as-usual (BAU) issues. Over five months, the site leadership teams were well underway moving beyond the resource sector's 'heroic leadership' to a more 'inclusive' way of working both within sites and across the organisation.

Learning on collaboration: We learned the importance of working with what was already present to break their paradigm. We deliberately mimicked 'heroic leadership' through the role of the team coach by giving them small experiments for the teams to collaborate and experience 'inclusive leadership' during the team coaching sessions.

Gender and cognitive diversity bias

Another opportunity to in-build 'inclusive leadership' was to address the diversity issue and engage teams around communication. At the beginning of the pilot, we discovered gender diversity was either ignored or subjected to protection bias. Equally, while cognitive diversity was seen as important to the inclusion and innovation agenda and more easily accessible than gender diversity, it was also undervalued in lieu of industry-specific expertise and a dominant leadership style.

Almost from the outset, one of the tangible outcomes of the team coaching programme was greater gender and cognitive diversity in team meetings. It created the space for female team members to provide feedback: "You guys just dominate the meetings – there is little opportunity for me to have my thoughts heard, let alone have them considered". This shift to inclusion is reflected in team comments such as, "the team coaching process gave everyone a voice, and those with a strong voice less impact", and "allowing others to speak and feel listened to takes practice. It can be awkward and means authoritative or extroverted team members do not have the opportunity to dominate". This related not only to women but those who had differing views, introverted natures, or were simply being passive when their participation was expected by the team.

Learning on gender and cognitive diversity bias: Using TD profiles helped individuals recognise their unique leadership traits and laid the groundwork for the team working together collectively. Creating a psychologically safe space, along with a team coaching process in which everyone was required to speak only once before contributing again, provided the stage for individuals to cut across their own bias, and to hear and consider others' contributions.

Systemic bias: From 'us and them' to 'we'

Key success measurements coming out of the TEAM Connect 360 data were to share information, save on costs, and eliminate redundancy across the Australian sites. As one team member commented, "All of IMC works in silos and there's no understanding of the business as a whole". Data further revealed that leaders didn't understand where the organisation was going, what IMC really needed, and why. Stakeholders and leaders from other locations commented that they didn't get the necessary information from sites to make informed decisions.

What success would look like post the team coaching pilot was primarily focused on the Australian business. One of the biases that appeared was when the Australian business head stated, "that in addition to exceeding operational objectives, the Australian teams needed to pivot to think collectively, lead professionally with a less directive style, demonstrate less fear of failure, and experience an absence of "us" and "them" language within and across the teams". Given both commercial and leadership advancement, team members were keen to engage in the 'once in a career' opportunity the pilot presented.

In contrast, as Hughes ventured outside of the Australian business, she was met by 'we have seen it all before' resistance, as stated by several overseas team members. Once again, our global sponsor's bias towards 'one IMC' as the systemic imperative wasn't shared.

At a team and site level, an 'us' or 'we' tribalism reigned. "Across the entire business there is a general lack of uniformity" and "team collaboration and development at the senior level is not valued if it takes longer and is not 100% focused on dollars or tonnes", shared one team member. This was compounded by the Australian imperative to engage with Canadian stakeholders only on an 'as-needed' basis.

Lacking direct involvement with the key Canadian stakeholder meant the team coaches relied more heavily on the system bias through other internal stakeholders. One of those Canadian biases was the comment, "what interests the boss fascinates me", compared with the Australian attitude, "it's better to ask forgiveness rather than permission". These mixed messages created risk in the engagement and anxiety in the system. As organisational disruptions occurred, so did the leader's prediction that without clearly expressed CEO support for the programme, it would have limited impact.

As the Australian teams had made progress on working collectively, we were then able to feed back emerging patterns. We noticed members collaborated with others when their expertise was required to solve their own challenges, rather than 'someone else's challenge'. They saw accountability only as the output of their functional teams, systemically contributing to an undercurrent of blame. We signposted that the absence of their leader holding team members to account was, in fact, indicative of how team coaching could assist them in collective decision-making, shared agreements and outcomes.

In a site leadership team's session 4, an opportunity to explore these concepts appeared. It was disclosed that members made agreements in the room but 'going back to site' did not uphold them. This opened the space to dialogue about how they could be accountable to each other, ensuring that their team agreements stuck. These included: a commitment to actions made in the team coaching sessions were followed through; each team member who was unable to attend the team coaching session was brought up to speed by one of their team members; and equally to ensure that they collectively contracted on the purpose of each session. In session 5 we introduced the 3 Factor RAA model to embed accountability, decrease the tendency to blame, and increase inclusion for a more accountable culture.

But systemic change was limited as the remaining three months were scuppered. We felt gutted. The broader Canadian leadership development programme was shelved due to an acquisition. In tandem, one of the Australian sites was shut down, the team coaching paused, major global disruption and a change in roles for our sponsor resulted in the full engagement being abandoned.

Learning on systemic bias: Bias was an unwelcomed partner in this engagement. Throughout the engagement, Hughes met monthly with the client sponsor for updates and further input. To understand the biases at play, Hughes and Turner met fortnightly for peer supervision. Turner also took team dynamics to professional supervision for further input. These inputs were important to give voice to this broad range of biases within the system.

Conclusion

The original programme design included another TEAM Connect 360, stakeholder interviews, and leader reflections to wrap up. Instead, key leaders were interviewed and all individual and team coaching participants were surveyed.

At this point, one of the site leaders concluded that, "from an Australian point of view, the whole process was a success. Both the site teams will experience greater benefits going forward. As an Australian team we can continue to increase trust and relationships by working together on this common goal (of inclusive leadership)". Data also indicated team coaches did not provide specific instructions and/or make the teams more accountable, perhaps indicating that the 'heroic leadership' tendency had not had as much traction as we thought. At a team level there was some progress: "The team coaching process was difficult for us all, but it helped build the trust in the team".

We ended the engagement knowing more about what to do differently in the future, what to be on alert to within a systemic team coaching context, and how to work under pressure using contracting skills to develop a solid coaching presence. Equally important, the collected exit data provided us and the client with a sense of gratification that although the project was cancelled owing to the business restructuring, we made a difference to their leaders and hopefully to a more collective approach to leadership in the times ahead.

Future applications

- Ensure you have clearly expressed buy-in and agreed accountability factors from the CEO and any other key stakeholders and the team itself.
- Budget in time and money for peer and professional supervision.
- Be aware of all biases – ours, theirs, internal and external stakeholders, sponsor(s), and systemic.
- Communicate team performance outputs from team coaching that are directly tied to business imperatives to key stakeholders and perhaps entire site employees.

References

Dresdner, L. (2019) Active Listening: Small Group Activity [https://ctl.byu.edu/tip/active-listening-small-group-activity].

Edmondson, A.C. (2012) *Teaming: How Organisations Learn, Innovate, and Compete in the Knowledge Economy.* San Francisco, CA: Jossey-Bass.

Hamilton, R.J. (2014) *The Millionaire Master Plan.* New York: Business Plus.

Hawkins, P. (2011) *Leadership Team Coaching: Developing Collective Transformational Leadership.* London: Kogan Page.

Hawkins, P. (2017) *Leadership Team Coaching: Developing Collective Transformational Leadership,* 3rd edition. London: Kogan Page.

Šimundić, A.-M. (2013) Bias in research, *Biochemia Medica,* 23 (1): 12–15 [https://doi.org/10.11613/BM.2013.003].

Turner, T. (2018) Excellence in Leadership: Responsibility, Accountability and Authority (3 Factor RAA model) [https://05596da6-a477-4459-a3ae-9e722ef14947.filesusr.com/ugd/11f34b_6ae0f2d809c84c6bb97a2a3dbe7f066f.pdf].

Foundations to sustainability: A leadership team coaching case study

Melissa J. Sayer and Colm Murphy

Leadership team background

This case study is about coaching the leadership team of a publicly quoted company (PLC) in the construction industry in Ireland. We were engaged, in 2015, to work with the leadership team by the CEO shortly after the company listed on the stock exchange. During the birth stage of the company (Greiner, 1998), the leadership team were entrepreneurially focused and worked excessive hours to raise the capital for the public share issuance. Consequently, the team's energy had been consumed with getting the company off the ground with little time for putting in place organisational processes and procedures. The CEO requested coaching for the senior leadership team as he recognised that the leadership team was about to expand. Their focus would need to shift to putting in place the required structures, processes, and procedures needed for the organisation in its growth phase.

We agreed to an initial programme of team coaching that would last 18 months. We began with a preliminary meeting with the team leader, followed by a meeting with the team leader and the team, to understand the team vision of success for team coaching and talk through the principles of team coaching. We used a team diagnostic tool, the Rocket Model (Curphy and Hogan, 2012), to obtain time 1 data (data at the commencement of the team coaching engagement) from team members and key stakeholders, on the performance of the team. We utilised the data and the team vision of success for coaching to co-create the agenda. We scheduled to work with the team for a series of two-day offsites spread over 18 months, with planned check-ins and support provided between the offsites. The key themes for team coaching centred on supporting the leadership team to take some time out to consider both teamwork and taskwork (Dinh and Salas, 2017).

Introduction to the case

When considering team coaching, potential clients often ask us about examples of how teams and organisations have benefitted from investing in this type of development. When you get behind the intention of such questions, it is often that leaders and organisations want a sense of what outcomes they can expect. The answer, of course, is never clear-cut. There are typically contextual factors, variations, and nuances that make each team intervention unique, and the answer can be broad and hard to pinpoint. That said, we appreciate that the curiosity behind such questions is often to help leaders and teams understand what the experience of team coaching might be like before committing, and also as a way of getting to know what it might be like to work with us.

We deployed the lens of critical moments as a means to understand the benefits of team coaching for leaders, teams, and organisations. De Haan et al. (2010) studied 'critical moments' in the context of one-to-one coaching, defining a critical moment as a turning point in the coaching journey. Such significant moments are often exciting and tense. We focused on what might constitute a critical moment for this leadership team in their team coaching journey by undertaking a co-inquiry with our client.

We began by asking the CEO and leader of the team to 'pinpoint' some of his experiences of team coaching and to share from his perspective what he perceived and felt were the tangible outcomes from engaging in team coaching. He remarked, 'As CEO, and particularly at the beginning, the role is very busy, and your time is consumed with trying to get a business off the ground. It is tough to plan, and the team coaching provided us with a structure. It allowed me to be pro-active'. Next, we collated our notes from interviews (with the CEO and team members) and further analysed our extensive field notes to help us to identify some potential patterns and insights from our work with this team. We were curious to understand if we could identify the critical moments that most contributed to the success of the team coaching engagement with this client, and what lessons could be learnt.

We honed in on the client's perspective to ensure that the stakeholder's voice guided the identification of the critical moment. We concluded from our analysis, and in particular from this comment from the CEO, that the team coaching sessions enabled them to 'work out our unique selling point, and get very clear on our philosophy' – that one such critical moment was the creation of their Big Hairy Audacious Goal (BHAG) (Collins and Porras, 1996).

Critical moment – BHAG

The origins of the critical moment came from a pre-call with the CEO before the first two-day team coaching session, when he mentioned using some of the session time to establish a BHAG. The data from the Rocket Model diagnostic supported this instinct, where it was clear from the results that the team also agreed that they needed greater clarity on their team mission and organisational goals. On day one of the first offsite, we coached the team to agree explicit norms for the two days and spent some time creating the environment for good conversations and listening. We shared the data from the Rocket Model diagnostic, and in the afternoon the team worked on developing and co-creating a BHAG. This work resulted in a draft vision/BHAG statement of:

> 'Transforming Dublin by being the best property company for our tenants, staff, and shareholders'.

We noticed that the energy in the room outweighed the feeling of exhaustion at the end of the first day. As coaches, we also sensed anticipation, excitement, and anxiety around how this 'stretch' goal could be translated into reality and a way of working.

The next morning, we shared with the team an idea of creating pillars as a way of operationalising the BHAG. We spent the day assisting the team in identifying and evolving the pillars to support their BHAG. Each pillar had an overarching goal; several tactics to achieve that goal; ways to measure the tactics; and a leadership team member sponsor. The five pillars that emerged supported strategy, culture, shareholder, customer, and product excellence in service of delivering on the BHAG. Having spent their first six months in survival and creation mode, the co-creation of a BHAG – and supporting pillars, tactics, and ownership – gave the team a focus beyond their day-to-day activities. It also got the individual team members thinking about the leadership of their teams.

The CEO noted that for him the BHAG meant that

> 'I could now see problems before they happened, and this is possible through the development of the pillars, which allowed for individual goals. This clarity contributed hugely to the organisation because our people could see how their contribution contributed to the overall, and this became highly motivating for them'.

The BHAG and pillars have been reviewed and adapted over subsequent years, with a sixth pillar (risk management) added, demonstrating how they have become central to driving the performance and culture of the organisation.

And so, it might be asked, why did the creation of a BHAG become so instrumental to this team's success and stick out as a critical moment in this team coaching engagement? In this case, the BHAG and pillars became the driving force for strategic decision-making in subsequent coaching sessions, but more importantly, outside of the coaching sessions. In other words, it became embedded in 'how they do things'. The clarity of the BHAG transformed the team's focus, roles, and identity and provided the platform for each of the team members to structure their functions and bring clarity in the communication with their teams.

As coaches, we work hard to support teams with developing clarity of purpose and often find that teams struggle with the oftentimes abstract aspect of such an exercise. Our most important role as coaches is staying with the team's discomfort of not knowing and the ambiguity such discussions bring about. As mentioned above, we experienced the excitement and tension in the room as the BHAG crystallised. We recall at times during the creation of the BHAG sharing doubts between ourselves about where it was all going, as we battled our own need for clarity and to see tangible actions. De Haan et al. (2010) describe that the provoking of tension by the coach in a coaching session can often bring about unease and doubt for the coach. In this case, we recall that our insistence of staying with the ambiguity sat in the air between the coach and client. We allowed it to be so and the team found their way past it.

Critical moments are often characterised by an understanding or a reflection after the event that the insight for the client became a turning point, a catalyst for change. We did not have an immediate appreciation as to the strength of the critical moment's ongoing influence on the success of this team. We have since reflected as coaches on the extent to which this moment became a catalyst and the foundation for the development and growth of the organisation's performance and culture.

BHAG driving performance and culture

Following the offsite, the leadership team did an all-hands with the entire company to share their BHAG and the new pillar structure so that they could invite feedback on how it could be improved and embedded. We coached the team through this process and attended the event as they wanted feedback on their performance. The pillars, in turn, shaped the weekly team meetings, and eventually became the framework by which departmental and individual roles and goals were set. The offsite outcomes were also shared with the company board. The importance and impact of the leadership team making leadership offsites transparent to key stakeholders not only breathed life into the vision and strategic direction, but it also created focus, accountability, and identity.

The development of the strategic pillars and a clear set of goals enabled the leadership team to determine standards for each of the functions, and more explicitly formalise a process to evaluate tasks and work. This process also allowed the team to thoughtfully consider how rewards would be distributed in alignment with goals set and the broader strategic vision. The approach enabled the organisation to be very clear on the organisational, team, and individual improvement, and the CEO described how it allowed staff to 'see their contribution and how it relates to the organisation they work in'. The team coaching enabled the team to consider the framework for all these varying and interrelated elements and to make decisions based on their espoused values and the culture they wanted to create. The execution and the nuts and bolts of its implementation happened with the support of external HR expertise.

The feedback from the first team diagnostic indicated to the team that the organisation wanted increased levels of communication from the leadership team. This was an area that the team also recognised when we initially contracted with them around success. The clarity of the BHAG and pillars empowered the leadership team to enhance communication through town hall gatherings, giving more significant consideration to the format and frequency of team meetings, and it provided a focus for one-to-one performance and developmental sessions. It also brought about a discipline of Monday leadership team lunchtime meetings, creating the space for the team to have lunch together once a week and 'talk about all the big things'.

Communication continues to be an area that the team works to improve and reflect on. One such example is the onboarding of new members to the senior leadership team. The original four-person team is now a team of seven. The CEO initiated a process that a team coaching offsite session would coincide with the onboarding of a new senior leadership team member. Using the team coaching sessions as part of the onboarding helped the new members, in the CEO's opinion, to 'know what was expected and to be a platform for all voices to discuss issues that might not otherwise be raised'. It was important that the new team member got to experience, early in their new role, the more open and strategic space of the team coaching session and the opportunity to get to know the team from the inside.

It is worth highlighting this team's commitment and discipline to improve performance, and the willingness to be coached. Most of our team coaching clients will experience a team diagnostic survey once or twice in the team coaching process. This team takes a pulse check with all their key stakeholders every nine to twelve months. One board member on the most recent diagnostic noted: 'the emphasis on team-building and morale is commendable. There is a genuine interest in the team members and how best to maximise everyone's potential'. Another board member stated, 'I think the team are highly effective performers and excellent communicators'.

Stakeholder perspectives on team coaching

The main insights from the CEO centred on people and how the BHAG and pillars helped define the required culture, which in turn focused the hiring and retention approach. He commented, 'When you build a strategy and have a defined ethos, you can quickly learn if you have buy-in or not. In the team coaching sessions, we identified the skills gaps and areas where we needed to strengthen. We knew who we wanted to join this organisation, retain, and we continue to keep benchmarking ourselves'.

A leadership team member, not initially part of the senior leadership team, shared her experience of the team communicating the BHAG and pillars with the company after that first offsite. She recalled the impact of their communication as 'reassuring': 'It was clear, understandable, and it made our values and culture, which were already there, very explicit. It was very transparent, it fed down well, and it was not fluffy'.

She also went on to describe her experience as a new member of the senior leadership team at her first team coaching offsite. Having no previous knowledge of team coaching, she was surprised that it was not more like a team meeting, working through documents and slides. Rather, she experienced it as a space created for the team to 'kick the tyres, in an environment where you could say what you wanted, a safe zone'.

When asked how she would describe team coaching to others, she remarked that it brought 'openness and communication in the team to a new level', and that it 'brought a deep-seated sense of clarity on our key priorities and a sense that we were all aligned and on the same page around achieving those goals'. She mentioned that there is a 'lot of noise' when you are a senior leader, and the team coaching helped them 'get rid of the noise'. She viewed the team coaching as allowing the team to guide themselves and commented that as coaches, we did not 'interfere' and only stepped in to provide light touch structure, ask questions, and make sure that everyone's voice could be heard.

Lessons learned

As team coaches, we have identified several critical learnings for our team coaching practice from working with this client. We appreciate the impact of a genuinely compelling, shared vision and team goals rather than a vision that often is just a list of words. This experience has helped us distinguish, in subsequent team coaching engagements, when a team has developed a purpose that truly energises the team or when there is still further work to be done. It is often a felt sense between us as a team of team coaches, a shared mental model of our acquired knowledge from working with this team that has improved our performance as coaches (Mathieu et al., 2000).

We are clearer that a team has the potential to take a few blocks of output from a team coaching session and build something substantial and transformative beyond the team coaching session. In our case study example, the BHAG and pillars evolved into a performance management system. We consequently are firmer in our expectations of teams to engage in defined objectives in between sessions in ways that are evident and, if possible, measurable. We are more exact about our role as coaches, which is to support teams to lay the foundations, and therefore it is the team's job to build sustainable practices and be self-disciplined to reach their fullest potential.

Conclusion

By engaging the voices of the team coaching client and the team coaches, we have looked at a critical moment in a team coaching case study. The significance of the moment is characterised by the energy and discipline of the team to share and create new and wide-ranging conversations with themselves and their stakeholders that transcend the original discussion from the team coaching session. The critical moment needs to be so compelling that the team want to evangelise it to others and breathe life into it. Spending the time to have genuine and robust conversations on purpose has the potential to invigorate a culture and a performance environment. This case study has enabled us to demonstrate what is possible from team coaching. It has also reminded us that the real impact and potential of team coaching remain firmly in the hands of the team.

Addendum

During the process of drafting and re-drafting this chapter, the case study team engaged us to do a review of the pillars to test out if the pillars remained fit for purpose and would see the organisation through a pandemic and post-pandemic world. The session enabled the leadership team to challenge the merit of each pillar robustly and to review the new pillar for Environment, Social, and Governance (ESG). Since the last review in 2019, the team has added new team members, and it was evident that this collective teasing apart of the pillars progressed their shared understanding and alignment. As coaches, we noticed that working virtually with the team did not impact the quality of the session, and we believe that this is because of the team's experience of using the coaching space, and the quality and depth of our relationship with the team members.

References

Collins, J.C. and Porras, J.I. (1996) Building your company's vision, *Harvard Business Review*, 74 (5): 65–77 [http://search.ebscohost.com/login.aspx?direct=true&db=bth&AN=9609167704&site=eds-live].

Curphy, G. and Hogan, R. (2012) *The Rocket Model: Practical Advice for Building High Performing Teams*. Tulsa, OK: Hogan Press.

De Haan, E., Bertie, C., Day, A., and Sills, C. (2010) Clients' critical moments of coaching: Toward a 'client model' of executive coaching, *Academy of Management Learning & Education*, 9 (4): 607–621 [https://doi.org/10.5465/amle.9.4.zqr607].

Dinh, J.V. and Salas, E. (2017) Factors that influence teamwork, in E. Salas and R. Rico (eds.) *The Wiley Blackwell Handbook of the Psychology of Teamwork and Collaborative Processes* (pp. 15–41). Malden, MA: Wiley.

Greiner, L.E. (1998) Evolution and revolution as organisations grow, *Harvard Business Review*, 76 (3): 55–67 [http://search.ebscohost.com/login.aspx?direct=true&db=edb&AN=547117&site=eds-live].

Mathieu, J.E., Goodwin, G.F., Heffner, T.S., Salas, E., and Cannon-Bowers, J.A. (2000) The influence of shared mental models on team process and performance, *Journal of Applied Psychology*, 85 (2): 273–283 [https://doi.org/10.1037/0021-9010.85.2.273].

Systemic team coaching essentials: Global Leadership Community case study

Michael Shell

Introduction

This case study is written to support team coaches and team leaders developing a multidimensional systems perspective in their work. While it is intended to help all teams, it will be especially useful for adaptive purposeful teams working towards a sustainable future.

I am cautious not to reduce systemic team coaching to a simple step-by-step process, as it is complex, adaptive, and evolving. Instead of speaking as the expert, I will weave in stories from the Global Leadership Community (GLC) integrated with insights from my coaching career. I am speaking from the role of a GLC founder, team leader, storyteller, and participant. These insights should by no means be considered whole and complete, but part of the journey in the discovery of teaming and team leadership.

The GLC is an intentional leadership community of coaches and change agents utilising coaching, World Café, Open Space Technology, Holacracy, and other collaborative leadership development methodologies to evolve society through conversations that matter. The GLC formed spontaneously and grew organically. While the original idea was to gain experience organising a single World Café conversation, it was clear at the first event a community had been formed and it developed a life of its own. It is understood that whatever is shared in the community is available to everyone. If someone has their own intellectual property, we ask them not to share it.

The GLC consists of four main stakeholder groups: society at large, event participants, the leadership team, and the individual leaders. We have held 22 events across four countries; collaborations with the International Coaching Federation (ICF) Manila, two Future of Leadership events, and we have hosted conversations with over a thousand participants. Our vision is, that through conversations and innovative ways of working together, to help shift society from the dominant reductionistic materialistic worldview to a holistic, sustainable worldview that recognises our true state of interconnectedness.

This is an unorthodox case study for the following reasons. The team coaching facet emerged organically from the inside out. We never contracted with an external team coach and as a non-profit organisation we had no financial responsibilities. We were all part-time contributors, and team members often changed from event to event. We were accountable to no one but ourselves. 'Our client was societal unmet needs', said leader Mick.

This case includes 11 essential qualities for team coaches and team leaders. Having been born into a family of five children to a mother who was a family therapist, I began systemic thinking at an early age. It builds on 20 years of study into the fields of human development, consciousness, conscious evolution, as well as leadership coaching, team coaching, coaching supervision, and community leadership.

The dream

It wasn't until later reflection that I realised the GLC was the fulfilment of a long-held dream to be part of an organisation of teams where the coaching was the common method of communication. Co-workers are learning and laughing together. Constructive feedback is integrated into regular interactions. People ask generative questions more than they direct. Conflict is embraced as an opportunity to grow; appreciation is the norm and we support one another to the best versions of ourselves.

The GLC team approach

Our process ensures all voices are heard. We build on each other's ideas and do our best to ensure balance between speaking with listening, doing and being, directing and reflecting, as well as convergent and divergent thinking. Our vision inspires us and our purpose serves as a foundation of trust that sustains us when things are difficult.

We experiment with ways to choose World Café conversation topics, how to design events and meetings, onboarding new leaders, and ways to give and receive feedback. We have no bosses. Instead, we created an innovative governance approach that grants teams full authority to make their own decisions given clear accountabilities, clear roles, and a purpose that aligns with the GLC purpose. This approach gives people the autonomy to make their own decisions and ensures the community is not dependent on individual personalities. New members are mentored and supported by an onboarding programme.

We created a manual to support other communities that might want to form emergent leadership communities. We created a mission statement, a purpose statement, guidelines for working together, and the 7 Principles, which follow below.

The 7 principles

1. **Effortless effort:** We practise working from choice in alignment with our values. We take action from joy instead of from obligation.
2. **There's nothing to fix:** We practise responding to life as it is rather than from how we think it should be.
3. **Assume best intentions:** We assume that the actions of others come from the intention to benefit the greatest good.
4. **Every voice matters:** We listen and value every voice, whether spoken or unspoken.
5. **Embrace emergence:** We enter conversations with curiosity and listening for what wants to arise in the moment.
6. **Distributed leadership:** Everyone has intrinsic leadership qualities. We support everyone's greatest qualities to shine in community and encourage leaders to align accountabilities with their leadership challenges.
7. **Playfulness, experimentation, and life-long learning:** We maintain a child-like, open attitude of curiosity and playfulness.

The 11 essential qualities of high-value teams

Our non-judgemental approach supported by a shared purpose created an atmosphere that supported accelerated learning. The insights gleaned from our leadership learning laboratory are shared below to support team leaders and team coaches.

> **Quality 1: A multidimensional perspective.** An effective team coach and team leader holds a multidimensional perspective. This means being able to sense the context and viewpoints in which the team members perceive their worlds. This creates the space for all voices to be heard, even contradictory voices. As Keith shared, 'we became skilful at suspending our preconceived notions from the past. We would share them, listen for how others would respond, let me them go and lean into what wanted to happen next. We learned not to ask who came up with a novel idea. We often didn't know and ultimately it didn't matter. It was as if the idea came from the field'. In my experience, each individual perspective is true, but is limited. To hear the fullest truth, one needs to hear all voices, both spoken and unspoken. This takes a beginner's mind.
>
> **Quality 2: The beginner's mind.** As we matured, the GLC team became more curious about divergent viewpoints and less attached to our individual points of view. By taking time to slow down and adapt a beginner's mind, new perspectives not previously considered emerge. As our curiosity grows, we develop the capacity to listen and our growth expands exponentially. 'When we let go of our limited perspective and

self-consciousness, spontaneity arose. Not knowing became a powerful reference point', shared Scarlett. We learned that the answer usually wasn't what we initially expected.

Quality 3: Creating the container. The container is a field of energy cultivated collectively with the team to create a psychological safe space. It allows team members to trust whatever is said will be listened to and respected even when not agreed with. Maintaining the container includes ongoing contracting ensuring people are comfortable sharing authentically, allowing deep insights and new wisdom to emerge.

In the GLC, many experienced being their true self with another, often for the first time. Yoshi, one of the early team leaders reflected, 'I will never forget my first leadership meeting. I felt so accepted. Everyone seemed interested in everything I said. There were no judgements. I felt safe to be myself and I experienced myself being seen for who I truly was'.

Our container often felt sacred. It created a space for quality conversations to take place which connect us at a deep level and create shared meaning. According to Yoshi, 'in some meetings I felt like we were jazz musicians. We were so tuned into each other; we truly didn't know what we were going to say and when it was said it was as if the conversation was happening through us'. These moments can be described as 'flow states', times of synchronicities where answers, connections, and gifts arrived at the moment they were needed. The outcomes were not predictable from conventional reductionistic frameworks and were not possible from independent thinking.

Quality 4: Reflective practice. We started meetings by checking in on how each person was feeling and how we imagined the team was feeling. We ended by reflecting on what was learned and what changes in process, if any, we wanted to make to our system. This reflective practice ensured mutual support and ongoing learning. By reflecting together, we became more aware of our biases, mental models and our beliefs. We also became better at letting go of our individual positions and we began to develop our systemic listening capabilities.

We developed the capacity of building on other team members' ideas and tapping into new intelligence. Kyoko shared: 'it was like weaving a tapestry, as we listened to each other we would add new ideas, then someone else would get inspired and weave in their thoughts, laying knowledge and creating synergistic ideas'.

We discovered in our vigorous reflective practice that the more vulnerable we became, the less time and energy was needed for defending or holding on to a position. We became a living system, which allowed us to work as a unit instead of working as individual parts. This brought us to effortless effort, which meant fewer 're-do's' were required.

Quality 5: Sensing. Sensing means being aware of what is happening in the room or a place in the present moment. We developed our sense-making capacities by listening to the spaces between words, noticing the emotional field, where people look when they speak, what was being said or not said, how people were sitting or standing, the pace of a conversation, which dimension and worldview of reality people were speaking from, and so on. We accelerated the team learning by asking team-based questions, such as: What do you sense is being asked of the team? What do you sense the team is feeling now? What metaphors describe the team today and into the future?

Another aspect of sensing is pattern spotting. We discovered that our discovery conversations often gave the perspective of the interior and exterior state of the individual as well as the collective, as outlined in Ken Wilbur's 4-Quadrant model.

Quality 6: Nested systems. Everything exists inside a larger system and systems can been seen in its parts. This means nothing is separate and everything we do impacts everyone else in some way. As a team coach entering a system you become part of that system. You are never separate. Like a fractal, each part reflects the design of the whole.

In the GLC team, we recognised ourselves as mirrors of each other. The qualities someone dislikes about another often are qualities we dislike about ourselves, or they are hidden or undeveloped qualities. Constructive feedback gives us access to our unconscious thoughts and behaviours. The system became a self-reflecting organism that supported individual growth as well as supporting the sustainability of the system itself.

Quality 7: Embrace diversity of diversity. To get the most out of each event, we formed leadership teams with the greatest diversity. We considered age, gender, religion, race, sexual orientation, emotional intelligence, personalities, processes for meaning-making, levels of self-awareness, levels of maturity, common-sense assumptions, leadership styles, ways of making decisions, personalities, cultural backgrounds, emotional states, relationships to change, communication styles, depth of self-awareness, system intelligence, ways of dealing with stress, personal shadows, maturity levels, and others. We learned as a team diversity is one of our core strengths.

Quality 8: Clear team roles. All teams have internal and external roles. External roles in the GLC included promoter, facilitator, logistics, survey tabulator, storyteller, and social media manager. Internal roles included peacekeeper, supporter, challenger, bridge, and disrupter. We learned to be aware of the nuances of roles, the fact that roles are not people, roles belong to the system and, when not occupied well, the team should discuss the role instead of attacking the person filling the role. To provide new perspectives, from time to time roles should shift between individuals.

We also considered ghost roles. They came from roles previously occupied by someone no longer on the team or team members' voices not being heard. It is the purpose of ghost roles to disturb the system until recognised. We noticed and listened for the ghost roles, and the team discovered new possibilities to help fill gaps in the system.

Quality 9: Holistic perspective on privilege. The reductionistic shame-based perspective on privilege needs to evolve to one that is more holistic and empowering. This perspective posits that there are many types of privilege, including the social, economic, spiritual, language, moral, psychological, economic, gender, and educational. Unconscious use of privilege can have devasting effects on people. It is time to understand our privilege and own it. Some is earned and some you are born into. Discovering your privilege is not easy though. It is obvious when you don't have it, but when you have it you are likely the last to know. We learned by helping team members recognise their privilege, and to be open and curious towards those without it, teams can benefit by its hidden gifts. Instead of feeling shame, they can share their privilege to benefit the team's larger system.

Through the GLC feedback, I learned that my fast-paced, Western style of communication sometimes disenfranchised others working in Asia. For example, I developed psychological privilege (feeling comfort in my own skin), supported by the cultural structures in which I was born into as a white middle-class male. Once the team made a decision, I often wanted to move to the next item under discussion. I hadn't realised some had agreed to a team decision to maintain harmony even though in reality they didn't agree with that decision. They were uncomfortable to speak up for themselves in the moment and felt marginalised. I learned to honour people's processes and to give them the time they need to make decisions.

Quality 10: Conflict as an opportunity to grow. Not everything was peachy keen with the GLC. As with every team I have worked with, we had our share of conflict. Our conflicts included how to engage with outside communities, choosing themes, and scheduling. However, because we had a clear purpose and the shared agreement to embrace conflict as an opportunity to grow, we were able to resolve any conflict quickly.

When we remembered to shift our attention to our purpose, we experienced better decisions, greater efficiency, and more learnings. We learned that most, if not all, conflict can be resolved quickly if people can expand their viewpoint to include larger versions of reality; seeing the issue from the other's perspective and from the perspective of the stakeholders. We learned from the harvest session of GLC V: Creative Conflict, 'there is no failure when the value of learning exceeds the cost of the failure'.

Quality 11: Context shifting. When we were stuck, often it was because we were operating from different contexts. Shifting from our personal or team perspective to a broader context helped us to see the interconnectedness of an issue, spot patterns, and solve the problem with new creative ideas.

Our first principle, 'Effortless effort', allowed us to relax around tension and sense what wanted to happen. More often than not, what needed to happen was a shift in perspective, instead of someone needing to change. By exploring our 'stuckness', we learned that context creates meaning. For example, at one event a leader complained about trash not getting taken out. Through reflection, he was able to see he was attacking the person by judging their intent instead of focusing on the issue and the deeper values at play. Upon realising this, not only was the issue resolved immediately but we created the Principle, 'Assume best intentions'.

Our shared agreements allowed failure, and team members transformed what was framed as a negative into necessary steps in their learning journeys. Questions that helped us shift context included: What is the perspective of our stakeholders? What is happening between us that isn't about one of us in particular? What is the bigger pattern? What is the story we are telling that keeps us stuck? In what ways is our story true and untrue? How is the opposite point of view also true? These questions helped reveal information not previously available. By reflecting on these questions, we began to realise there are many different layers to life and to truth. We learned that nothing is ever black and white, and we rarely have the full truth. We developed the capacity to spot patterns that reveal deeper truths in the system.

Conclusion

The GLC experience taught me that by cultivating diverse and divergent viewpoints, we can co-create new perspectives we hadn't considered in the past. Given the breakdown of systems, the speed of work today, the growing complexity and interconnectedness in our work, as well as the increased social isolation, it is clear team coaching will play a central role in the evolution of humanity. Its growth is coming at just the right time. We are at a turning point. I believe we can continue operating from the ageing materialistic, reductionistic operating system, which includes working for short-term results, living as separate entities with individual mindsets, while ignoring our impact on the planet. Or, we can upgrade to a holistic, systemic operating system that recognises our interconnected nature and embraces the unknown. As we do this, I believe we will cultivate our imagination and create families, organisations, and communities that are sustainable. My hope is by sharing what was learned in the GLC, problems that previously seemed unsolvable will begin to dissolve and we become custodians of a sustainable future that works for everyone.

Team coaching in a professional services firm: A case study of internal and external team coaching in a complex adaptive system

Angela Wright and Sarah Tennyson

Introduction

The North American practice of a global law firm was experiencing high levels of interpersonal conflict, burnout, and turnover coupled with low levels of engagement, motivation, and productivity. The firm was divided along hierarchical lines with a strong 'us' and 'them' mentality operating to create mistrust and a lack of cohesion between lawyers and non-legal staff. This impacted how work was getting done within the firm and the maintenance of important client relationships.

Conceptualising the firm as a complex adaptive system (CAS) – a dynamic network of interacting systems that adapt and respond to both the internal and external environment – this case study describes how a team coaching engagement led by an external and an internal coach helped shift the firm's culture and enhance collaboration, motivation, and performance across the firm, thus improving both client engagement and staff retention.

Despite some very positive results, the coaching was not without its challenges and missteps along the way. Viewing the experience in terms of complex and dynamic patterns, the management of anxiety was identified as one of the core themes that emerged during the process. Moreover, the coaching illuminated some of the critical differences of coaching within a professional services context.

First, this case study describes the context and the broader system as critical considerations in the coaching process. Next, it provides an overview of the contracting, inquiry, design and development phase. Selected components of the coaching engagement along with key learning are highlighted. Finally, this case study shares key insights emerging as a result of the coaches' supervision and reflective practice.

Context and broader system

The legal service industry is experiencing unprecedented, radical, and disruptive change. Lawyers face a fundamentally different legal landscape – one characterised by a myriad of interconnected internal and external challenges.

Within law firms, low levels of wellbeing and resilience, elevated anxiety, depression, and burnout have traditionally been accepted as inherent in the practice of law. Despite growing international concern about wellbeing in the legal profession, significant challenges still remain, including poor management, achieving billable hours, managing work–life balance, and navigating often competitive and perfectionist cultures that have historically worn 'overwork' as a badge of honour (Wright, 2020).

These internal challenges are compounded by external pressures such as increasing client demands, discounted prices, shrinking margins, disruptive technologies, shifting demographics, outsourcing of legal services, global mergers, and the collapse of a number of large law firms resulting from the sweeping structural changes since the Global Financial Crisis in 2008.

At the International Bar Association's 17th International M&A conference in 2018, in-house counsel observed that resolving complex legal issues is necessary, but no longer sufficient. Today's lawyers need the capacity to think more strategically, more systemically, to 'connect the dots'. They need to respond to tomorrow's challenges today, to be proactive, not reactive, and to work collaboratively and innovatively based on an intimate understanding of a client's business and environment.

Contracting, inquiry, design and development phase

The external coach had been coaching at the firm for more than two years. 'Harvesting the learning' from multiple coaching assignments indicated that there were some significant and reoccurring issues that were impacting the firm's relationships with clients and contributing to low levels of engagement and increased staff turnover. These issues had been shared with senior members of the firm and members of the HR team. Various developmental initiatives were explored with a focus group who had been brought together for the purpose of addressing these concerns and steering the design of the intervention ultimately delivered. Initial discussions about team coaching created a heightened level of anxiety in the group. What would this look like? What would it mean? What would it require? Visions and rumours of intimate group therapy type sessions requiring personal disclosures ran riot.

Ultimately, it was agreed that the results of a 'future-back/outside-in' inquiry would determine the most appropriate type of intervention. This included environmental scanning, review of client feedback, and semi-structured interviews with selected members of the firm. During the interviews it became apparent that there were some very different, seemingly irreconcilable views across the firm about the firm's future strategic direction, its culture and leadership, and consequently what the requisite development would need to look like.

Eventually, the focus group agreed to pilot a team coaching intervention. The external coach initially suggested that social network analysis (SNA) be used to identify a diverse group of team members based on their connectivity and relational influence within the system. The aim of SNA is to understand a system by mapping the relationships that connect them as a network.

However, the focus group was concerned that this approach would result in a team comprising individuals holding different positions within the firm, with potentially very different perspectives. They requested the team comprise practice group leaders only. After extensive discussions, it became apparent that certain power dynamics and tensions might create too much anxiety within the team, thereby eroding trust and limiting possibilities for change. Given this, a compromise was reached: partners who were not practice group leaders were also included in the team.

Overview of the programme and purpose

The programme comprised an initial two-day workshop followed by monthly team coaching sessions over a 12-month period. A number of theoretical perspectives, tools, techniques, and skills were shared during the two-day workshop, including but not limited to complex adaptive systems (Cavanagh, 2013; Stacey 2011), broaden-and-build theory (Fredrickson, 2001), and dialogue (Isaacs, 1999). These were identified, highlighted, and explored during the coaching sessions. The team purpose was also co-created during the first part of the two-day workshop:

> *To learn to create and maintain a culture of engagement, high performance, learning, and wellbeing, while proactively meeting the current and future needs of external stakeholders.*

The firm as a complex adaptive system

Key characteristics of a CAS were used to help team members understand firm dynamics, behaviours, and attitudes. In a CAS, cause and effect are not linear; properties such as behaviour, roles, practices, processes, engagement, performance, culture, etc. emerge from complex relationships and interactions within and beyond the system. A system is more than the sum of its parts; it is a complex set of interconnected interacting subsystems that self-organise into characteristic patterns of interaction. For example, the concept of emergence helped the managing partner understand his role in enabling unhelpful behaviours that permeated across the firm: 'Our most demanding partners are also our biggest rainmakers, they bring in a lot of work. These individuals demotivate others, which leads to lower levels of performance and wellbeing across the firm. In trying to keep everyone happy, I have enabled this'.

A number of approaches were used to scaffold systems thinking. For example, network mapping became a useful tool to bring the relational elements of personal challenges or goals to life. The concept of feedback loops was also explored. Team members were asked to draw a representation of a work-related challenge or relationship issue – identifying the reciprocal relationships between their thoughts, feelings, emotions, behaviour, and actions. One team member observed: 'Suddenly it became clear, I was part of the problem. My responses were causing others to react defensively, which irritated me. We were in a vicious cycle, so I experimented with small changes to try to break that cycle'.

Through reflecting on patterns and themes, the team also began to recognise *attractors* in the system (such as rules, assumptions, processes, people, knowledge, structures, practices, conversations, power dynamics, and outside influences), which shaped choices and exerted a powerful influence on both individual and collective behaviour. Certain attractors were trapping the firm into rigid patterns of thinking, leading to lower energy and performance. For example, a senior partner commented: 'We shared everyone's billable hours weekly so that we could better utilise those that were not busy. This resulted in competitive behaviour and holding on to clients and new work. This unintended consequence was an unseen attractor that was demotivating many'.

Disruption, change, disagreement, challenge, conflict, and uncertainty all cause anxiety within a system, which often elicits defensive or reactive responses that aim to return the system to a stable equilibrium or homeostasis. Understanding and acknowledging these processes as they were occurring 'in the room' and recognising such processes at play in the broader system became a critical component of the coaching endeavour. It was important that anxiety be managed not removed. To this end, the coaches introduced exercises to enhance positive emotions and create a positive emotional climate.

Creating a positive climate

The coaches attempted to help the team manage negative affect through normalising it, reframing it as an opportunity for growth and development and through providing scaffolding for efforts to develop new perspectives. Exercises to enhance positive emotions (e.g. gratitude exercises and the use of strengths) were also used to help undo the effects of negative emotions, broaden cognitive and behavioural capacities, and to build personal resources for coping, such as optimism, social relations, and resilience. The coaches also attempted to facilitate the expression of positive affect as an integral part of the dialogue, drawing on elements of appreciative inquiry and solutions-focused coaching. Consistent with research on positivity, the team reported that this enhanced creativity and improved interpersonal relationships.

Relevantly, experiencing positive emotions also assists the concordance of personal goals and values with the emerging outcomes of the team, and boosts personal meaning and transcendence so that strengths and goals are enacted in the service of something bigger than self. This was noticeable in the team as their language began to change from 'I' to 'we'.

Practising dialogue

The team found Issac's (1999) conceptualisation of dialogue particularly useful. During dialogue we must be able to suspend our own point of view long enough to understand another's perspective. This creates a 'tension', not least for lawyers who have been trained to 'win' in an adversarial legal system. Using real and hypothetical situations, the team practised asking questions and becoming curious instead of providing an opinion and letting go of, or at least quietening, their inner critic. They were encouraged to notice, test, and question their assumptions. One team member shared: 'At times it was virtually impossible for me not to jump in to defend my position. I realised that I did this in all my conversations, and I began to see the broader negative impact it was having'.

They practised reflective listening, not only to hear what others were saying, but to understand their point of view – what deeper meanings were being expressed and why this was important to the speaker. The team were asked to reflect on failed or stuck conversations, identifying the relevant choices they had made and where that led the conversation. The coaches shared examples of common derailers (e.g. holding back, prematurely rushing into action, making assumptions), asking team members to reflect on the part they played in their conversations.

The team also practised listening for strengths and value in other perspectives, advocating or presenting the perspectives of others and engaging in dialogue on paradoxes. This helped them discover new and more useful options to improve their collective learning and to see multiple perspectives, both inside and outside the team. They began to co-create joint understandings, shared meanings, and strategies for action, including coming up with more creative and innovative ideas to support employee engagement and for generating new business across practice areas rather than through the traditional silos.

Reflections and implications for practice

Supervision and fitness for purpose

Supervision and reflective practice were a critical part of the engagement. For the first couple of months, the coaches came together to reflect on the previous session and the patterns that were emerging across sessions. The coaches also worked one-on-one with their own supervisor. It became apparent, however, that more was needed. The internal coach did not have the same level of experience as the external coach and found their one-on-one supervision insufficient, since its focus was on the development of skills and competencies. This highlighted the critical importance of joint supervision for team coaching pairs and choice of supervisor.

For the remainder of the engagement, the coaches worked jointly with a supervisor who practised as a team coach, had a sophisticated understanding of the dynamics of CAS, and worked from a systemic, developmental perspective. This allowed the coaches to increase their capacity to take multiple systemic perspectives, gain a greater appreciation of the predispositions of their own system, see various stakeholder perspectives and the complexity of interpersonal dynamics, including those in the coach–client relationship. We have argued elsewhere that this is essential if coaches are to remain relevant and fit for purpose (Wright et al., 2019). Joint supervision also became a useful forum to explore the dynamic between the coaches and for practising, and agreeing, ways of working more effectively as a coach team.

Attractors: Context matters

While many significant insights emerged during the supervision process, the most powerful related to the importance of recognising attractors in the system and the critical differences of team coaching within a professional services context. During supervision, the coaches were able to explore attractors and subsequently engage in discussion around those attractors with the team. Recognising that attractors can occur at many levels (intrapersonal, interpersonal, team, organisational, industry, market) and across time was crucial. For example, law firms face disruption and complexity in the present, a fight to stay relevant and a fear for survival in the future, and hundreds of years of tradition that pull towards the homeostasis of the past. Being mindful of these attractors and the interrelationships and interplay between them became vitally important for the team. Team members provided feedback as follows: 'We began to see that our history as a profession was holding us back. There was an unspoken hierarchical culture that was inconsistent with our espoused culture'. The team also acknowledged that they, like many members of the firm, were highly sceptical and often problem-focused – and identified these as attractors that were at play within the team and across the firm.

A microcosm of the bigger system

Most professional services firms operate as a partnership, resulting in a distinctive leadership model. This has many implications in terms of hierarchy, power dynamics, and feedback loops. During the coaching, for example, it became evident that different levels of expertise, seniority, and credibility were being attributed to the coaches. The team often tried to defer to the assumed 'expertise' of the external coach while downplaying the contributions of the internal coach. In turn, the internal coach tended to show deference to the team members who were partners in the firm. By naming the pattern, the coaches helped the team see how it paralleled a broader dynamic across the firm.

This situation was also compounded by the fact that the internal coach wore multiple hats, which caused a number of potential conflicts of interest, confidentiality issues, and ethical dilemmas. This highlights the critical importance of supervision for both internal and external coaches. The external coach noticed and commented on this dynamic during the contracting stage. With hindsight, however, this may have caused less resistance if this had been done once some of the fundamental concepts of CAS had been shared with the team. Moreover, perhaps this dynamic would not have been so focused on the internal coach if the team had comprised members with different roles and functions. No doubt this would have created more tension in the team but may have brought new and valuable information and perspectives. In future team coaching assignments, we would recommend introducing CAS concepts at the focus group stage.

Coach contracting: Differing philosophies

It also became apparent that the coaches operated from different philosophical perspectives. For the internal coach, using a coaching model was fundamental to the coaching process. The external coach preferred a more emergent process. During supervision, the internal coach reflected that 'supervision helped me reflect on my behaviour during the coaching sessions. I felt a sense of responsibility to the partners, which resulted in a greater discomfort with ambiguity, so I would often jump in to try to create a sense of order'. Conversely, the external coach was more comfortable with the ambiguity, and as such, welcomed chaos a little too often. Balance was key. This emphasises the importance of a level of alignment, shared expectations, and contracting between the coaches.

Conclusion

This case study has attempted to demonstrate how adopting a CAS approach in team coaching built awareness of the multiple complexities in a system, which challenged existing frames of reference producing a tipping point – crystallising the need for change. Specifically, the team coaching design and process introduced new attractors, which resulted in slow, yet marked, changes in the way the team members thought, acted, and engaged. As role models of new behaviour, team members also became new attractors in the broader firm, which resulted in some significant shifts in levels of engagement, performance, and wellbeing. This also led to new innovative approaches to work practices and client relationship-building.

For the coaches, an appreciation of the broader context and the dynamics of operating in a professional services firm was crucial, not least in terms of being able to recognise and work with the attractors in the system. Moreover, if coaches are to assist clients in the co-creation of new perspectives, helping them recognise patterns within the interconnected web of their complex experience, this case study highlights the need to be mindful of the part the coaches play in co-creating that dynamic and pattern of interactions. This is particularly important for the internal coach, who may be recreating familiar organisational patterns within the coaching engagement. In this context, reflective practice and coaching supervision become a critical component of any team coaching engagement, an essential part of a coach's professional and ethical responsibility, and crucial if team coaches are to become and remain relevant and fit for purpose.

References

Cavanagh, M. (2013) The coaching engagement in the 21st century: New paradigms for complex times, in S. David, D. Clutterbuck, and D. Megginson (eds.) *Beyond Goals: Effective Strategies for Coaching and Mentoring*. London: Gower.

Fredrickson, B.L. (2001) The role of positive emotions in positive psychology: The broaden-and-build theory of positive emotions, *American Psychologist*, 56 (3): 218–226.

Isaacs, W. (1999) *Dialogue: The Art of Thinking Together*. New York: Doubleday.

Stacey, R.D. (2011) *Strategic Management and Organisational Dynamics: The Challenge of Complexity*, 6th edition. Harlow: Pearson Education.

Wright, A. (2020) Enhancing Lawyer Well-Being & Performance Through the Coaching Ripple Effect, *Law Practice Today*, 14 January [https://www.lawpracticetoday.org/article/enhancing-lawyer-wellbeing-performance-through-the-coaching-ripple-effect/].

Wright, A., McLean Walsh, M., and Tennyson, S. (2019) Systemic coaching supervision: Responding to the complex challenges of our time, *Philosophy of Coaching: An International Journal*, 4 (1): 107–122.

Unfolding team power and increasing psychological safety by effectively addressing a taboo subject

Robert Wegener

Team coaching assignment

In September 2019, I received a call from an institution that helps men suffering from various addictions to find their way back into society. This means helping them to control their addictions, to organise independent living arrangements, and to find a job, thereby becoming financially autonomous. The call was from the head of professional integration and, at that time, the institution's ad-interim managing director. (Since he became the full-time managing director during the team coaching assignment, I will no longer use the term ad-interim manager but managing director instead.) He wanted me to organise a team coaching session with him and his eleven colleagues, including therapists, job attendants, job coaches, and a social worker.

I was interested and asked what the objective of team coaching was exactly. After apparently experiencing difficulties with a former managing director, team coaching was intended to help the team come up with a suitable vision and strategy for the coming years. In a follow-up call, it became clear that the once successful and prosperous institution had encountered some problems in the past. Furthermore, the managing director spoke of ongoing tensions between the therapists and the job attendants. He, nonetheless, insisted on focusing on the future and on working together effectively.

Due to the various topics and me not being fully aware of how much the past still influenced the team and the level of psychological safety within it, I decided to first get an impression of the challenges based on individual sessions with all the team members: the managing director, his assistant, the administrator, the social worker, the two therapists, and the five job attendants. This would be an important starting point for a bespoke team coaching process and additionally help to rapidly build working alliances with all the team members. My argument was that since coaching would eventually take longer, the one-to-one sessions would be a cost-effective investment. I summarised that the assignment was about clarifying the vision and strategy of the institution and, as such, the process should help strengthen the team.

One-to-one sessions and first team coaching session in November 2019

During the one-to-one sessions, I wanted to learn more about the individual perspectives of the team members. I was particularly curious about their opinions related to the need for a vision for the institution as well as already existing ideas on this. Furthermore, I wanted to discover more about what had happened in the past and its effect on current team dynamics, as I was unsure about this aspect based on the managing director's descriptions alone. The interviewees were all open, curious, and precise in their statements as well as in their descriptions of the institution. It was quite striking that the participants' perspectives were biased somewhat due to their individual roles but still relatively homogeneous and compatible concerning emerging topics.

Initially, I invited each team member to reflect on individual and collective strengths, as it seemed important to strengthen the team's self-confidence first. Moreover, identifying its strengths was also essential in terms of clarifying the institution's future vision:

> 'Offers specifically aimed at men'.
>
> 'Well-trained specialists (therapists, job attendants, job coaches, and a social worker)'.
>
> 'Strong commitment to work, and an acute understanding and sympathy for the residents'.
>
> 'Working in a privileged institution that does a good job for its residents'.
>
> 'Very meaningful work for the residents in addition to therapy' (= building/renovating homes).
>
> 'Dealing honestly with each other within the team' (saying what annoys you).
>
> 'A team that shows perseverance, resilience, and patience' (coping with difficult situations).
>
> 'Diversity of characters as well as of knowledge, skills, and attitudes'.
>
> 'A small, tight-knit team'.

Answers regarding important challenges were clustered in the following four team dimensions: (1) goals, (2) resources and skills, (3) performance processes, and (4) internal and external relations (Loebbert, 2013). Examples of topics under each heading include:

1. **Goals**
   - Changing goals in relation to changing work conditions, such as increasing political uncertainty, changing residents (e.g. double diagnoses), increasing expectations of referrers, residents (individualisation), and society (e.g. towards drug addiction).
   - Uncertainty about who will benefit from the institution's services in the future.
2. **Resources and skills**
   - Currently there are only two therapists for 17–18 residents instead of the previous four.
3. **Performance process**
   - Increasing the relevance of team self-regulation skills after a long period of dominant team leaders.
   - A need to update an outdated addiction treatment concept based on an ongoing change from 'phase plans' to 'individual treatment plans'.
   - A need to act proactively instead of simply reacting to a changing 'addiction landscape'.
4. **Internal and external relations**
   - Constant tensions between the therapists and the job attendants ('inexplicable competition'). The following challenges were mentioned:
     - How can we, as specialists, work better together?
     - How can we focus more on our residents?
     - How can we work together more easily?
     - How can we work better together as a team?

Three major *hypotheses* resulted from these one-to-one sessions:

- The institution's vision was already relatively clear; namely, that the team wanted to remain the leading institution for the comprehensive integration of drug-addicted men.
- Achieving this vision has become a complex challenge because of major external changes, whilst the organisational model was still rather hierarchical instead of more agile. The team, therefore, had to become more self-organised when developing individualised solutions for its residents and referrers.
- The remaining tensions between the therapists and the job attendants were a real threat to the institution and its modernisation process. These tensions seemed to go along with an implicit accumulation of power: the therapists were responsible for therapeutic work, case management, and contact with external authorities, while the job attendants were 'only' in charge of the residents' working and living arrangements.

The team would only be able to find its way out of this challenging situation by addressing relevant topics without unnecessary risks in a psychologically safe environment. Consequently, my idea was to submit the first two hypotheses to the team to determine whether they would agree to them or not. If they would, my intention was to invite the team to work on relevant aspects of a more modern 'addiction treatment concept' (e.g. characteristics of future clients and referrals, dealing with competitors, unique selling points). Secondly, as a solution to the tensions between the therapists and the job attendants, and in relation to the third hypothesis, I wanted the team to examine the idea of an 'inclusion coach'. This idea had emerged during the one-to-one sessions and led to a positive resonance. The role of the 'inclusion coach' would be to support the residents in their development regarding the three integration dimensions, 'addiction', 'work', and 'living'. Depending on each resident's individual needs, available measures and experts would be activated accordingly. Theoretically, anyone in the institution, including the job attendants, and no longer just the therapists, could be considered for such a role if the necessary criteria were met. The effects of this (unusual) coaching approach of introducing a potential solution to an existing problem were very intense, as we will see later.

I discussed my agenda with the managing director, and he agreed with it – as did the team at the beginning of the first team coaching session. An important result of this first session was that all the team members agreed on both hypotheses and worked committedly in subgroups on a more 'modern addiction treatment concept'. As a final point of this first session, I invited the team to examine the idea of an 'inclusion coach'. This led to the session taking a decisive turn. Whatever the advantages of an 'inclusion coach', the disadvantages outweighed them. The issues of additional effort and costs prevailed above all else. I was somewhat surprised by this and offered the team my perspectives: if this new role were not implemented, it would be virtually impossible to overcome the ongoing tensions between the therapists and the job attendants, as an asymmetry of power would continue to exist. After a productive and interesting day (the team said they had not been so productive and enthused for a long time), the team's mood changed radically: 'Not the topic of power again!'; 'We've already had all that! We should be looking ahead!'; 'Power, that's, above all, a lot of responsibility'; 'Finally, an important topic has been raised!' The (unusual) coaching approach of introducing a potential solution to an existing problem had activated a dynamic dialogue that indicated the existence of an as-yet unaddressed topic; namely, how the organisation and the team deals with power and responsibility.

As the agreed end of the first team coaching session was quickly approaching, I initiated a short discussion on what had just happened. I expressed my feeling that we had activated a deeper underlying process. Then I proposed to return to this dynamic dialogue and topic during a follow-up session, as it would most probably stand in the way of any vigorous teamwork. The team agreed, but the heavy atmosphere was palpable to everyone. The managing director, who was also present, said that he felt that this had been an effective session. He seemed satisfied that a hidden topic – namely, dealing with power and responsibility – had finally become visible.

Second team coaching session in February 2020

When preparing for the second team coaching session in February 2020, I was concerned with the question of how the team could deal with the irritation from the previous session. I wanted to increase the possibility of the team working on the said topic, as I guessed that this was highly relevant to unlocking the team's full potential. If they would agree, I had considered various methodological approaches, including Robert Dilts' SCORE model (Dilts and Bonissone, 1999), which, in contrast to many other solution-oriented approaches, also gives room to the clients' problems, in particular the symptoms they currently suffer from and subjective explanations for this. From my point of view, this was an interesting approach, as there appeared to be a bit of a taboo about speaking openly about 'dealing with power and responsibility within the team'. A second option was Steve de Shazer's 'miracle question' (de Shazer and Dolan, 2007) – that is, the question of how the team would recognise that they no longer had a problem in dealing with 'power and responsibility'.

Based on an exchange with the managing director, I developed a final programme for the second team coaching session. We agreed to address the issue of 'power and responsibility', as well as to offer room to work on the vision, strategy, and concept, all in line with the original assignment. Like the first session, there was time to chat before the second session started. After a brief introduction by the managing director, I greeted everyone warmly. All the team members received a handout with the programme overview. When asked whether it seemed appropriate, there was broad approval. I then inquired if the team was willing to reflect on what had happened last time and, in particular, on what had irritated them so much. They were quick to respond:

> 'We're unable to take an impartial view of power'.
>
> 'We've already experienced sufficient abuse of power in the past'.
>
> 'I perceived a pejorative reaction when I spoke positively about the inclusion coach'.
>
> 'The power games have been going on forever. We have to stop this'.
>
> 'We're uncertain about who is responsible for what and who actually wields the power'.
>
> 'There was an increasing awareness last time related to the dual role of power and responsibility'.
>
> 'Power and responsibility are not balanced equally here'.
>
> 'We've never addressed our past experiences'.
>
> 'We urgently need to receive clarification of responsibility'.
>
> 'We have to question how we deal with power in our team and our work with the residents'.
>
> 'What is actually a good way of dealing with power?'

Without fully understanding every aspect of the views, I noticed something valuable was happening. In retrospect, I would describe this as a collective opening of perception to an important taboo subject that had not been touched upon for a long time. The psychologically safe environment allowed every statement made to have new associations. During the first break, I thought an even more in-depth confrontation with 'handling power and responsibility within the team' could now be achieved – that is, how the current situation had come about. The SCORE model seemed ideal for this purpose. I therefore asked the managing director for his opinion and whether he would assist me in this process. He was convinced of the method and was also willing to help by making a note of the statements from the team members. After the break, I introduced the team to this method and asked if they were willing to give it a go. They were.

At first, there was a certain reluctance to describe the 'symptoms' the team members were currently suffering from as a result of 'power and responsibility'. This applied especially to the team members who had previously emphasised the importance of looking forward and not staying in the past. I remained quiet and offered them sufficient space and time. Suddenly, the team started mentioning some severe symptoms: stress, uncertainty, fear, demotivation, helplessness, fatigue, loss of quality, bad moods, feeling misunderstood, and prejudices. When I felt a certain saturation, I invited the team to go to the next point 'causes', referring to individual explanations for the current situation. During a 45-minute exchange, something I perceived as healing and connecting took place. Highly personal experiences were shared, such as manipulation, abuse of power, power vacuums, resignation, deceit, unclear structures, vague roles, structural gaps, and so on. As a meaningful moment (Wegener, 2019), one team member shared with us how much he had actually suffered from existential fears under the previous management, as there were always concerns about being fired suddenly and without any cause.

After lunch, the team continued working on the points: 'outcome', 'effects', and 'resources'. All the points had a clear, positive, and significant impact for the future. This confirmed that the team was on the right path. It also helped the team to accept that all other planned topics would have to be left for another day. As a last assignment, I invited the team to come up with the working steps needed to achieve the stated goals. This resulted in specific self-assignments for the team. At the end, I asked the team to rate the current quality of the team, something they had already done in the morning. As suspected, there was a clear improvement compared with the early morning rating.

The second team coaching session was successful because it allowed the team to participate in a collective experience; namely, to speak openly about problematic experiences and critical aspects of the organisation. Experiences that had never been shared before, thus unleashing an emotional outpouring of pent-up frustration. This allowed me to make the team aware of the importance of psychological safety for the overall success of the team. In other words, the ability to speak openly, honestly, and without unnecessary risks about goal-relevant topics (Clutterbuck, 2020). The positive experience of the quality and the noticeably positive future-oriented attitude of the team made me confident that they had achieved an important result. In line with the systemic idea of change (Schiersmann and Thiel, 2018), I was fully aware that a new equilibrium had not been reached but an important step in this direction had been taken. The next session scheduled for April 2020 was unfortunately cancelled due to Covid-19.

Learning outcome and conclusion

This coaching engagement, based on individual one-to-one sessions and two team coaching sessions, is not yet finished and will continue after a longer break. I have, in the meantime, spoken to the managing director, a job attendant, and the social worker to find out how things are going and how the process has been perceived.

From the discussion with the managing director, it became clear that the team coaching sessions had helped the team to regain its strength and to reduce existing tensions. He wanted to go on with these sessions, as a rational follow-on to what had happened so far, and to further improve the self-organising skills of his team. For him, this is a crucial aspect of working on the institution's future vision, strategy, and goals. He described the team coaching sessions as 'professional and process-oriented events that cover a range of highly relevant topics'.

In comparison, the job attendant I talked to still saw the current situation as challenging. He deeply regretted that the planned team coaching session had been cancelled due to the coronavirus pandemic and was looking forward to addressing additional topics during the next session.

Finally, I spoke to the social worker who has worked at the institution for several decades. He was positive about the team coaching sessions and said that he believed the aforesaid tensions had been overcome and a lasting change in the team had taken place. In his eyes, the sessions had helped to stop ongoing difficult discussions between the therapists and the job attendants, and he too was looking forward to the next session.

As a German saying goes: 'Disturbances take precedence'. This saying summarises what has been the essence of these team coaching sessions so far: helping the team to safely share difficult experiences related to power (abuse) and responsibility, thereby allowing the team to regenerate itself fully. Thanks to the individual one-to-one sessions, a good rapport, well-planned and structured team coaching sessions, and sufficient transparency, the team has been able to open up and overcome difficult past experiences. It appears that the team now has more energy to cope with ongoing changes as a more agile and self-organised team that can deal adequately with rapidly changing requests.

On a personal learning level, I was impressed with how much impact it can have when you offer a team a potential solution ('inclusion coach') to an identified problem ('tensions'). Since it is not ideal to work like this as a team coach,

I will be alert to such issues in the future. Instead, I will try to examine how such an idea can help develop powerful questions that allow a team to generate suitable solutions by itself. Nevertheless, confronting the team with this idea highlighted a taboo subject which might otherwise not have been addressed so quickly.

References

Clutterbuck, D. (2020) *Coaching the Team at Work*, 2nd edition. London: Nicholas Brealey.

de Shazer, S. and Dolan, Y. (2007) *More than Miracles: The State of the Art of Solution-Focused Brief Therapy*. New York: Routledge.

Dilts, R.B. and Bonissone, G. (1999) *Zukunftstechniken zur Leistungssteigerung und für das Management von Veränderungen*. Paderborn: Junfermann.

Loebbert, M. (2013) Coaching von Teams, in M. Loebbert (ed.) *Professional Coaching – Konzepte, Instrumente, Anwendungsfelder* (pp. 259–275). Stuttgart: Schäffer-Poeschel Verlag.

Schiersmann, C. and Thiel, H.-U. (2018) Was wirkt eigentlich in der Beratung? Auf dem Weg zu einer allgemeinen Theorie der Beratung, in R. Wegener, A. Fritze, M. Hänseler, and M. Loebbert (eds.) *Coaching-Prozessforschung. Forschung und Praxis im Dialog* (pp. 175–193). Wiesbaden: Springer.

Wegener, R. (2019) *Bedeutsame Momente im Coaching. Eine explorative Untersuchung zur Weiterentwicklung der Prozessforschung*. Wiesbaden: Springer Research.

The good, the bad, and the unexpected impact of internal coach on a high-performing team development journey

Helen Zink

Introduction

A team is a complex adaptive system (CAS), described by Cavanagh (2006) and Hawkins (2019) as a group of interdependent parts, which, when combined, create something more than the sum of their parts. Where a team has a coach, the coach is part of the team system too.

In most team coaching engagements, an external coach physically enters and leaves the system to support specific interventions. However, in this case the coach is internal to the organisation and a member of the team being coached. This unique system dynamic presents many challenges and insights.

This case covers a one-year period from the time the coach joined the team to the time this case study was written. Good, bad, and unexpected implications of this unusual coaching engagement are considered. (Note, this case is ongoing at the time of writing, and future opportunities have been incorporated within the team's development plan going forward.)

Context

The subject of this case is a senior leadership team (the team) within a large organisation (the organisation).[1] The team provides key support functions and comprises seven members, including the C-suite leader (the leader) and the coach. The team was newly formed following a restructure, with the coach being the only external appointment. There were many aspects to the coach's role; however, for the purposes of this case, the focus is on coaching.

The first six months of the engagement were challenging for the team. In addition to embedding the new structure, they faced significant system and process changes during a peak delivery period. The team describes this time as a 'perfect storm'. Nine months into the engagement, the worst of the storm was over and the environment was more stable.

Team development purpose

The five-year strategic goal of the team is to become world class within their functional area. The first year of implementation focused on system and process changes. The second year began with the new structure described above, and an increased focus on the people and leadership aspects of change. Enter the coach, and the start of the coaching engagement.

To begin, the coach took time to understand the strategic drivers for change and the organisational and functional context. Around month three, the coach suggested a simple team development goal of 'becoming a high-performing team' (HPT), the rationale being: 'Leaders role-model, set the tone, create culture, and enable others to perform at their best. For the function to be world class, focus must be on the leadership team first'.

The coach created a team development plan based on this goal involving the 'development and delivery of coordinated interventions, based on agreed priorities that would have the most significant impact'. Interventions were aligned with the organisation's culture and development strategy, and the coach's own experience and knowledge. The team development goal and approach were endorsed by the leader and the organisation's HR team.

Effective team coaching needs to work at multiple levels of the system, and here the team development plan is activated in three streams. The first stream is monthly team development days. Interventions and focus topics forming the content of these days are outlined in Table 1. Table 1 also identifies how interventions broadly align with Clutterbuck's (2019) HPT PERILL model, with the addition of wellbeing.

Agendas for development days were created by the coach based on their own judgement. To begin with, the interventions were more foundational, such as strengths and personality profiling. Later, the interventions were more relevant to 'hot topics' the team were facing. For example, during the 'perfect storm' the team's reputation with stakeholders was low, and interventions to address this were selected.

The coach made use of a spectrum of styles when facilitating interventions:

- Teaching at one end of the spectrum, where content was planned in advance and delivered by the coach.
- Facilitation in the middle of the spectrum, where the coach managed the process with a predetermined outcome.
- Team coaching at the other end of the spectrum, which Clutterbuck (2007) and Turner (2019) suggest is an environment where the team, including the coach, collaboratively create content and outcomes in the moment.

Table 1 Interventions and focus topics for team development

Interventions/focus topics	Development area (based on PERILL)	Month 1	2	3	4	5	6	7	8	9	10	11	12
Team development plan	Learning processes												
HPT theory	Learning processes												
Wellbeing and resilience	Wellbeing												
Mindfulness practice	Wellbeing			T	T				T			T	T
Team ground rules	Internal processes		T+F		T+F								
Team delivery plan and prioritisation	Internal processes		T+F		T+F		T+F	T+F	T+F				T+F
Sharing personal stories	Relationships			T+F									
Sharing personal development areas	Relationships									T+F			
Celebrating success	Internal processes						T+F						
Understanding stakeholders and reputation	External processes												
Future vision for team and function	Purpose and motivation												
Describing best self, stressed self (using animals)	Relationships		F										
Myers Briggs/MBTI personality profiling	Relationships			F									
Reflecting on application of previous interventions	Learning processes				F	F	F	F	F	F		F	F
HPT questionnaire and outcomes	Learning processes				F	F		F	F	F			F
Positive leadership theory and application	Leadership					F							
Understanding roles in team (using Lego Serious Play)	Internal processes							F					
Strengths theory, including individual/team application	Internal processes										F+TC	F+TC	F+TC
Leading through change	Leadership												F+TC
Accountability	Relationships										TC	TC	
Collective leadership	Leadership												

Spectrum of teaching (T) vs. facilitation (F) vs. team coaching (TC): T | T + F | F | F + TC | TC

Sometimes a team coaching style of intervention was anticipated and other times it emerged as 'hot topics' came up. The shading in Table 1 broadly outlines styles applied to the interventions selected. In reality, boundaries between teaching, facilitation, and team coaching were often blurred or combined, also reflected in Table 1. The coach observed that over time the team became more willing to take risks, resulting in more opportunity for team coaching style.

The second stream of activity was one-on-one coaching of team members. This included formal prearranged coaching sessions with some, and informal spontaneous coaching conversations with others. The coach also provided direct advice to team members as appropriate.

The third stream of activity was one-on-one coaching of the leader. This played out as day-to-day ad-hoc coaching style conversations, along with direct guidance and support as required. The coach encouraged the leader to create a personal leadership development plan, including formal coaching. However, the leader repeatedly declined, to the frustration of the coach.

Team development outcomes

When the team development goal was established, two objective measures of performance were also established by the coach. The first was the team engagement score, measured using the organisation's own tool. The team score was 8.3 out of 10 at the start of the year, 7.4 during the challenging 'perfect storm' period, and 8.6 at the one-year mark, all versus a benchmark of 7.8.

The second objective measure was a HPT questionnaire based on the organisation's own HPT model, expanded by the coach to be more in line with Clutterbuck's (2019) PERILL model. The overall score moved from 3.1 out of 5 at the three-month mark, to 3.2 at the nine-month mark. Both the coach and leader were disappointed by the modest increase. Increases in some components of the measure were offset by a reduction in team members' perception of leadership quality. Interventions focused on this area were included in subsequent development sessions as a result.

The coach also solicited subjective feedback from the leader and team members one year into the engagement. The leader described improvements in his own leadership style, citing improvements in delegation, collective decision-making, self-awareness, ability to communicate and share long-term vision. The coach thought the most significant changes were an acknowledgement that he needed to lead change himself, manage his leadership style with intent, and role-model the change he expects to see in others. (Note that these observations are the leader's own rather than 360-degree feedback from stakeholders.)

Individual team members' responses to how they had changed over the year included improvements in self-awareness, confidence, and accountability. They also thought the team had improved in the following areas: their understanding of one another, their collective decision-making, trust, learning together, and challenging one another. Also, all agreed benefits gained at the team level were trickling through the wider functional team and wider system. O'Connor and Cavanagh (2013) refer to this as the coaching ripple effect and the coach was pleased the team could see this impact for themselves. Team members and the coach also agreed that although significant progress had been made, some things could have been done differently and there were further opportunities for team development going forward.

External stakeholders were not specifically questioned around changes observed during the engagement period. However, anecdotally the coach believes overall reputation and quality of team deliverables improved.

Learnings: good, bad, and unexpected

Learnings from this case are a combination of insights gained by the coach in practice and reflection, through one-on-one supervision, group supervision, feedback from the leader, and feedback from the team members. As the title of this case study suggests, some learnings were good, some bad, and some were unexpected.

An 'inside job'

The coach thought good aspects included a first-hand understanding of levels within the CAS, including industry, organisation, team, and individual levels. Team members appreciated this too, expressing that:

> 'Having an internal coach meant the coach got to know us really well, how we tick, and how our workload and day-to-day issues affect us. There was no hiding'.

> 'There was first-hand experience in understanding what my development requirements were, and this was incredibly valuable'.

The system and its layers were accessible to the coach throughout the engagement, avoiding reliance on second-hand system understanding.

The coach felt that as a team member they were able to make well-informed judgements on appropriate intervention content and delivery styles. As explained above, interventions often related to real-life 'hot topics' the team were facing. The leader agreed, saying that: 'The coach had a strong understanding of deep dynamics and the interactions across the team system and was able to adapt'.

As the coach interacted with team members on a day-to-day basis, strong relationships and trust were formed, allowing flexibility to experiment with various interventions, in a 'safe to fail' environment. The leader often used the term 'high risk, high return' in relation to team development, which the coach appreciated.

The proximity of the coach made visible how well interventions were 'sticking' in real life. The coach provided ongoing reminders of agreements team members had made and offered adjustments in the moment to support the team's development journey. A team member shared: 'The coach was closely involved in day-to-day activities. This opened a door and opportunity to provide input and support to help us build and grow every day'.

The coach and the leader worked closely together, providing opportunities for the coach to advise, influence, and provide feedback in the moment. This allowed the leader to better align his leadership style with the team's development journey and embed interventions.

The coach, as part of the team, had the opportunity to role-model appropriate and agreed leadership styles and behaviours every day, again reinforcing the development journey.

Blurred lines

Bad aspects of the system dynamics included a lack of clarity of the coach's role. As a result, particularly at the beginning of the engagement, boundaries and scope were blurred, resulting in confusion and frustration for all, including the coach. Although the leader described the coach's role as 'an experiment' and the coach was on board with this, basic scope and boundaries were lacking.

In hindsight, the coach believes the team were not ready for coaching at the start of the engagement. Although the team coaching approach was endorsed, the team may not have understood what they were agreeing to, and early team coaching interventions were of limited success. Team coaching before a team is ready is unlikely to stick.

As the coach's knowledge of the system increased over time, the coach took a stronger leadership role within the team, filling a void left by the leader due to a lack of focus and capacity. Clutterbuck (2017) refers to this as a vacuum trap, and the coach stepped right into this 'blind spot'. The team expressed frustration around role confusion, with 'Who is the boss?' becoming a team catch phrase. Some clarity was gained through subsequent team discussions. However, tension around this area remains at the time of writing.

The coach, as a team member, contributed content as part of team interventions. Sometimes this worked well, with a team member commenting that, 'What could have been an awkward situation was not. Due to ability to juggle many hats, it felt very natural to see the coach as facilitator in some circumstances and as team member in others'. However, the leader did not express the same opinion, saying: 'It sometimes felt as if the coach was holding back somewhat on their team member perspective to enable effective coaching. This left a sense that some things were not addressed at the table'. The coach found the dual role in development sessions extremely difficult to maintain at times.

The bad aspects of the case outlined above would have been mitigated by explicit and ongoing contracting between the coach, the leader, and the team at the beginning and throughout the engagement. Increased clarity of respective roles, expectations, and boundaries within the system would have been beneficial.

Coach to the rescue!

Unexpected aspects of the system dynamics in this case include a lack of accountability of team members to regulate one another. One year on, team members still look to the coach to rescue the situation if agreed ground rules are violated.

The coach has a supportive nature, wanting the best overall outcome for the team. As a result, the coach often took on responsibility for resolving matters rather than coaching team members to do so for themselves. By behaving this way, the coach encouraged a lack of responsibility for leadership within the team, a significant 'blind spot'.

The coach, in the role of team member, felt a lack of support from the rest of the team, particularly at the start of the engagement. A member of the team shared: 'We were all guilty of leaning on the coach as a coach and forgetting they also needed support as a team member'. The leader also expressed he was 'not expecting the need to support the coach during team development sessions'. Sometimes the coach did not feel as though they were part of the team at all.

The relationship between coach and leader was, and continues to be, complicated. As part of their role, the coach is coaching and advising the leader. The leader also coaches the coach in his capacity as line manager. The interplay between the roles results in tension and conflict at times as both struggle to switch between appropriate roles.

Unexpected 'blind spots' within the system outlined above were the focus of regular and ongoing one-on-one and team supervision sessions. The coach was supported with reflection, self-awareness, system awareness, and development of mitigation options.

Future opportunities

The ongoing nature of this case enables the following opportunities to be included in the team's development plan going forward.

The most significant opportunity in this case study is explicit ongoing re-contracting between the coach and leader, coach and team, and the team members with each other. Clarification of expectations, responsibilities, and boundaries of all parties would mitigate many of the bad aspects of the case outlined above. Contracting should also include how parties will support each other to maintain contracts made.

The coach could support the team to collaboratively refresh the team's development plan. This could involve the coach outlining possible interventions to experiment with and the team selecting those they wanted to try. This would create more ownership of and responsibility for interventions, potentially creating an environment for further 'safe to fail' experiments.

There is opportunity for the leader, with support from the coach, to more explicitly embed interventions into day-to-day activity, further reinforcing change. For example, explicit reference to intervention outcomes in team meetings and one-on-one conversations with individual team members.

Clutterbuck (2019) points to the significant impact leadership has on team development in the PERILL model. As mentioned, the leader now recognises his own important role in the team's development journey. The coach should seize this 'ah-ha' moment and support him to create a personal leadership development plan that aligns the leader's own aspirations with the team development journey. The coach, being part of the team, is in the unique position of being able to support the leader with his development on a day-to-day basis. A similar opportunity exists for all members of the team.

The team has observed that their own team development journey has a ripple effect on the wider functional area they lead. This positive impact could be accelerated by widening the scope of successful interventions across other teams and the wider system.

Conclusion

The unique system aspect of this case is that the internal coach is part of the team being coached. There are good, bad, and unexpected outcomes from this arrangement. Good aspects of the 'inside job' include a first-hand understanding of the team system in play, selecting impactful interventions at the right time, and the ability to influence the system on a day-to-day basis in the moment.

Blurred lines between the coach, the leader, and team members are the bad aspects of this case. The main insight is the need for explicit and ongoing contracting between the coach, the leader, and the team throughout the engagement. Contracting is a vital part of any coaching or team coaching arrangement, and even more critical for an 'inside job'.

Unexpected aspects of this case involve the coach coming to the rescue, filling vacuums, and taking on more responsibility for outcomes than they should. These 'blind spots' within the system were the focus of regular and ongoing supervision sessions which the coach heavily relied on throughout the engagement. Supervision is recommended for all coaches and is even more important during complicated engagements such as this.

Although this case is unusual and challenging, the coach believes the benefits of an 'inside job' outweigh blurred lines and the coach coming to the rescue. The leader agrees, saying: 'Having someone embedded in the team ensures that development time is well spent, and learning is constantly connected with real-world execution'.

The leader, the team members, and the coach all agree that significant progress has been made towards their HPT goal. However, this case includes many recommendations for future development areas. As Hawkins (2017) points out, the team development journey should never be seen as a place of arrival, as the nature of a CAS implies that the environment, subsystems, and interrelationships between them are constantly changing. There is a lot that team coaches, internal team coaches, and teams can learn from this case, and the journey continues.

Note

1 The names of the organisation and team members that form the basis of this case are not disclosed to protect confidentiality. The content of this case study, including references to internal organisational information and quotes from team members, have been approved by the organisation for publication.

References

Cavanagh, M. (2006) Coaching from a systemic perspective: A complex adaptive conversation, in D. Stober and A.M. Grant (eds.) *Evidence Based Coaching Handbook*. New York: Wiley.

Clutterbuck, D. (2007) *Coaching the Team at Work*. London: Nicholas Brealey.

Clutterbuck, D. (2017) The leadership vacuum trap and how coaches and mentors can avoid it [https://www.coachingandmentoringinternational.org].

Clutterbuck, D. (2019) Towards a pragmatic model of team function and dysfunction, in D. Clutterbuck, J. Gannon, S. Hayes, I. Iordanou, K. Lowe, and D. MacKie (eds.) *The Practitioner's Handbook of Team Coaching* (pp. 150–160). London: Routledge.

Hawkins, P. (2017) *Leadership Team Coaching: Developing Collective Transformational Leadership*. London: Kogan Page.

Hawkins, P. (2019) Systematic team coaching, in D. Clutterbuck, J. Gannon, S. Hayes, I. Iordanou, K. Lowe, and D. MacKie (eds.) *The Practitioner's Handbook of Team Coaching* (pp. 36–52). London: Routledge.

O'Connor, S. and Cavanagh, M. (2013) The coaching ripple effect: The effects of developmental coaching on wellbeing across organisational networks, *Psychology of Well-Being: Theory, Research and Practice*, 3: 2 [https://doi.org/10.1186/2211-1522-3-2].

Turner, T. (2019) Team coaching: Passing trend or organisational staple?, in D. Clutterbuck, J. Gannon, S. Hayes, I. Iordanou, K. Lowe, and D. MacKie (eds.) *The Practitioner's Handbook of Team Coaching* (pp. 443–454). London: Routledge.

Models & Tools

Foreword: Maps, models, and muddles!

Peter Hawkins

I am pleased to introduce these fascinating case studies of different practitioners from different trainings, working in many countries and varied sectors, each sharing their learning journey. I have long been an active promoter of team coach practitioners sharing the journeys they have gone on with teams who are undertaking the challenging work of reflecting on their own purpose, patterns, and working, and then attempting to develop them, not just for their own benefit but to better serve all their stakeholders (Hawkins, 2014, 2018, 2022). Case studies help us see how other team coaches link theory and practice, models and interventions, but also how they deal with the muddles when the maps and models don't help.

Team coaching is a relatively new field but growing and expanding rapidly. Although the approaches to team coaching have mainly been developed in the last 20 years, its roots go back much further and deeper. This is because it draws, not just on the fields of executive and leadership coaching, but also on the longer traditions of team facilitation, process consultancy, and organisational development (Hawkins, 2021: 74–83).

The best models for team coaches draw on and integrate the best aspects of all these strands, in a way that provides a framework for both understanding the complexity of teams and teaming, and also for the journey and stages of the team coaching process. Some frameworks also draw on other parallel professions such as family systems, systemic theory, cybernetics, ecology, or social psychology (see previous section).

There can often be confusion between different terminologies and how the following terms are used: an approach, a framework, a model, a map, a technique, a tool. These are the building-blocks of a coherent team coaching practice, so I will offer my clarification of these different terms.

> **An approach** is a pre-existent perspective that is brought to the field of team coaching from another field, such as a 'psychodynamic approach', a 'relational approach', or a 'systemic approach'. Two of the cases ('Team coaching for communication continuity' by Michelle Chambers, and 'A case study on team coaching using an appreciative inquiry approach in an educational institution' by Paul Lim) found in this section use an appreciative inquiry approach which emphasises ways of building on the positives.

A framework is a meta-model, a scaffolding. Some frameworks also draw on other parallel professions such as family systems, systemic theory, cybernetics, ecology, or social psychology (see previous section). One case study ('The HR-Partner team at the Swedish Migration Agency' by Peter Englén and Anders Troedsson) used the Team Coaching International (TCI) diagnostic, which was developed from the framework constructed by Philip Sandahl (Sandahl and Phillips, 2019).

A model is a structure for sorting and separating the different aspects of team functioning or the team coaching activities as well as showing the interconnections. The best models for team coaches draw on and integrate the best aspects of all these strands, in a way that provides a framework for both understanding the complexity of teams and teaming, and also for the journey and stages of the team coaching process. Some of the cases here use the systemic team coaching 5 Disciplines model (Hawkins, 2021) or the PERILL model (Clutterbuck, 2020), showing how it informed their focus and design.

A map is a way of capturing the different stages a team may go through in its evolution and development, or the stages in the journey of a team coaching assignment. Some of the case studies have developed their own map of the team coaching stages (e.g. 'Into the void: Building leadership through team coaching in the executive team of a government agency' by Declan Woods and Georgina Woudstra), others have used established process maps such as the CIDCLEAR process (Hawkins, 2021) or Peters and Carr's (2015) six phases of high-performance team coaching.

A tool and technique is a method the team coach can utilise to diagnose or orchestrate a team exploration to help him or her to intervene effectively in a team process. The best tools and techniques are ones that are co-created or developed live with the team and continue to be useful after the team coach has departed. In Jacqueline Peters' case study ('Team coaching for culture change'), we can see an example of a technique she used called 'check-ins and check-outs'. She made use of a series of questions as a specific tool when using this technique.

The best approaches to team coaching provide a **nested approach**, which shows how the tools and techniques are nested in the maps and models, which in turn are nested in the framework and approach. This enables the practitioner to see where the tool or technique is best applied on the team coaching journey, as well as which parts of the model are addressed by which techniques.

Good case studies also provide these nested connections, showing how their approach, framework, and model connect and inform their process design as well as the tools and techniques they use. A good example of this is the way that Chambers uses 'The wall of pride' with her team, a tool that is based on the appreciative inquiry approach.

But we should also recognise that, in the words of Korzybski (1933), 'The map is not the territory'. Neither is a model or framework. Good maps and models help us to explore and open up areas that we and the team may well otherwise be blind to. But maps and models are built on the collective experience of the past, which can blinker us to the unexpected and newness in the emerging future.

Teams are complex and changing systems, as much created by their context as by their members. My colleague and best-selling author, Margaret Heffernan, warns us: 'The temptation to try to simplify complex systems is how you get them wrong; just like profiling, just like any kind of model, what gets left out or what changes can turn out to be vital' (2020: 88).

Good cases studies also show how what emerged in practice also challenged the framework the coach(es) started with – how the journey changed the map. What is very useful about these cases is the reflections the coaches offer on what went well, what did not work, and their learning from both the work and their reflections, including understanding how the journey changed the team's map.

Some clear lessons emerge from both within and between these case examples. Here are some I could glean:

1 **The importance of starting with a clear, well-chosen diagnostic**, which is easily understood by the team members, and which is repeated at the end of the team coaching assignment to both measure progress and to identify where more work needs to be done. At the same time, we need to be alive to what is left out and not focused on, by whatever diagnostic is chosen.
2 **The importance of team buy-in.** Several of these writers realised in retrospect they over-relied on the commitment of the team leader and HR partner to the team coaching and did not spend enough time and attention on getting the buy-in of the whole team. This buy-in needs to be a commitment and not just an agreement to passively go along with the process. This can only be achieved by the team collectively realising that the work is a business imperative and not an optional extra. The more 'successful' outcomes were in the cases where there was a clear and immediate need for change as the team were leading a wider transformation.
3 Many of the team coaches realised they **focused too much on the internal functioning of the team and what the team felt they needed, and did not focus enough on the stakeholders' needs.** Woods and Woudstra realised that although dissatisfaction among key customers and stakeholders was a key driver of initiating team coaching, 'they were largely out of sight during the coaching'. Chambers realised that her work would have been stronger had they started with 'quantifiable as well as qualitative measures from external stakeholders'; a clearer understanding of the team's purpose; and if she had coached the connections and partnership alliances between the team and their stakeholders.
4 **The importance of challenging the assumptions you are constantly making about the team.** These include assumptions you may make about

who the team members are, what the team's purpose is, and what will help the team improve. This is where supervision is so critical and essential, and it is a shame that there is little in the cases about how the team coach took their work to supervision and changed their perspective about ways of working from having done so.

Maps and models are important, but also potentially dangerous. They help you explore areas you might well have not considered without them, but they also shape your thinking, and cause you to see what you expected and experience merely what others have already found. We must never forget that the real learning and the most exciting and scary work in team coaching happens in the midst of muddles, where the team does not have the answer, the team coach does not have the answer, the models, frameworks, maps, diagnostics do not have the answer, but it is clear life is requiring us to find a new response.

We cannot do this important work alone, simply learning at the speed of our own experience. This is where the generous writing and reflection of our colleagues in case studies such as these, enriches the collective collaborative inquiry process that must always be at the heart of team coaching. We, as team coaches, must also be an effective, fast learning, constantly adapting, value-creating team.

References

Clutterbuck, D. (2020) *Coaching the Team at Work*, 2nd edition. London: Nicholas Brealey.
Hawkins, P. (2014) *Leadership Team Coaching in Practice*. London: Kogan Page.
Hawkins, P. (2017) *Leadership Team Coaching: Developing Collective Transformational Leadership*, 3rd edition. London: Kogan Page.
Hawkins, P. (2018) *Leadership Team Coaching in Practice*, 2nd edition. London: Kogan Page.
Hawkins, P. (2021) *Leadership Team Coaching: Developing Collective Transformational Leadership*, 4th edition. London: Kogan Page.
Hawkins, P. (2022) *Leadership Team Coaching in Practice*, 3rd edition. London: Kogan Page.
Heffernan, M. (2020) *Uncharted: How to Map the Future Together*. London: Simon & Schuster.
Korzybski, A. (1933) *Science and Sanity: An Introduction to Non-Aristotelian Systems and General Semantics*. New York: The International Non-Aristotelian Library Publishing Company.
Peters, J. and Carr, C. (2015) *High Performance Team Coaching: A Comprehensive System for Leaders and Coaches*. Calgary, Alberta: InnerActive Leadership Associates.
Sandahl, P. and Phillips A. (2019) *Teams Unleashed: How to Release the Power and Human Potential of Work Teams*. London: Nicholas Brealey.
System for Leaders and Coaches. Calgary, Alberta: InnerActive Leadership Associates.

Navigating crisis with integrative systemic team coaching (ISTC)

Radvan Bahbouh and Pauline Willis

Introduction

Systemic approaches to team coaching offer a sustainable and effective approach to team coaching interventions. Systems impacting on a team are multi-levelled and complex, operating at the individual, team, organisational, as well as the market and societal levels. This set of interrelationships can be misunderstood or key elements ignored or neglected simply because they are not easy to measure, monitor, or manage. Addressing the systemic forces impacting on individual, team, and organisational effectiveness is, however, critical to the success of any coaching intervention, especially during times of change and when the team is facing a crisis.

Using data analytics to reveal the most important influenceable elements of the whole system, in a way that is easy for the team to comprehend and work with, is a new and fundamentally different approach to the way coaches have historically used diagnostics.

In this case study, we will provide only key highlights from the diagnostics to illustrate how the tools were integrated within the coaching process together with a small selection of key outcomes. Readers interested in a detailed overview of the tools and data underpinning this case are referred to Bahbouh and Willis (2020).

Integrative systemic team coaching for an agile SME

An integrative systemic team coaching (ISTC) approach, covering individual, team, organisational, and stakeholder levels, formed the basis of the team coaching process applied within a medium-sized coaching consultancy to support the whole organisation and its sub-teams through crisis. The company of 25 core employees was an agile 'team of teams'. The leader was expert in team coaching and team members skilful as 'peer-coaches'. External support was also provided for the team leader in the form of peer consultation. Together, these elements were critical success factors underpinning a strong state of readiness to switch into 'alert mode'.

Switching up into 'alert mode'

Alert mode was initiated for this team when external pressures required transformation of its design and mode of working together into a virtual hybrid team, rather than a co-located team within a physical office environment. A structured intervention to support the team through change using 'sociomapping' was launched by the team leader. The leader, together with team members as 'peer-coaches', were responsible for delivering the main team coaching functions for this team.

Sociomapping

What is a sociomap and what makes sociomapping different?

Data presented in the form of a sociomap is a unique type of graphical representation of the team based on mutual relationships. It is a type of network map, not an xy plot of data, which is why there are no axes in the following illustrative diagrams. Sociomaps are usually shown in colour and an interactive viewer is employed to reveal different layers of the analysis dynamically within the team coaching session. Team members learn to read and interpret sociomaps, so all team members are fully engaged with both the analysis and decision-making when sociomapping is used as part of the team coaching process.

Sociomapping as the launch point for a systemic team coaching intervention

Sociomapping was an appropriate team coaching intervention during a crisis because it is a scientifically validated approach designed to support teams of different types in extreme contexts using immediate short-term, focused measures that can be repeated to track team dynamics (Bahbouh, 2012a; Fabianová, 2020). This has included aircrews (Bahbouh, 2012b), military teams in active combat (Bernardová, 2012), as well as teams being prepared to perform in extreme isolation or prepare for future events, such as space flight to Mars (Bahbouh, 2020). The methodology has also been translated successfully for teams where the objective is high performance, such as management teams, leadership teams (Franc et al., 2019), sports teams, as well as 'teams of teams' in agile organisations.

How sociomaps were used in real time to support the coaching process

Sociomaps are based on a new form of data visualisation for networks and used to create a shared mental model of underlying team dynamics, where data are integral to the coaching process and track changes to reveal success or failure. A key objective of the coaching process was to support the team in focusing on positive, effective communication, enabling the team to respond to the crisis in psychologically healthy ways whilst taking appropriate effective action in support of business needs.

Data were collected from each team member and shared in real time as part of the coaching process to support decision-making and action planning. Engaging with the sociomaps synergised and catalysed the processes of action planning, performance, and evaluation. The team could see which actions for change were being effective, as current and optimal state maps moved into alignment. The team was able to focus on the critical performance-enhancing behaviours (CPEBs). Complementary data for performance and wellbeing were also collected. Using triangulated, repeated measures provided insights into key relationship dynamics and provided the team with the information needed to drive a steep trajectory for ongoing development.

Examples from the sociomapping process used with the team

The first sociomap (Figure 3) shows communication dynamics within the sub-team of five team members holding managerial responsibilities. Each person is represented by a dot and labelled with a letter. Each map is like a landscape with the hills showing the highest points (height). In black and white, black shows the highest point. In this map, height shows evaluation of current communication on a 5-point scale. The position of each dot on the map shows how frequently each team member communicates relative to their colleagues.

It is possible to identify whether a team needs interventional support when a sociomap of current communication is compared with an equivalent sociomap of optimal communication. If there is a significant gap between the two states, this indicates a need to explore specific changes at individual and team levels, to improve effectiveness.

Sociomapping commenced for this team at the beginning of 'alert mode' because it was not clear whether the impact of the crisis would be positive, negative, or neutral. At the beginning of the process, the assessments quickly revealed a significant gap between current and optimal states emerging for this team. The decision to conduct sociomapping at weekly intervals was then driven by the team as a whole and based on what they felt would be the most appropriate option to support their work. Three team coaching sessions were then conducted at fortnightly intervals to evaluate, explore, and develop action plans for immediate development needs.

Figure 4 is also drawn from the analysis. Communication frequency is shown for the 25 company team members and illustrates one of the common patterns encountered, which is when one team member is central to the communication dynamic for the team. An individual in this position is often overloaded by

Figure 3 Current frequency of communication for team members with managerial responsibilities ($n = 5$)

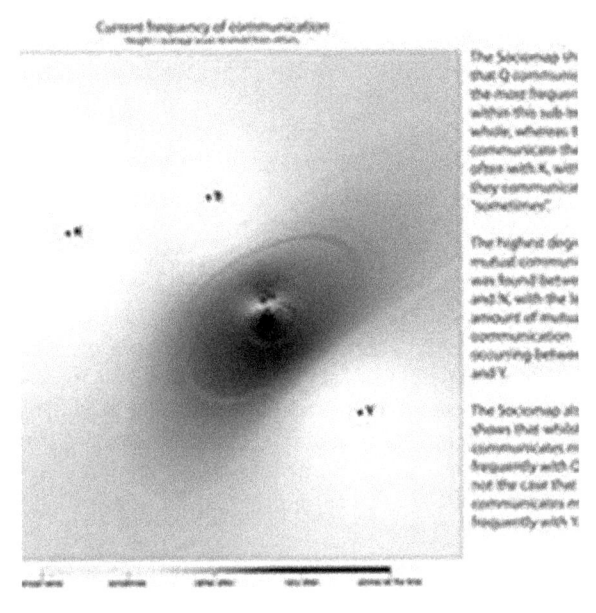

Figure 4 Current frequency of communication at week 15 for the whole team ($n = 25$)

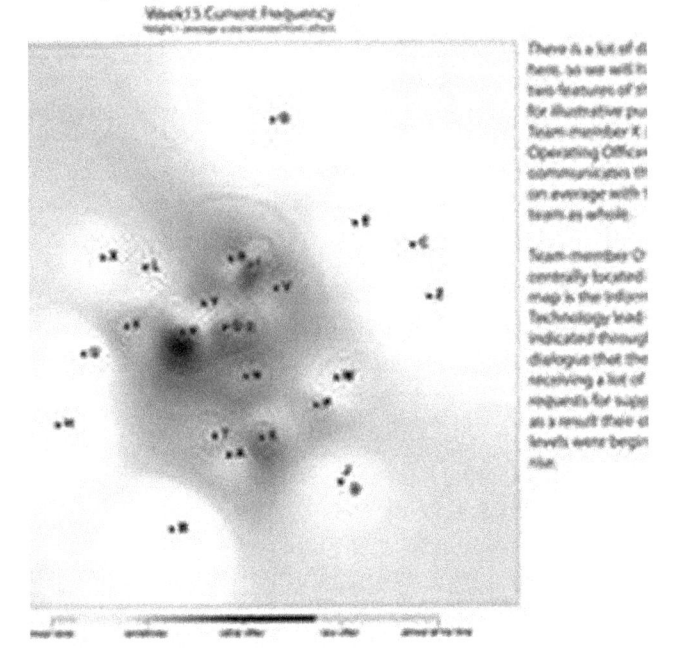

requests from others. In Figure 4, the IT lead (team member O) was central to the map. Dialogue within the team coaching process confirmed that work overload was an emergent issue needing attention.

How does the coaching process work?

During each team coaching session, the team familiarised itself with descriptive statistics for wellbeing and performance as well as the sociomaps. Team dialogue was facilitated by the team leader to explore the differences between the current and optimal levels of communication quality and about the possible actions or changes to be taken for the gap to be reduced. One of the key coaching questions explored by the team was whether they were surprised by anything revealed by the sociomapping.

When comparing results from the latest sociomaps with previous administrations, coaching dialogue focused on whether the current situation was satisfactory or whether actions should be taken for improvement. The whole team was engaged in this process. Action plans were formulated for each team member as well as the team as a whole that specified how all team members would ensure that the required changes would occur. The whole process was a sequence of elements as shown in Figure 5.

Figure 5 Team coaching with sociomapping

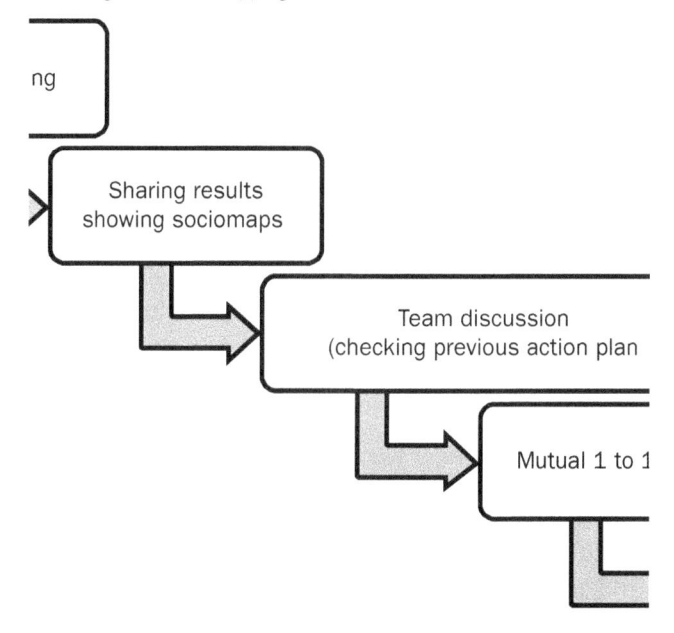

ng

Sharing results showing sociomaps

Team discussion (checking previous action plan

Mutual 1 to 1

Summary of key outcomes from sociomapping

Over time, gaps between current and optimal communication steadily decreased until the maps were aligned showing that team communication had been optimised. Similar positive trends were also captured on metrics of mood, perceived team performance, and work overload. These critical indicators were measured each week as part of the team coaching programme, forming an important source of data for calibrating team feedback and behavioural norms.

There were many outcomes. However, there are three key outcomes we would like to highlight. In each of these instances, sociomapping, together with the subsequent debriefing, led to specific actions which optimised the situation for the team and improved their effectiveness.

Outcome 1: Successful identification of psychosocial risk from work overload for individual team members and implementation of an action plan for the team as a whole. One goal of the coaching process was to identify which members of the team were most at risk of overload, so action could be taken to prevent team members from being overwhelmed. The person identified as being most at risk was the information technology lead. Appreciation of this risk early in the process enabled the team to produce and implement a plan to prevent a derailment. They took appropriate action coordinating and prioritising requests for information and support. Behavioural change was then sustained and calibrated through leader and team coaching with identification of existing and new CPEBs informed by repeat sociomappings. As a result, no one on the team was overwhelmed, critical relationships were calibrated, and both technical and psychosocial resources focused on areas of highest need. Team success followed because the CPEBs were fully focused and aligned with mission critical tasks and activities.

Outcome 2: Successful onboarding of a new team member and effective rapid integration within the team. The coaching process also supported the need for rapid onboarding of a new team member. Leader and peer coaching supported by the repeated sociomapping led to identification and implementation of actions specific team members could take to integrate their new colleague within several established sub-teams. Over time, the new team member was strategically involved in activities that made best use of their skills and delivered most impact for the business.

Outcome 3: New skills in working virtually as a team were developed and refined. At the beginning of the process, virtual formats for meetings and delivery of services were used very rarely, if ever, by team members and were also the least preferred option. Virtual forms of communication are now a key feature of the way this team works together and considered to be fundamental to the future success of the team, even though face-to-face meetings have been resumed.

Role of the team diagnostic survey and peer consultation

There were two reasons for implementing the **team diagnostic survey (TDS)** towards the end of the coaching programme. First, it was used to provide a scientifically validated diagnostic (Wageman et al., 2005) for evaluating the success of the coaching process. Secondly, it was used to provide feedback to inform future team design and development activity. Inclusion of a TDS as an additional measure at week 15 introduced a set of complementary systemic indicators that were completely new to this team.

A summary of key elements from the TDS analysis shown in Figure 4 offers a snapshot of both the 6 Team Conditions Framework and the data that were collected for this team in relation to the input–process–output (IPO) framework for coaching effectiveness created by Hackman and Wageman (2005), which underpins the design, launch, maintenance, and evaluation of team coaching programmes using the 6 Team Conditions (Hackman, 2011; Wageman et al., 2008) and use of the 60-30-10 rule (Wageman and Lowe, 2019). A detailed report was also provided to the team which broke down each of the conditions into constituent elements together with additional information on team learning orientation, psychological safety, and type.

Feedback was delivered to the team in two stages. First, as part of a peer consultation process involving the team leader and two senior colleagues holding managerial responsibilities. Secondly, the team leader and colleagues integrated key insights from the TDS analysis into the final team coaching session that included both sociomapping and key information from the TDS.

Results from TDS analysis and what this means for the team

When the team is in good shape, the results for each dimension are close to the perfect score of five (5) and the inner triangle is a closer fit with the outer triangle.

These results, taken together with the sociomapping data and supplementary measures, demonstrate that sustaining team effectiveness whilst preserving the wellbeing of team members was achieved. Whilst there were some areas of team design that needed attention, there were no significant challenges to the team stemming from the essential conditions for team success, which had been embedded through the team coaching process.

Exit from 'alert mode' in the team coaching process

Improvements in communication effectiveness, performance, and wellbeing, together with the fact that the key challenges associated with the crisis abated

Figure 6 TDS Team report page 3 – Overall snapshot: What is the team's standing on the 6 Team Conditions, the 3 key task processes, and the 3 criteria of effectiveness

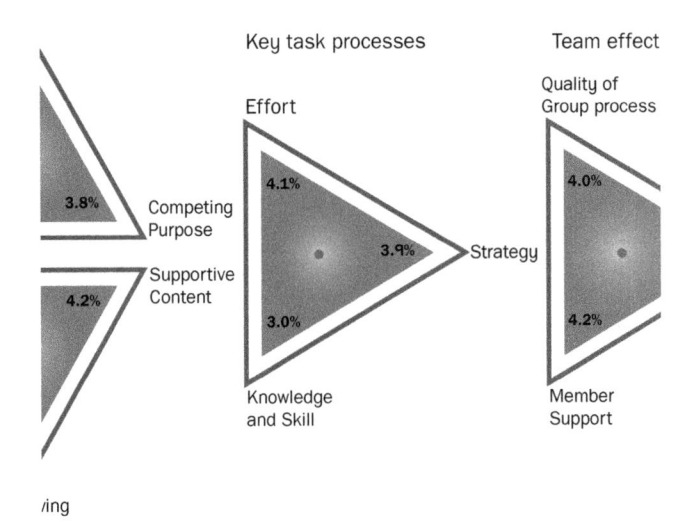

;ks

Key task processes
Effort
4.1%

3.8% Competing Purpose

3.9% Strategy

4.2% Supportive Content

3.0%
Knowledge and Skill

Team effect
Quality of Group process
4.0%

4.2%
Member Support

/ing

as the team pivoted into new ways of working, signalled that it was time to exit from the intensive cycles of weekly sociomapping and fortnightly team coaching sessions. At week 18, the team decided to use the time scheduled for sociomapping as an opportunity for a final debriefing of the whole coaching programme, which included key feedback from the TDS.

The final debriefing was formulated as a reflective session where each team member shared either single words or short phrases to highlight key learning through the team coaching process. The most common theme was appreciation of how successful online modes of service delivery had proven to be, together with the value of virtual meetings as a new and effective way of working.

During the final debriefing as a means of finalising and celebrating the conclusion of the programme, individual team members wrote personal messages of gratitude to each other. Three messages summarise feedback to the leader:

> 'Thank you for how well you set up the team's functioning in these unusual times. I also appreciate the team's TDS results'.
>
> 'I would like to thank you for how you approached the current situation, your willingness to adapt to the possibilities we presently have, and for the sociomaps'.
>
> 'Thanks for always being there for us, for believing in us, and for the massive support I feel from you!'

Reflections and conclusion

The context for this case was the need for team coaching to support radical change in the way a business operated, whilst preserving team effectiveness and the wellbeing of individual team members, which has been achieved.

In this instance, it was a natural step to escalate and formalise an emergency response to the crisis because the team was trained and experienced with both the coaching process and the sociomapping diagnostics. Integrating team coaching skillsets (Willis, 2013) and tools before during and after a crisis, in a way that did not overload the team, ensured that both familiar and new diagnostics were successfully and seamlessly embedded in the team coaching process.

Engagement of an external perspective was also timely when the team was out of the immediate crisis. The TDS analysis was new to the team, but appropriately timed and useful both as an evaluation to confirm broad success in the way the team has been reformulated, and as a reflective tool to support ongoing dialogue about the process. This big picture view informed team decision-making for the cessation of 'alert mode' as well as providing critical data to support ongoing coaching and team design.

Ultimately, the success of the ISTC process at the heart of this case shows that when facing a crisis, either for a single team or the whole company 'team of teams', it made sense to monitor the team development process using focused short-term measures such as team communication, wellbeing, and performance. Taking longer-term design characteristics of the team into account using the TDS provided a more complete assessment of the team, verifying successful team re-design and providing essential data to focus attention on continuing design needs.

Bringing in company performance data in the form of productivity, redundancy, and lay-off figures together with stakeholder feedback rounded off the evaluation of success for this systemic approach. Further evaluation of company performance six months after the beginning of the crisis confirmed that changes in team design and the move to virtual products and services was successful. Capacity to meet company objectives has continued to improve and has been verified by client and partner stakeholder feedback. Team size has also remained constant during this time whilst demand on financial and human resources increased.

Final thoughts

Using assessments and data within a coaching process can be controversial, maybe because assessment in coaching either does not capture the whole system or sits alongside, rather than being seamlessly integrated within, a team coaching process. Identifying and implementing appropriate systemic measures for factors that influence team performance is critical to an integrative approach to systemic team coaching. In this this case, we have shown how a set of scientifically valid and reliable tools and metrics can optimise both team coaching processes and outcomes.

One final reflection is that external support may have been valuable to this team at the beginning of the process as well as at the mid-point and end, offering the leader a sounding board to sense-check the approach being taken and provide peer psychosocial support during a stressful period. A brief scoping session before the next alert mode is initiated, will ensure the coaching process designed represents the most appropriate response to the next crisis.

References

Bahbouh, R. (2012a) Using sociomapping when coaching teams, in R. Bahbouh, E. Rozehnalová, and V. Sailerová (eds.) *New Perspectives of Psychodiagnostics* (pp. 63–70). Prague: QED Group.

Bahbouh, R. (2012b) *Sociomapping of Teams*. Prague: QED Group.

Bahbouh, R. (2020) Psychosocial aspects of a flight to Mars, *IntechOpen* [https://www.intechopen.com/online-first/psychosocial-aspects-of-a-flight-to-mars].

Bahbouh, R. and Willis, P. (2020) Creating effective virtual & hybrid teams with Integrative Systemic Team Coaching (ISTC). Oxford: Lauriate [https://www.lauriate.com/article/cevt].

Bernardová, K. (2012) Using sociomapping with the Czech Army, in R. Bahbouh, E. Rozehnalová, and V. Sailerová (eds.) *New Perspectives of Psychodiagnostics* (pp. 71–82). Prague: QED Group.

Fabianová, I. (2020) The effectiveness of team coaching using sociomapping. Unpublished doctoral dissertation, Charles University, Prague.

Franc, M., Bahbouh, R., and Kubík, R. (2019) The effect of manager's frequency and quality of communication on team's performance, in J. Procházka, T. Kratochvíl, and M. Vaculík (eds.) *Work and Organizational Psychology 2019: Proceedings of the 18th International Conference* (pp. 44–52). Brno: Masaryk University Press.

Hackman, J.R. (2011) *Collaborative Intelligence: Using Teams to Solve Hard Problems*. San Francisco, CA: Berrett-Koehler.

Hackman, J.R. and Wageman, R. (2005) A theory of team coaching, *The Academy of Management Review*, 30 (2): 269–287.

Wageman, R., Hackman, J.R., and Lehman, E. (2005) Team diagnostic survey: Development of an instrument, *Journal of Applied Behavioral Science*, 41 (4): 373–398.

Wageman, R. and Lowe, K. (2019) Designing, launching, and coaching teams: The 60-30-10 rule and its implications for team coaching, in D. Clutterbuck, J. Gannon, S. Hayes, I. Iordanou, K. Lowe, and D. MacKie (eds.) *The Practitioner's Handbook of Team Coaching* (pp. 121–137). Abingdon: Routledge.

Wageman, R., Nunes, D.A., Burruss, J.A., and Hackman J.R. (2008) *Senior Leadership Teams: What It Takes to Make Them Great*. Boston, MA: Harvard Business School Press.

Willis, P. (2013) Introduction to team coaching skills and competencies for team leaders. Oxford: Lauriate [https://www.lauriate.com/article/itcsctl].

Team coaching for communication continuity

Michelle Chambers

Background

The team coaching objective was to enable a senior leadership communications team within a large municipal government organisation to improve their effectiveness and achieve their business goals. The team had multiple strategies to achieve within the year, including: the integration of two siloed departments within their division; to improve relations with client stakeholder groups to be their supplier of choice; to improve team dynamics; and to develop and implement a new service delivery model. The team comprised one director, two managers, and five supervisors.

Initial request for team coaching

I was contacted by the project manager, Corporate Strategic Projects & Services, to meet with her and director of the communications leadership team. I conducted a 'discovery process' to better understand the team; their business objectives, their team, and organisational culture; their strengths as a team and their opportunities for development. Finally, I wanted to understand their desired future state.

Later, I met with the rest of the leadership team to hear their viewpoints and to answer their questions on the proposed solution of team coaching. It was a good opportunity to build a relationship and gain their support and buy-in. It also enabled me to clarify that team coaching was an intervention designed to coach the team as a whole system and that it required a minimum of a six-month commitment to create sustainable changes in behaviour. Furthermore, it was going to require their commitment to change and it would be hard work!

Issues presented

Historically, this was a team that did not work well together. A new organisational structure was being implemented to merge the two different departments under the leadership of the director. There was low trust, poor morale, siloes, and independent work efforts. In addition, productivity was poor and toxic communication, including blaming, were evident to all within the organisation. The team had also experienced three changes of director within the previous four years and had participated in several leadership development interventions, including 360° feedback, team-building and other workshops with no real evidence of change. Furthermore, they had been assigned a project manager from the chief administrator's office to make the team more effective and to help them implement a 'service delivery' transformation, as many of their stakeholders were choosing to work with external partners. Imagine outsourcing the 'communication' function within your organisation!

Approaches used

A team diagnostic assessment was chosen to collect data, as the team needed to move quickly to make changes and it was more likely the team would accept assessment data since it is more objective than interview data. The team diagnostic assessment (TDA) by Team Coaching International was chosen, since it was designed using team research, emotional intelligence, and appreciative inquiry. The TDA assesses seven positivity factors (qualities that optimise the team's ability to collaborate such as trust and communication) and seven productivity team performance factors (qualities that optimise a team's ability to get the job done, such as team leadership and decision-making) (Sandahl and Phillips, 2019: 5–9). The assessment enabled us to benchmark the team's current performance and identify strengths and opportunities for development.

A one-day offsite was designed to introduce the team to the process of team coaching, share the assessment results, develop team norms, and create an action plan to guide ongoing sessions. The team decided to focus on roles and responsibilities, decision-making, accountability, trust, and constructive interaction. Their overarching purpose was their 'service delivery transformation'. Transformation started that day. The director shared that 'she was encouraged by the leaders taking ownership and making commitments to work on items'.

Initially, the team contracted to do six in-person team coaching sessions on a monthly basis. The format of these 90-minute sessions included a check-in, confirmation of the coaching theme, an update on team norms, an accountability follow-up from the last coaching session, team coaching to address a team performance factor and/or relevant business issue, and training on a team tool or process.

Experiential coaching exercises, such as constellations and coaching wheels, were used to enable the team to embody their experience and to tap into their emotional side of the brain versus their logical side. For example, a constellation was used to tap into the voices present in the system and to get a snapshot of the system by having the group 'vote with their feet'. The initial inquiry question asked them how engaged they were with the transformation. Next, an 'unfolding' question probed how important it was to be aligned as a team around the transformation. Finally, the resolving question asked them what they needed to fully support the transformation. Team members loved the 'no judgement' concept and were able to share that they needed a clear vision, more frequent communication, better understanding of their roles, and greater involvement in designing the strategy. The director expressed how helpful this exercise was for her to see the team as a 'system' and to make changes to better support them.

In addition, various tools, including assessments, feedback and decision-making models, role and responsibility clarification tools, and conflict protocols were provided to inspire and enable team members to change their behaviours. For example, they learned their primary conflict styles and strategies on how to better handle conflict. They developed a conflict protocol to address the behaviours they wanted to see emerge within the team when conflict arose. They also practised giving one another positive and constructive feedback. I also observed the team at work making a real business decision to share with them what I was observing and to teach them a more effective process of decision-making. In between sessions, the team read HBR articles, chose a positivity factor to pay attention to, or practised using a new tool or process within their work.

The end goal of the team coaching process was to ensure that this team was functioning more effectively and would be able to hold one another accountable as a system and become the supplier of choice for communications within the organisation as per their service delivery transformation. In the final coaching session, the team also developed an action plan to support one another and to ensure sustainable change through time – this included sharing their learnings and tools with their own teams and stakeholders. They also agreed to do a team 'health check' one year down the line.

Specific outcomes

One year after the journey began, the team was reassessed using the TDA to create a second benchmark and to measure their progress. The team transitioned from a 'low positivity, low productivity' (Sandahl and Phillips, 2019) team into a higher performing team (high positivity, high productivity). Goals and strategies saw a 68% improvement, with alignment showing a 63% increase and team leadership a 40% increase. With respect to positivity factors, significant increases were demonstrated in respect (80%), optimism (83%), and constructive interaction (64%). There was no formal measurement of their service delivery transformation, as the timeline for attaining this was

Figure 7 Polar diagram: Before and after team coaching results

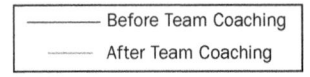

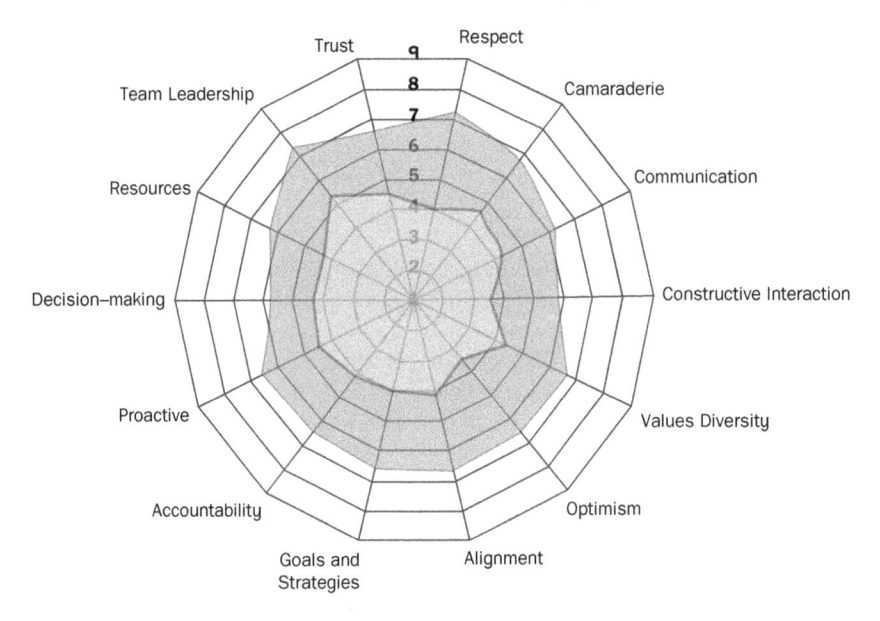

longer than the initial contracted team coaching engagement. Informal progress was measured through conversations with the project manager and stakeholder team debriefs. As a result, not only did this senior leadership team transform itself, but it supported its division through a significant business transformation.

Benefits realised by the team and team leader

The team learned that the process would take them out of their comfort zone and would require an intentional effort to change behaviours. Team norms were great to help hold team members accountable to one another and to build trust. Their team norms included: 'respecting each other by communicating openly', 'considering relationships as well as desired outcomes', and 'speaking positively about their team and supporting one another'. Team norms were referenced and assessed in key leadership meetings and ongoing coaching sessions. This team also created a shared purpose, which gave them a clear goal and higher levels of engagement. The process also enabled them to connect with their stakeholder groups to ensure they were being client centric in driving their change. They also improved inter-departmental cooperation through the reduction of 'silos' and enhanced relationships with their key stakeholders.

It became clear to the team that it takes time to build trust and develop relationships. This required open, honest communication and giving one another positive and constructive feedback. There were times when there were perceived setbacks and when team members were frustrated and struggling to have their voice heard. They also learned that effective teams need to focus on both business outcomes and team performance simultaneously. Being able to communicate effectively and trust one another is just as critical to team effectiveness as having clearly aligned goals. The 'how' was just as important as the 'why'. Taking the time to have the difficult conversations, improve decision-making, and clarify roles significantly improved their effectiveness. Furthermore, team members experienced the joy and positive energy that comes from a team that works well together, team members who appreciate one another, and achieving one's goals. They learned how to manage their team culture and orient new team members successfully. Furthermore, they shared their learning from the team coaching process with the teams they supported to increase organisational learning. As one member shared a year later, 'we have more open, honest dialogue and we're working collaboratively together to achieve the division's goals'.

The director recognised the need for additional support, as she felt vulnerable and needed to build trust with the team coach. At times, the leader needed support around the team coaching process itself, when to provide performance coaching, and how to support the team in their execution of their action items, even when times were challenging. The director also benefited from the coaching processes and tools shared with the team so that they could role-model the expected behaviours both with the team and their stakeholders. Furthermore, using an assessment pre and post coaching was invaluable to support the sponsor's' request for a return on their investment with both qualitative and quantitative data. This was particularly important as the director was under organisational pressure to ensure the 'service delivery' transformation was successful and that the organisation was utilising its own communication department versus external vendors. In addition, feedback from the stakeholder groups via the project manager was also helpful in gaining support for additional team coaching sessions. Even the project manager noted that the team learned to speak in 'open, honest, and non-threatening ways. This is a big step for this team'.

Key learnings for the team coach

As team coaches, we learn that we must meet the needs of our clients in the present moment, even if we come with a plan in mind. I never expected to spend most of the first ongoing team coaching session helping the team come to align and agree on a word choice to represent their 'team norms'. To a 'communications team', this was more critical than agreeing on principles and moving forward on their action plan. To a team coach, it was completely frustrating, although it provided great insight into the team. It demonstrated their challenge in making decisions which would hold them accountable. It was my opportunity to be a 'reflective observer' and to inform the team of their behaviours and challenge them to try doing things differently. It is so important as a team coach to be fully present and to focus on the system's needs. Advice I often share with new team coaches is never forget the power of curiosity and the art of a powerful question.

Furthermore, I was also reminded that a team's learning journey is often cyclical, not linear. A team may be changing their behaviours and moving forward in a positive direction while taking a step backwards in other ways. This often happens when change is difficult or there is an absence of coaching for a period (e.g. summer vacation). I will never forget a team coaching session after summer vacation when the director, a normally very positive individual, was exhibiting signs of despair and frustration. Other team members also modelled similar behaviour. I therefore suggested an appreciative inquiry exercise known as the 'Wall of Pride' to help them recall all of their 'proud moments' and what they had achieved as a team. What a game changer! The emotional field completely changed and everyone indicated how much more energised and committed they were despite their ongoing challenges.

At times as team coaches, we also doubt our own abilities. Consequently, I think it made me look for different ways to serve my client better. I did not have the benefit of a co-coach to share the process of facilitation, to observe the client when I was not able to, or to debrief after each experience. As a result, I built in a process whereby after each team coaching session, I wrote down and debriefed myself in my virtual office (car in parking lot). I noted what went well, what did not seem to go well, and what could be done differently in my role as a team coach. I also built in processes to debrief with the team leader around the effectiveness of the team coaching after each session, and to build in design time prior to each session to discuss cultural and team issues that might impact our session. This was done with transparency and the team knew that I would not be discussing individual team members. Also, I built in a 'pulse check' or debrief at the end of each coaching session to inquire what each member of the team felt was effective, what they were going to do differently back in the workplace, and what they wanted to focus on in the next team coaching session. This was incredibly worthwhile to ensure all voices were heard and to increase my insight into the team. We truly co-designed the processes as we went along!

Things I would have done differently

- Confirm the team's understanding of their purpose and key strategies to ensure alignment at the beginning of the team coaching process. For example, it did not become evident that the team had different interpretations of

what a 'service delivery' transformation meant, nor did they have a common vision until it came up in a coaching session.
- Co-design with the project manager, quantifiable as well as qualitative measures from external stakeholder groups (e.g. number of departments that switched from external vendors to internal communications department). This would have served to inform the team of their success and their ability to be a more credible function within the organisation.
- Meet with the external groups directly and encourage systemic team coaching as well for them and to coach the connections between the teams.
- Coach the team members to develop partnership alliances with their respective client group.

Application of lessons learned in my practice

I now contract for more formal opportunities to engage and collect data from the client's stakeholders to provide more of a systemic team coaching perspective. This has been valuable as we move to a more digital environment in which being client centric will be even more critical in enabling teams to achieve their business objectives. I have also engaged in further reading and training around 'systemic team coaching'. This has reinforced for me the value of coaching teams as a 'system' over time and the value of coaching the connections between teams. Systemic team coaching works on strengthening the interrelationships amongst team members and research indicates that connectivity between team members is strongly correlated with business performance (Losada and Heaphy, 2004).

Issues and insights brought to, and gained from, supervision

Although I did not have formal supervision, I did engage in mentoring with Phil Sandahl and conversations with other team coaches. This reinforced for me the value of having different lenses and enabled me to increase my objectivity around the team and their behaviours. Also, I learned to bring the perspective of other stakeholders into the room even just by adding chairs and asking the team to consider what those stakeholders would say. Finally, it increased my confidence as a team coach in supporting my client throughout the team coaching process.

This particular client and their team coaching journey was such a memorable one that I asked the director to co-present and share our learnings at a national Canadian HR conference. Subsequently, it also sparked an article in *Municipal World* magazine. Watching the team change their behaviours and adopt new ways to work collaboratively was immensely fulfilling. I truly believe that everyone should be engaged and enjoy their work and the people they work with. I always consider it an honour and a privilege to serve teams and to bring coaching and process skills that enable poorly functioning teams to become higher performing to achieve their business results.

References

Hawkins, P. (2017) *Leadership Team Coaching: Developing Collective Transformational Leadership*, 3rd edition. London: Kogan Page.

Losada, M. and Heaphy, E. (2004) The role of positivity and connectivity in the performance of business teams: A nonlinear dynamics model, *American Behavioral Scientist*, 47 (6): 740–765.

Sandahl, P. and Phillips, A. (2019) *Teams Unleashed: How to Release the Power and Human Potential of Work Teams*. London: Nicholas Brealey.

Team intelligence (TQ™) assessment that informed effective team coaching approaches and generated improvements in financial performance

Solange Charas

This case highlights a coaching engagement with the pharmaceutical division of a Fortune Global 500 organisation. The case is transformative because it was based on the results of a team-level assessment tool (based on my PhD research). This assessment compares the team's dynamic quality 'current state' to the team's 'desired state'. Both the current and desired states reflect the collective experience of team members. What makes the team assessment unique is that it measures the team at the 'team level' versus consolidating individual assessments as a poor proxy for the team. Teams are systems and need to be evaluated as such (Cardon, 2008). When working with team assessment instruments, you should ensure that the assessment has high reliability and validity and the results generated are statistically significant (Gallo, 2016). Without this, the team assessment may not be adding value to the process, and may be as unscientific and unreliable as 'guessing' about the team, sight unseen. The results of the assessment informed the coaching roadmap used to guide the team to achieve its self-generated desired state. The assessment also allows the team coach to model the critical positive or negative impact the team, in this case the top management team (TMT), has on corporate financial performance. This is critical, as the organisation will be less inclined to invest in team coaching if the financial benefit of team coaching cannot be quantified – and the results of the assessment tool make this possible. This brings a different kind of relevancy and urgency to improving teams – not only can the interventions generate qualitative benefits but the financial benefits to the organisation can be quantified (Redman, 2008).

This case study will cover the following topics:

1 Understanding the challenges faced by the client
2 TQ™ – the assessment instrument
3 Results of the TQ™ assessment and implications for effective team coaching
4 Resulting coaching engagement insights.

Understanding the challenges faced by the client

The organisation (fewer than 100 employees) was the US division of a large global pharmaceutical company, headed by a rotational executive from the company's home country (an 'expatriate'). The TMT consisted of the function heads from each of the 10 functions in the organisation reporting into an expatriate executive. The TMT was highly diverse, representing six different nationalities and four different races and balanced gender representation. Due to the high level of team diversity, the team coaches (myself and the TMT's individual coach) expected that the team would be open to team coaching. However, we quickly learned that, either for cultural or personal reasons, the individuals on the TMT did not place value on the effectiveness of either the individual coaching they were receiving or team coaching they were about to receive. This was a significant hurdle we had to overcome.

The expatriate division president and the American head of HR identified the following as critical to improving performance in the organisation:

1 Behavioural issues in the organisation across functional teams were creating a 'silo-ed' work environment incompatible with the culture and climate the division president wanted to create. According to the division president, 'The TMT wasn't working well together, members were often rude, aggressive, and hostile to one another, which was often observed by others in the organization'. This resulted in diminished cross-functional coordination and a general sense of dysfunction: 'when the parents are fighting, the children don't get along'. This was the highest priority for the division president – to improve the relationships between the TMT members so that there would be a more 'unified' leadership profile for the organisation (Slagter and Wilderom, 2018).
2 Financial performance was declining, which was attributed to the dysfunctional TMT. Academic research indicates that a workplace filled with unaddressed conflict (Wei et al., 2020) is costly to an organisation (Cram and MacWilliams, 2011). Based on human capital analytics performed on this company, we identified that there was a 25% decline in employee productivity due to employees being focused on disputes instead of work-related activities, and there were high levels of stress, frustration, anxiety, absenteeism, and attrition. The division president confirmed that the financial performance of the division had been on a steady decline for two years.

The division president confirmed that the deteriorating productivity cost the organisation over $3.5 million in profits.

Our approach was to assess the TMT and each functional team in the organisation and then move forward with team coaching. The assessment would provide information about where a team coaching intervention would be needed and what coaching would address (Clutterbuck, 2020). The assessment provides information on the current state of the team's TQ™ and the team's perceived gap between the current and the desired level of TQ™. Coaching would address behavioural areas where there were large gaps between the assessment's identified current and desired state.

The following steps were undertaken in conducting this engagement:

1 The division president met with his TMT prior to the distribution of the assessment instrument to get their buy-in and support and informed them that team coaching might be the recommended intervention.
2 The online assessment was distributed to the entire organisation with communications from the division president about the initiative. Assessment-takers were instructed to focus on the 'team' and not themselves in responding to the survey questions. All data was treated as confidential and presented in the aggregate – reflecting the health of the system, not the individuals in it. We did not have any contact with any of the employees prior to distributing the assessment.
3 The assessment results were analysed and interpreted, and feedback reports were created for each team.
4 In 11 separate meetings, each team had an opportunity to understand the unique profile of their team and their level of TQ™. We used the feedback session to highlight where the teams had done well and where they could improve their 'system of working together' (Gorman et al., 2017). Despite four of the 11 teams needing coaching, the division president decided to start with the TMT.
5 Team coaching was delivered. There were two team coaches for this engagement. We asked for a 10-coaching session commitment by the TMT, delivered once every two weeks during their regularly scheduled TMT meetings. The process of team coaching was to allow the team to do their regular work with the team coaches present, providing coaching when issues related to specific areas identified by the TQ™ arose. These were not special meetings with a specific focus on coaching, but meetings in the normal course of business. The second coach continued to work with the individuals on the TMT on a one-on-one basis, while the team coaching engagement was in force. The expatriate division president decided to exclude himself from the process as he knew he would be returning to his home country within the next two to four months and he wanted the team to learn to work effectively with one another without the president's influence.
6 After seven coaching sessions with the TMT, we administered the assessment tool again to measure and provide feedback to the team about their

improvements in critical areas. Because teams learn, it is important to administer the assessment again. This allowed the coaches, as well as the team, to get quantitative evidence of TQ™ improvements.

TQ™ – the assessment instrument

Intuitively, we know that high-performing teams generate better financial results, and my doctoral research provided a way to understand team quality and quantify the team's impact on financial outcomes. Thousands of board directors and C-suite executives participated in the research as well as lower-level teams in the organisation.

The instrument assesses three fundamental dimensions: team dynamic quality, team agreeableness, and team effectiveness (Charas, 2015).

1. **Team dynamic quality (TDQ):** Measures the 'white space' between people generating team ethos. Attributes that make up this variable include engagement, active listening, individuality, understanding, planning, power and influence, and openness.

   The assessment compares the current experience of the team with the desired experience of the team and generates a measurable 'gap'. Teams with more than a 15% gap between current and desired are considered dysfunctional teams.

2. **Team agreeableness (TA):** Measures the tendency to be compassionate and cooperative towards others based on the Big 5 Personality Indicator. Attributes measured include trust, morality, modesty, altruism, team-mindedness, and pro-social behaviours.

   The assessment compares the current experience with the desired experience of the team and generates a 'gap' measure. Teams with more than an overall 15% gap between current and desired are considered disagreeable teams.

3. **Team effectiveness (TE):** Measures the ability of the team to generate desired outcomes (Collins and Parker, 2010). The five attributes measured include: skills, synergy, innovation, quality measures, and team self-efficacy.

   The assessment captures the current level of TE and benchmarks this performance against more than 1,300 teams in the assessment database.

All attributes taken together are an indicator of the team's intelligence or TQ™. When the overall gap is more than 15% between current and desired state, the team is considered dysfunctional and is likely to have a deleterious impact on corporate financial performance.

Results of the TQ™ assessment and implications for effective team coaching

The coaches reviewed the results of the assessment to craft a team coaching strategy. This was shared with the division president and the head of HR.

The main findings of the assessment were as follows:

Organisation-wide assessment: TDQ, TA, and TE (excluding the TMT) for the entire organisation had average gaps ranging from 13% to 22% and therefore near or above the threshold of 15%. The organisation as a whole was only marginally dysfunctional. As mentioned above, only 4 teams in total had TQ™ levels that would benefit from team coaching. It was determined that coaching the TMT would be the highest priority. If the TMT improved, we believed that the other 3 teams would improve organically and not need a coaching intervention. The biggest gaps for the TMT were in areas that reflected interpersonal attributes (relationality, solidarity and understanding) and personal behaviors (altruism).

TMT assessment: When we reviewed the overall team dynamic profile of the TMT, we identified that the TDQ and TA gap was close to **40%**. Significant gaps existed in many areas (engagement, active listening,

Figure 8 Top management team initial assessment: Team dynamic quality

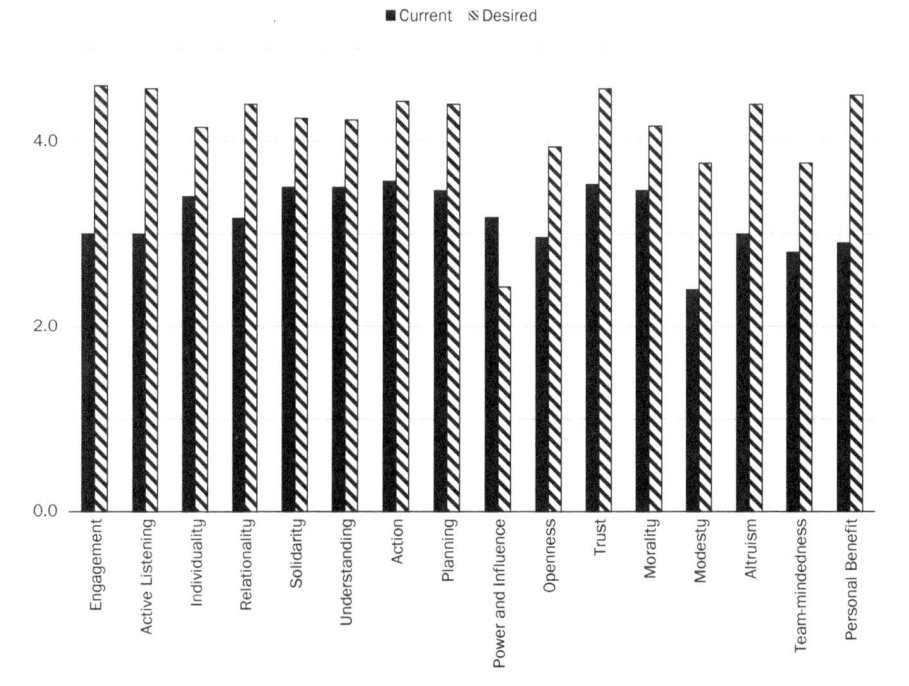

Figure 9 Top management team initial assessment: Team effectiveness benchmark results

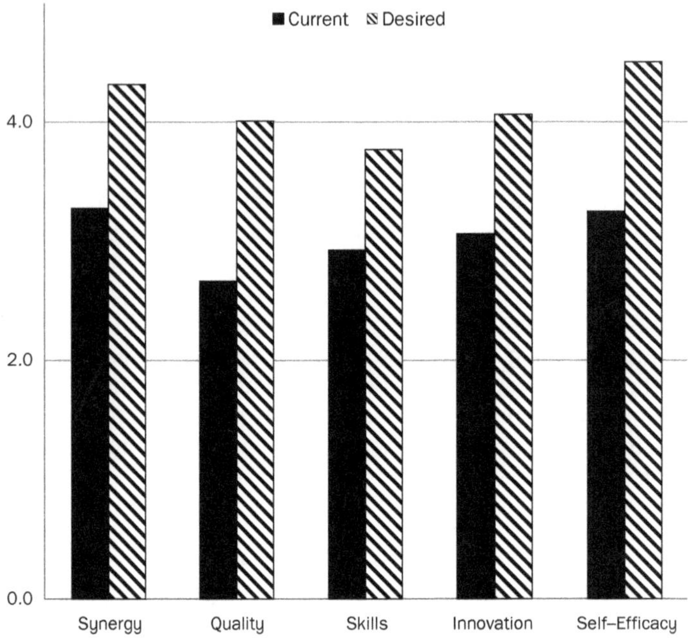

openness, trust, modesty, altruism, and personal benefit) (Figure 8). When assessing TE, we found that the team performed below the benchmark by about 36%, specifically in the areas of quality and self-efficacy (Figure 9). The low team self-efficacy score was of concern as team self-efficacy (or self-belief) is one of the strongest predictors of team success. We needed to get the team members to believe that they could work effectively together.

These overall findings confirmed the observations of the division president and head of HR. More importantly, the assessment provided information about the source of the TMT dysfunction – indicated by the large gaps between the current and desired experience (or how the team believes it needs to be), so that it can achieve success. The gaps that exist between current and desired inform the team coaches on behavioural aspects that should be the focus while coaching the team at work.

Team coaching sessions: Focus and format

Team coaching followed the protocols of accepted approaches – namely, that the coaches participated in regularly scheduled team meetings and identified opportunities during these dynamic live sessions to address areas for improvement in TQ™, as identified by the assessment results. The value of the assessment was identifying where coaching was required. This benefited the team, as the coaches used the assessment to pinpoint precisely where the team had gaps. The team coaches listened and observed conversations and body language while the team held their regular management meetings. The coaches interrupted the dialogue/discussion among TMT members to correct for behaviours that had been identified as high-gap areas.

During the first TMT session, we established ground rules and built consensus about their objectives for team coaching. These included:

- Decreasing the gap between real and ideal experience in TDQ and TA.
- Improving TE scores against the benchmark.
- Supporting the team in seeing one selected strategic initiative to completion, as determined by the team. The reason we focused on a shared initiative was to allow the team to focus on a project, and to avoid the conversations becoming a complaining session about others' individual behaviours.
- Enhancing cross-functional cooperation and collaboration below the TMT level.

Seven team coaching sessions were completed over a period of three months. By focusing on the attributes with the largest gaps, we helped the team be more aligned on the other attributes, as teams tend to self-correct once the most contentious areas are resolved. This is a consistent pattern we observed in other coaching assignments, supported by post-coaching assessment results.

Despite the acknowledged progress with the team, the coaching engagement was stopped once the division president returned to his home country. The team felt that they did not have to continue the sessions, since their 'boss' was no longer there requiring them to participate in team coaching. Individual coaching was also terminated, which was expected because the individuals were not inclined to participate in any form of coaching to begin with. What was gratifying for the coaches was that in the final coaching session, each of the TMT members communicated that they felt the team was functioning better, that their own personal experience on the team had improved, and that the organisation was working better. They felt that the coaching was too confrontational for them and pushed them too far out of their 'comfort zone'. As coaches we learned that the team must want to participate in team coaching, but even if they don't want to participate, they can still get value from the process.

Findings from the post-coaching assessment

The TMT agreed to complete the post-coaching assessment to quantify if and where improvements were made in the team's TQ™. We found that the overall gap between current and desired went from 40% to less than 20%! This improvement occurred over a six-week period. The greatest improvement occurred in our focus areas (engagement, active listening, modesty, altruism).

When considering TE, we observed an average of 30% improvements against the benchmarks.

Resulting coaching engagement insights

The TMT and the coaches gained many insights from this engagement.

Organisation/team insights

1. Team members found value in the quantitative approach (they were all scientists). The most valuable benefit from a quantitative approach is the proof of improvement by comparing the results of the pre- and post-coaching assessments. This reinforces team self-efficacy – so vital to team performance.
2. The TMT went into this process with a great deal of resistance. They did not want to participate, and they communicated that team coaching was not a familiar or welcomed process in their respective ethnic cultures. Despite their resistance, they acknowledged that the coaching was effective, and they felt that the pre- and post-coaching assessment results were an accurate representation of the team's quality and the progress they made. Individual team members communicated to the coaches, and to the head of HR, that they were working better together (as a team), felt that they had more personal satisfaction working on the team, and that there was increased cooperation cross-functionally in the organisation. Each team member acknowledged the value in the process even though it was uncomfortable, confrontational, and at times frustrating. They admitted that post coaching, they were working differently together and that the shift in their team experiences were helping to generate collective desired outcomes. When reviewing the original objectives of the team coaching, they agreed that the outcomes set at the start of the coaching process were achieved. However, they were uncomfortable with the coaching process itself.
3. The head of HR confirmed positive organisational results six months after the coaching was terminated. These benefits included:
   - Employee engagement scores improved: reflecting a more relaxed and less confrontational and stressful culture. Absenteeism dropped approximately 30% per month post coaching.
   - Attrition rate declined: because the TMT was working better together, the rest of the organisation was experiencing a less confrontational working environment. This had saved the company approximately $300,000 in headhunting and recruiting fees.
   - Job acceptance rate improved: the employer brand of this organisation improved (confirmed by improvements in Glassdoor ratings), which made it easier to recruit employees. The overall Glassdoor score for the organisation improved by 0.4 points (from 2.7 to 3.1).
   - Percent of projects completed on time improved: as a pharmaceutical organisation sensitive to timelines, a review of performance

against project plan for most of the projects in the organisation improved. There were fewer missed deadlines because of improved cross-function coordination. There was an estimated positive financial impact of $1.5 million over the six-month period post-coaching.
- The division's financial performance had improved over the six-month period, which was attributed to the team coaching. The improvement in financial performance was estimated to be close to $2 million.
- Return on investment in team coaching was approximately 425%, based on the beneficial financial return compared to the cost of the coaching engagement.

Coach insights gained

1. Sponsor support is critical. The TMT leader should be part of the process and an active participant in the coaching. Overall results are enhanced when all team members participate.
2. It is important to obtain buy-in and commitment from all team members participating in the coaching process. If there are any perceived barriers to coaching, cultural or otherwise, these should be addressed before the process begins. Periodic check-ins with team members about their continued willingness to participate in the coaching process is critical.
3. Articulate mutually agreed-to goals for coaching at the start of the engagement and revisit them periodically with the team.
4. Use human capital metrics to 'baseline' selected performance indicators of the organisation – namely, attrition and absenteeism, retention, employee engagement, financial performance – as a way to measure the residual impact of coaching the TMT, and calculate the return on investment of team coaching.
5. Do not be discouraged if the team discontinues the team coaching engagement. In the end, you can still make a significant difference to the organisation and the coached team, even with a truncated engagement.

References

Cardon, A. (2008) Systemic Organizational Coaching, a Case Study and Methodology. Paris: Metasysteme Coaching [https://www.metasysteme-coaching.eu/english/systemic-organizational-coaching-a-case-study-and-methodology/].
Charas, S. (2015) Improving corporate performance by enhancing team dynamics at the board level, *International Journal of Disclosure and Governance*, 12(2): 107–131.
Clutterbuck, D. (2020) *Coaching the Team at Work: The Definitive Guide to Team Coaching*, 2nd edition. London: Nicholas Brealey.
Collins, C.G. and Parker, S.K. (2010) Team capability beliefs over time: Distinguishing between team potency, team outcome efficacy, and team process efficacy, *Journal of Occupational and Organizational Psychology*, 83 (4): 1003–1023.

Cram, J.A. and MacWilliams, R.K. (2011) The cost of conflict in the workplace. [http://www.crambyriver.com/coc.html].

Gallo, A. (2016) Analytics: A refresher on statistical significance, *Harvard Business Review*, 16 February [https://hbr.org/2016/02/a-refresher-on-statistical-significance].

Gorman, J.C., Dunbar, T.A., Grimm, D., and Gipson, C.L. (2017) Understanding and modeling teams as dynamical systems, *Frontiers in Psychology*, 8: 1053 [https://doi.org/10.3389/fpsyg.2017.01053].

Redman, T.C. (2008) *Data Driven: Profiting from Your Most Important Business Asset*. Boston, MA: Harvard Business Press.

Slagter, M. and Wilderom, C. (2018) Team coaching and effective team leadership, in S. Greif, H. Möller, and W. Scholl (eds.) *Handbuch Schlüsselkonzepte im Coaching* (pp. 593–602). Berlin: Springer.

Wei, W., Fang, Y., Li, J., Shi, J., and Mo, S. (2020) The impact of conflict on performance: The moderating effects of individual and team agreeableness, *Acta Psychologica Sinica*, 52 (3): 345–356.

Inspiring collective leadership at an Australian public sector organisation

Pauline Lee and Sarah Cornally

Context

An Australian public sector department (the department) was under pressure to change. The department was not 'future-fit' for a complex and volatile environment. There were inadequate governance arrangements and strategic planning, while decision-making was largely done at the senior level. Risk aversion and siloed working was the norm. These factors created inefficiencies and a disengaged workforce. The department was given a clear mandate to transform – in particular, to address culture and leadership capability.

The chief operations officer (COO) leadership team (the Team) was responsible for leading the change effort while simultaneously running current operations. The Team was chosen to lead the change, due to their shared accountability for the change initiatives and their ability to mobilise the entire organisation. The Team had more influence than any one individual functional team.

The COO leader knew that the success of their transformation would be based on the effectiveness of their leadership team and engaged us to coach the Team. We were selected as their team coaches because of our deep experience of working in the public sector, coaching senior leadership teams and our willingness to challenge.

This chapter tells the story of coaching the COO leadership team over an 18-month period. We describe three different approaches used to unlock their potential.

Understanding the systemic landscape

After initial contracting discussions with the COO leader on the scope and desired outcomes, we inquired about the Team and its context. We used the PERILL model (Clutterbuck et al., 2019) and the Leadership Circle (Anderson and Adams, 2016) suite of diagnostics to reveal the underlying issues and dynamics of the Team in its organisational context.

The PERILL model provided a systemic perspective of the factors that underpin team performance. It identified five factors on which teams may function well or poorly and showed the moderating effect of leadership on all these factors. The factors were: 'purpose and motivation', 'external processes', 'relationships', 'internal processes', and 'learning'.

We interviewed each member of the Team and five deputy secretaries who were customers of their corporate services. The PERILL model, which provided the structure to our interviewing process and diagnosis, revealed a systemic picture of the Team's functioning. The positive and negative interactions between all the factors were highlighted. We mapped where the Team was functioning well and where it was currently challenged.

Given the transformation called for shifts in mindset and behaviour, we wanted to learn about the behaviours, habits, and patterns of the Team. We used the Collective Leadership Assessment™ (CLA) to measure the current and ideal culture of the Team. It indicated where the most energy for change was and illuminated their focus areas.

This survey was a powerful partner to the PERILL model because it revealed the beliefs, assumptions, and behaviours that were hindering and facilitating team performance. For example, their tendency for 'passive behaviour' (identified from the CLA) explained their dependency on the team leader to drive team projects and their hub-and-spoke approach.

Exploring the data and co-designing

The workshop design principles were to create engagement, energy, and ownership, be active inquirers rather than be told what to do. We didn't want the Team to feel judged or criticised. This first workshop focused on contracting on how we would work together, discussing both sources of data (survey and interviews), and co-creating a team coaching plan.

We explored their 'collective leadership' and shared challenges. In preparation for them receiving their feedback, we provided an overview of the PERILL model. We shared interview themes alongside asking powerful questions to stimulate their involvement in co-diagnosing its meaning. Questions asked included:

1 What resonates with you about this data?
2 What do you think is unclear that you need to find out more about?
3 How do these results show up in the system?
4 Can you see how the effectiveness of one factor impacts on another? What do you make of this?
5 What resources are available to you as a collective that you haven't fully mobilised towards this factor?

Team view using PERILL

- **Purpose and motivation:** they had a clear sense of team purpose, but this was not translated into clear team goals and performance measures. Performance was measured through individual business lines. Participants' responses included: 'We are not working as a team, but as a group of individuals with our own agendas ... we are unclear about what constitutes high team performance'.
- **External processes:** while their reputation was good, 'Business partners' service was patchy and sometimes of poor quality'.
- **Relationships:** members enjoyed positive, open relationships and psychological safety.
- **Internal processes:** decision-making was inclusive and directive when needed. 'However, we don't make many decisions as a team, we strive for consensus. The team leader acts as the umpire ... we avoid conflict and play it nice with each other'.
- **Learning:** the Team focused on individual learning, rather than team learning.

Collective Leadership Assessment™

The CLA assessed two primary cultures: the creative culture consisting of behaviours and internal assumptions that empowers and delivers outcomes; and the reactive culture that reflects inner beliefs and behaviours that limit effectiveness and engagement. The Team scored 86% on the reactive-creative scale (see Figure 10). This indicated that their leadership culture focused on bringing the best out in others, acting with integrity and courage, and leading with vision. However, their tendency to comply or control was limiting the full expression of their collective leadership.

This reinforced the PERILL findings that while this was a harmonious team who cooperated in service of their individual roles, they left potential on the table by not working to their full collective capacity.

The gap between the current culture and the desired culture revealed opportunities for development. They aspired to be more customer-focused, to think systemically, and be less reactive (arrogant, driven, and passive) under pressure. The Team expressed a deep longing for the aspired culture because they were responsible for focusing on whole-systems improvement and serving their internal customers. Their controlling and complying tendencies put the brakes on collective leadership. Under pressure, they played nice with each other, to ensure approval: 'If I don't please [approval seek] and give them (i.e. the Team, peers, and customers) enough of what they want, then I will be isolated', and 'If I don't stay in control, and on top of it all, then I will never get it back under control'. Setting demanding performance standards and driving hard-to-get results were habitual patterns.

Figure 10 COO leadership team culture survey

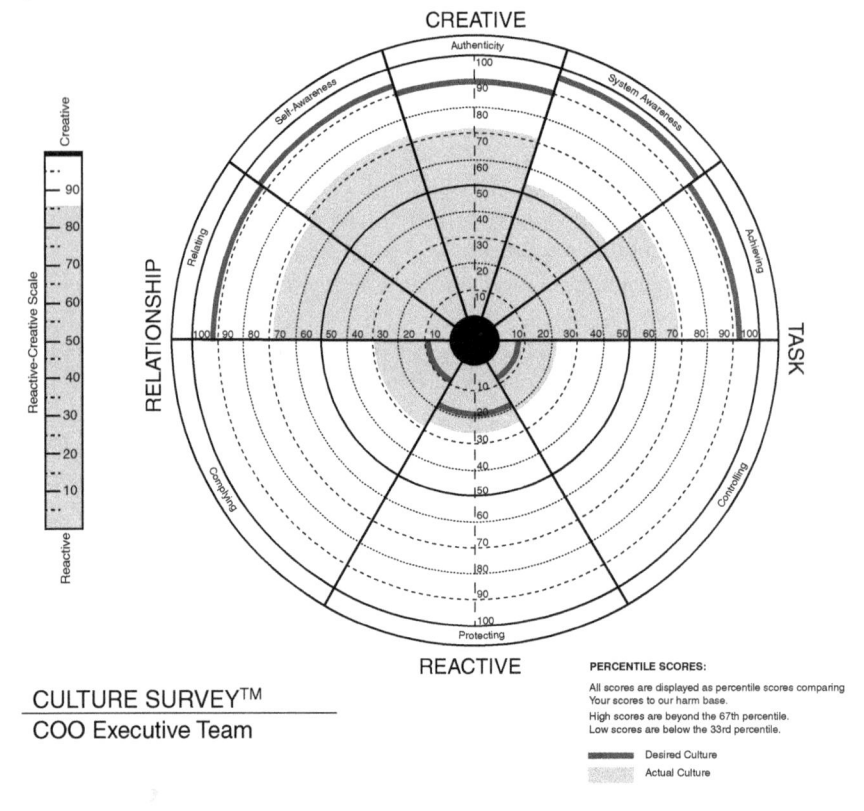

CULTURE SURVEY™
COO Executive Team

PERCENTILE SCORES:
All scores are displayed as percentile scores comparing Your scores to our harm base.
High scores are beyond the 67th percentile.
Low scores are below the 33rd percentile.

— Desired Culture
▓ Actual Culture

Seeing systemically

We discussed the interdependencies of the PERILL model with the Team. Table 2 presents a summary of COO leadership team performance and dysfunction using the PERILL model. It showed how one part can either facilitate or inhibit another part in team performance. For example, the team's goals and priorities were vague (*purpose*) and therefore members pursued their own individual accountabilities (*internally facing processes*). Meetings (*internally facing processes*) were ruled by lengthy agendas and status updates. The weekly team meeting didn't occur if the leader was absent. The Team identified that their overvaluation of harmony and avoidance of conflict impacted the quality of their meetings (*relationships*). They noticed the results systemically: 'Our meetings lack structure and focus. What kind of conversation are we having? Which ones are outcome focused?'; and in particular how their individual mindset and behaviour impacted their external results created a breakthrough. They were surprised to see the interdependencies of the PERILL factors, and accepted that this was true.

Models & Tools **101**

Table 2 Summary of COO leadership team performance (clear boxes) and dysfunction (shaded boxes) using the PERILL model

Leadership Quality Behaviours (LQB)	Purpose and motivation	Externally facing processes	Relationships	Internally facing processes	Learning
Purpose and motivation	LQB	Unclear how the leadership team as a whole engages the wider system	As team goals are vague, people pursue their own individual accountabilities	Lack of clarity on performance standards, shared goals, and processes for running team projects	Is learning more focused on the individual than the team?
Externally facing processes	High reputation among stakeholders. Senior leaders have easy access	LQB	What are our stakeholder performance expectations – could we raise our performance?	Lack of key resources. Federal budget considered more important than rest of COO services	Slow to innovate. Lack strategic dialogue
Relationships	Working enthusiastically towards individual goals. Desire to work towards shared goals	Team leader has strong collaborative relationships with stakeholders	LQB	Dependency on the team leader to drive team projects. Passive tendency; avoid conflict	'Too busy' syndrome; no time for reflection
Internally facing processes	Meetings are valued, clear individual roles, high clarity of mission linked with wider political drivers	Rapid and effective response to concerns, quality, and priorities	High levels of trust and honest feedback. Positive feedback encouraged. Psychological safety	LQB	Inadequate systems for review
Learning	Appetite to seek ways to leverage and expand team strengths	Team members focused on improving individual functional services	People support active responsibility for one another's development	Culture of continuous improvement	LQB

There was also tension and disagreement as they explored the impact of the team's behaviour on performance. One team member offered: 'we don't feel authorised to lead collective projects and we are dependent on two team members to make shared projects happen ... they seem to have more power and funding'. This was passionately disputed by another team member. While there was discomfort and unease in the Team as they explored the data, at the end of the session one team member said: 'this was the conversation we needed to have, the one that we have been avoiding for fear of upsetting others'.

The Team now had expanded awareness of themselves and a way of discussing the team's performance. 'We developed a language (through the leadership circle framework and PERILL) to communicate with each other'. They chose to develop as a true team. They asked themselves, 'what does performance mean for this team?', 'how and when should we be a team?', and 'how can we stop using our team leader as the focal point for cross-divisional collaboration?'. This insight sparked action and commitment to developing themselves for the future.

Together they co-created a team development plan focused on optimising their creative leadership and connecting collectively with the wider stakeholder system. The plan consisted of three streams of work to achieve these development goals:

- Quarterly team coaching sessions.
- One-year individual coaching programme for each member of the Team.
- Leadership breakthrough programme for middle managers to scale leadership.

Approaches to developing the Team

The effectiveness of our team coaching engagement was as a result of four design features:

- Focused on both collective and individual development in parallel. Individual coaching focused on team members' improvement goals to help achieve the collective outcome.
- Adopted a developmental perspective recognising that mindsets shape behaviours and results. We focused on upgrading team beliefs and assumptions on current issues so that behaviour change stuck.
- Balanced a mix of different learning modalities: experiential learning, educational input, facilitation, team coaching, and supplemental reading were used throughout the programme.
- Explored issues that emerged during the contracting phase, as well as working with 'live' issues that emerged during the sessions.

We describe three approaches that wove in team coaching, individual coaching, facilitation, and experiential methods:

1 Supporting the reactive–creative shift
2 Creating individual breakthroughs to support collective leadership
3 Experiential methods to embody creative competencies.

Supporting the reactive–creative shift

The reactive–creative shift is a process of moving the Team from being fear-based, problem-focused, and reactive towards being creative, open, and solution-focused. The creative mind starts with purpose and vision, not with a problem. While fear is naturally present when creating what we want, it is not running the show. We coached the Team on making a reactive–creative shift by practising Hawkins' (2011) CID-CLEAR coaching process of listening, exploring, and enacting new action with the Team. It was done iteratively building on the insights that were evolving throughout the programme.

We demonstrate this approach below.

1 We started with helping the Team get a clear sense of purpose and vision of what they wanted to create: 'We want to be a united team focused on the customer, think systemically, and be deliberate about the long-term health of the department', something they cared about and was worth taking risks for.
2 We explored their view of current reality, without illusions or distortions to see things clearly.
3 We clarified the Team's focus and investment moving towards their vision.
4 We worked iteratively on what mattered most, catalysing their creative tension, noticing what moved them towards their focus and what did not. We encouraged the Team to share their hopes and fears before exploring ways forward.
5 They defined their behaviour, underlying beliefs, and assumptions driving their reactivity and managed the consequences.
6 They defined the behaviour, mindset, and indicator of success for each creative competency.
7 They identified conscious practices the Team needed to embed to become habits, such as bringing issues to the Team to tackle collectively.
8 The Team practised these commitments and reviewed their progress at their regular team meetings.

Creating individual breakthroughs to support collective leadership

In between team coaching sessions, we coached individuals towards their improvement goals to enable team success. Using the Immunity to Change coaching methodology (Kegan and Lahey, 2009), we targeted adaptive change (Heifetz, 2003), a shift in mindset and belief systems.

The Immunity to Change surfaced the stories that kept the fears alive, challenged the accuracy of their assumptions, and ultimately overturned their psychological immune system. One team member offered: 'Individual coaching allowed me to break down my assumptions about the Team; the reframing has created richer relationships in the Team'. The team leader shared: 'I learned so much about my direct reports, how they ticked, what triggers them, their orientation to life when we shared our individual Leadership Circle Profile graphs and Immunity to Change maps. I was better able to play to their strengths and support their development'.

Experiential methods to embody creative competencies

We used a variety of experiential techniques to explore team dynamics. To prepare them for a team coaching session, we used a somatic technique to connect their head and heart, consequently shifting the internal state in the Team. Here is an example of a collective somatic process:

- We asked the team to stand apart from each other and asked: 'In the context of the purpose and vision, connect to your role and responsibility. As you stand alone, feel into this as an individual. What do you notice?' Team members felt isolated: 'If I try to do it on my own, it feels very hard'.
- Joining with one other person we asked: 'What difference do you notice when there are two of you versus one only?' Feelings of support, diversity, and safety were shared.
- We invited two pairs to form a group of four and explored
  - What difference does this make?
  - What is the implication for your leadership?
  - What does this highlight for supporting each other to achieve the new culture?

This was another breakthrough moment for the team where they could feel it in their body (not just in their heads): 'We have so much more to give by joining up together'. They now understood what it meant to work collectively and be in a team: 'We could approach the corporate strategy as a whole system, rather than that is your project, and this is mine'.

Our learnings

We were reminded about the *importance of contracting between team coaches*. In this case, one of the coaches conducted all the briefing and debrief meetings with the team leader on her own. The coach assumed that her co-coach was too busy to attend, and it would be an unnecessary burden for her. This resulted in the co-coach not being fully connected to the client and having a partial picture of the context and dynamics. In contracting with each other, key questions to consider are:

- What do we need from each other to be at our best?
- How will we prepare the team leader for each team coaching session and how will we debrief him after each session?
- How do we work each other's strengths and support each other's weaknesses?

Given the demands on the team, *focusing them on changing One Big Thing* or a few small things, rather than a long list of behaviours and actions, was engaging and effective.

By sequencing the individual coaching work to occur at the beginning of the team work, members are more familiar with the models being used, having greater insight into themselves, and bringing their development work into the team from the outset.

We missed the opportunity to do *'live' coaching* in their regular team meetings, and to provide feedback on how they were working together in real time. The team leader shared that 'the team behaves themselves when the coaches are in the room'. 'Live' coaching may have surfaced hidden dynamics and challenges, providing an opportunity to enhance their development by challenging them to stretch into working with their areas of focus.

Impact of team coaching

The impact of the team coaching work was examined at two levels, inside the team and outside the team. We interviewed four team members to learn about their experience of the programme and its impact. Their verbatim comments are provided below.

Inside the team

The team coaching journey moved the needle on their effectiveness as a leadership team. Collectively, they were client centric, thinking more systemically and strategically. Increased trust and psychological safety in the team allowed for more generative dialogue and collaboration on both shared and individual projects. One team member commented: 'We were more purposeful in our time together. We went from being friendly to understanding each other at a deeper level and were prepared to be vulnerable in the team'. They were now a real team, not just in name only.

Outside the team

Our stakeholders experienced a more seamless integrated corporate service: '71% of our stakeholders agree that we are providing a high-quality corporate service … From the Ministers to our APS staff, we are receiving positive feedback'.

The team presented as a united team and engaged as a whole team to their wider stakeholders: 'We presented visually as one team at the COO group All Staff Town Halls, we consistently spoke about our corporate vision and the behaviours expected of staff. We role modelled teaming to our people'.

The department is more 'future-fit' and adaptable, evidenced by its rapid and effective response to Covid-19.

Conclusion

This case study shows that team coaching accelerates a team's ability to achieve breakthrough results through collective leadership. There are two key insights that helped facilitate this breakthrough. First, using sufficiently broad frameworks like PERILL and the Leadership Circle captures the complete system, minimising the risk of a partial understanding of the team dynamics and/or working on the wrong challenge. Secondly, the importance of regular coaching conversations with the team and peer supervision makes sustainable systemic change. It is the iterative cycle of exploring, listening, experimenting, and reviewing that makes the changes stick.

References

Anderson, R.J. and Adams, W.A. (2016) *Mastering Leadership*. New York: Wiley.

Clutterbuck, D., Gannon, J., Hayes, S., Lordanou, L., Lowe, K. and MacKie, D. (2019) *The Practitioner's Handbook of Team Coaching*. London: Routledge.

Hawkins, P. (2011) *Leadership Team Coaching: Developing Collective Transformational Leadership*. London: Kogan Page.

Heifetz, R.A. (2003) *Leadership Without Easy Answers*. Cambridge, MA: Harvard University Press.

Kegan, R. and Lahey, L.L. (2009) *Immunity to Change*. Boston, MA: Harvard Business Review Press.

The HR partner team at the Swedish Migration Agency

Peter Englén and Anders Troedsson

Background

This case study describes a team coaching process with the HR Partner team at the Swedish Migration Agency from February 2019 to January 2020, performed by two team coaches. It was a systemic approach, using Team Coaching International's Measurement Team Diagnostic™ and Patrick Lencioni's Playbook model for creating clarity and alignment.

The agency is a Swedish government entity for evaluating and making decisions on applications from people seeking temporary residence and citizenship in Sweden. There were 8,600 employees in 2018.

The pressure on the agency has been extreme. The influx of migrants seeking asylum exploded in 2015, primarily from the war-torn parts of Syria. During the peak, approximately 160,000 refugees came to Sweden over a period of a few months. Sweden was, along with Germany, the largest receiver of refugees per capita in the EU. The challenge was immense for the agency to increase the capacity for asylum management, while maintaining a legally secure and efficient process with many new administrators.

In 2016, the inflow slowed. Consequently, the agency had to reorganise and lay off 3,000 staff.

The HR partners (HRP) play an important role in supporting managers and management teams throughout the agency. They are organised as an HRP-team, which is part of the 60-person HR department. When this process started, there were eight members on the team, but during the process vacancies were filled and we ended up with 17. This was a huge challenge for us.

Before the process started, we were told the workload for the HR partners had been high for some time. They had had an acting manager for over two years and staff turnover on the team was high. There were some interpersonal conflicts brewing and significant differences in what HR partners did and offered locally.

The HR competencies on the team were very high and they were very much appreciated by the organisation. The newly appointed director of HR was willing to invest in the team and allocated resources for a process of 10 days over 11 months, with two team coaches. In addition to the team coaching, the team members were to be offered three individual coaching sessions each.

The expected outcome of the team coaching was a better psychosocial work environment, improved team cohesion, and consistent deliveries across the agency. In addition, the goal was to make the team self-sufficient, motivated, and able to continue their own team development after the process.

As a benchmark and to measure results, we suggested the Team Diagnostic Assessment™, or TDA, from Team Coaching International, both before and after the process. The strength of the tool is that it focuses on the team as a *system* and is not an amalgamation of individual assessments.

We wanted the team to have something tangible to take away and to continue working with after the process. There was also a need for a backbone to tie the sessions together. We chose to let the team create a Playbook along the lines outlined by Patrick Lencioni in his book *The Advantage* (2012).

Our approach to the process, aside from using the Playbook as the backbone, was to follow the team. As the need arose, and based on what the team considered necessary, we integrated interventions and training.

The process

We started the process with a two-day session offsite in February 2019. The first thing we did after the introductions was to agree on the rules for the session. What behaviours do we want to see and what don't we want in our session? This created safety and was something to practise holding each other responsible for. We drew the outline of one of the participant's body on a large piece of paper on the wall. Everyone then got to write behaviours they wanted inside, and behaviours they didn't want outside, of the outline. A clarifying discussion was necessary to aid understanding and come to agreement. This generated a lot of laughs and some very good discussions on how to behave towards each other. 'We never talk about this, but it important', one person commented. With the agreement of all members, these became the Rules of Conduct.

Then it was time to introduce the idea of systemic thinking. We explained that we were there to work with the team, not its individual parts. This caused both confusion and curiosity: 'How will you do that?'. To demonstrate how the focus was to be on their collective behaviour, we used the 'Helium-stick'. This is an exercise where the team together must lower a long, light rod, or stick, to the floor. The rules are that the stick must rest on both forefingers held horizontally and the fingers must not lose touch with the stick. At first the stick will appear to rise by itself, and then, as the team begins to cooperate, they can lower it to the floor. 'Okay, so a "systemic approach" is how we work together', commented one member.

A group discussion was initiated on what defines a team and what high-performing teams have in common. We asked them if they saw themselves as a team or a group and followed up with a discussion on what they wanted to be and what the value was in one or the other. Some said, 'I belong to my regional management team, not this team' and questioned why this process was needed. Others said, 'I don't know the others on the team or what they can contribute, so why should I ask them for help?', or argued: 'We keep doing double work and rules are interpreted differently depending on region, we should be the aligning force here'.

The conclusion was that they didn't view themselves as a particularly good team. The majority saw great value for the agency if they could become a team: better alignment, higher value deliveries locally, and generally 'more bang for your buck'. We also explored how their team performance affected their stakeholders.

When they had agreed on their desire to be a team, we revealed the results of the Team Diagnostic Assessment™ (TDA). The TDA measures 14 strengths, or team performance indicators (TPIs). These are strengths required to be a high-performing team. The TPIs are divided into two groups: Productivity and Positivity (www.teamcoachinginternational.com).

The results showed a wide spread in the TPI results. Respect (6.8), trust (6.3), and team leadership (6.0) had high scores, while goals and strategies (4.3) and decision-making (4.3) had markedly low scores.

The main value of such measurements is the discussion to be had about the team's day-to-day work. The question we asked was: 'How do others see this?' The answers took a long time in coming, but eventually one person pointed out: 'We don't have any clear goals for our team', and another said, 'maybe this is why we deliver different things in different places'.

Putting words to what the low decision-making score represented was even harder. Asking them to set goals for the process made them aware of their behaviour as a team. The discussion went in circles and as soon as they came close to a decision, they went off on a new tangent. Reflecting this back to them allowed them to see the pattern. After reflecting back their inability to decide, the goal-setting became easier as they began to notice when they were diverging.

Another practical outcome of this epiphany was that they planned a full day on their own to decide on what meetings to have and what to do at the different meetings – they called it the 'Meeting-Meeting'.

Delving deeper into the data in the report, the questions with the lowest and highest scores became apparent. The team used this to see what they needed to work with and what strengths they possessed and could build on. One team member said, 'we really need to practise giving and receiving feedback', and 'we never celebrate, why is that?'. This was great input for us as coaches to plan for the following sessions, and to create 'homework' for in between sessions.

As a next step, we introduced the Playbook model. It consists basically of six questions to be addressed by the team:

1 Why do we exist?
2 How do we behave?
3 What do we do?

4   How will we succeed?
5   What is most important, right now?
6   Who must do what?

When we presented the model to the team, they liked it: 'This sounds good and not too hard to do'. But when we grappled with the first question, 'Why do we exist?', it proved to be harder than expected. The team wrestled with the question for a full afternoon, without being able to go beyond platitudes. We, as coaches, had to keep asking 'what does that mean?' to get to the core.

Team members' frustration was high as the day's session came to a close without a clear answer. The next morning, with fresh eyes, and a good night's sleep, it was much more straightforward. They found an answer that really meant something to them. The relief and joy in the room was palpable as they agreed, 'we coach and guide the managers in creating the greatest value in all operations at the agency'. This answer was the foundation against which all the others could be gauged.

An answer to the second question, 'How do we behave?', proved easier. It could be distilled from the Rules of Conduct that they already had agreed upon. The team quickly formulated their first version of an answer. But agreement at this stage was very general. The team had to go back to this question several times during the process. They started out with 15 'dos' and 8 'don'ts' that after eight months were whittled down to: 'prestige', 'inclusion', 'active participation', and 'generosity'.

The key question now became what they should do as a team when a rule is broken. The reason for agreeing Rules of Conduct is to allow the team to know what to hold each other accountable for, and how to communicate this in a constructive way. One team member observed: 'We have done this kind of exercise before but never talked about how to hold each other to account. Now, this will make a difference!'

The third question, 'What do we do?', revealed that the team had very different views on what to deliver. Everyone was working differently and expressed unique needs. To find the answer, we brought the team back to the first question, 'Why do we exist?' What the team does – and doesn't – do needs to be directly related to why it exists. This helped the team to set up a first version. The question stayed with the team throughout the whole process and was gradually refined over time.

Closing the first two-day session, we coached the team to set goals for where they wanted to be in 11 months. The team was tasked with defining what TPIs they saw as the ones most requiring improvement, and what score to aim for at the end of the 11-month process. They agreed on the following:

- Decision-making   6.0 (vs. 4.3)
- Goals and strategies   7.0 (vs. 4.3)
- Communication   7.0 (vs. 6.2)
- Resources   8.0 (vs. 5.6)

Throughout the following three sessions, from March to June 2019, our coaching was aimed at strengthening the team's capabilities around decision-making, feedback, and how to deal with stress. The coaching was intertwined with answering questions 4 and 5: 'How will we succeed?' and 'What is most important, right now?' The team assigned themselves homework to do between sessions to be followed up the next time we met.

It became apparent that by allowing the team to assign their own homework, they were entering into agreements they didn't intend to keep. We reflected this back to them and asked what other agreements they ignored: 'We never thought about this before, now it is obvious. Why do we do this?' Over the course of the process, we saw marked improvement in this area and more than once we heard, 'Is everyone on board with this?' when assigning themselves tasks.

There was a fair deal of apprehension on the team as August neared. The team had been understaffed and the new manager had made a huge effort to fill the positions. The result was that the size of the team doubled by the next session. We asked ourselves, 'Do we start over and regard this as a new team?' We decided to ask the team for its views, but they wanted to keep the process going: 'We have a great tool in the Playbook, let's use that to bring the new members aboard'.

The last session before September was devoted to work on how to on-board the new members. We let the team describe what their needs were when they were new. They created a plan for on-boarding where the team coaching was a major part.

In a two-day session in September, nine new members were added to the team. Much of the on-boarding was built on the Playbook and getting to know each other. Addressing the sixth question, 'Who does what?', gave everyone the opportunity to express their interests and expertise. The discussion resulted in agreement to reap the benefit of everyone's expertise. After the two days, one of the new members said, 'Wow, this is the best introduction I have ever had! It is like what you read about, but I never expected it to exist. Now I can be productive from day three on the job'. Another stated: 'Now I know who to contact, and I feel it is okay to call'.

We were surprised to see just how powerful the Playbook was in introducing the new members, and how quickly they came together as a team. The successful on-boarding was noticed in the organisation and the team leader was asked such questions as, 'What did you do to have everyone on board so quickly?'

Coaching a team of 17 members was hard. There are too many relationships to keep track of. This was taxing on us and slowed the process down. The result was, however, a team where they all know and trust each other, helping and bringing each other in. We learned to trust the team and the process. We were impressed by how the simple act of reflecting what the team says about itself starts the process of improvement.

In the next three sessions, between October 2019 and January 2020, the team worked on clarifying, integrating, and committing to the answers in the Playbook. We focused the dialogue on how they could utilise the learnings from the process and how to hold each other to account for further team development. In the final session, the focus was on evaluating, setting new goals, and celebrating.

The HR director, who came to the last session we had with the team, said: 'I am so pleased to see how you have become a team and how you use each other's skills now'.

Results

Jaqueline Peters and Catherine Carr (2015) state in their study of team coaching effectiveness that there are basically three types of coaching outcomes:

- team process improvements,
- results/outputs, and
- individual learning improvements.

The *team process improvements* for the HRP team were significant. Before the last workshop, the team took a new TDA. All TPIs showed improvement, not least the areas prioritised by the team in the first session.

Several other members of the team agreed when one said, 'Before we were *organised* as a team, now we *work* as a team!' Another major improvement on process was the Meeting-Meeting that defined all the meetings, what to do and what to decide in the different meetings.

The individual coaching was greatly appreciated: 'It gave me a chance to work on both professional and individual improvement areas like stress management, leadership development, and communication with the managers I support'.

The successful development of the team got a lot of attention both within and without the HR department. As a result, two second-level management teams have chosen to work with the combination of the Playbook and TDA measurements. Several project teams in the organisation have made their own Playbooks with the help of the HRPs.

In a follow-up meeting in May 2020, we received a testimonial that the HR Partner team, thanks to the team coaching process they had undertaken, was

Table 3 Goals and end results

	First score	Goal	End score
Decision-making	4.3	6.0	**6.6**
Goals and strategies	4.3	7.0	**6.9**
Communication	6.2	7.0	**7.6**
Resources	5.6	8.0	**6.9**

better functioning, more self-motivated, and better suited for working from home than other teams in the organisation when the Covid-19 pandemic struck.

As for the *results/outputs* of the team, they had a hard time defining any measurable result of the team's work. As a service function it is hard to quantify the direct impact on the output of the agency. As coaches this was a little frustrating. Although we were results-focused, we had to keep reminding ourselves that it was the team that needed to find the solutions and improvements.

A tangible outcome was that the team made a service level agreement (SLA), and negotiated it with all the teams they were part of. This was work that the team took upon themselves to do and was proof of their improved capacity to make decisions. The SLA was very useful for both clarifying what they could and could not deliver: 'I am so relieved because now I can point to the SLA and say, "This is not what we agreed I should do," and I don't need to feel bad about it!'

Another output was that the team became more aligned: 'Now we know that a question asked in one place gets the same answer as if it was asked here', was one comment from the team.

Regarding *individual learning improvements*, the members testified that they had increased their personal capability to help improve other teams, both as members of the team and as internal consultants. The individual learning also manifested itself in posture and how they went about their daily work: 'I am better at saying "no" now. Now I can get help in areas I am not really good at, without feeling that I can't do my job properly'.

References

Lencioni, P.M. (2012) *The Advantage*. Hoboken, NJ: Wiley.
Peters, J. and Carr, C. (2015) *High Performance Team Coaching: A Comprehensive System for Leaders and Coaches*. Calgary, Alberta: InnerActive Leadership Associates.
Sandahl, P. and Phillips, A. (2019) *Teams Unleashed: How to Release the Power and Human Potential of Work Teams*. London: Nicholas Brealey.
Team Coaching International (TCI) (2020) The TCI Team Diagnostic™. [https://team-coachinginternational.com/programs/program-team-diagnostic/].

A case study on team coaching using an appreciative inquiry approach in an educational institution

Paul S.H. Lim

Introduction and background

The team coaching assignment that is the focus of this case study started very positively with a team leader who was keen on team coaching, yet despite promising circumstances, ultimately failed. Here is the context and lessons learnt.

I was coaching leaders of several different educational institutions, following a leadership development programme. They were a mix of relatively new and experienced leaders. Some were in their first cycle (averaging 3–5 years per cycle) of leading an institution while others were into their second cycle, leading more established and larger institutions. My client, the team leader, was six months into his second cycle leading an established institution. In our earlier coaching sessions, he shared that, in his previous cycle, he avoided being seen as making too many changes as a new leader by operating more as 'first among colleagues', and failed to exercise the leadership expected of him. He had opportunities to initiate important changes but had let them slip away.

Six months into his second leadership cycle, he noted many of his management team and heads of departments had become complacent and jaded by the constant pressure of producing academic results. They were working hard, but were not always aligned, nor taking enough ownership of their work. The 'school' (his preferred terminology) was highly respected and had a long history with an active alumnus, many of whom were significant leaders in industry and public service. An alumnus himself, he felt building core school values and character were overshadowed in recent years by the focus on academic results. He wanted to engage his team in re-visioning an exciting future for the school and to take greater ownership.

He believed a strong team was far more effective than a single leader. His aspiration was to co-create a shared vision that would energise his staff, students, alumni, and parents, while also meeting the needs of other stakeholders, including HQ and the board. He wanted to reinvigorate and inspire his staff to serve with greater pride, collaboration, and purpose. He was keen to develop them as part of this project. Consequently, I proposed the idea of a systemic team coaching framework based on the 5 Disciplines of Team Coaching (Hawkins, 2011) coupled with an appreciative inquiry approach (Cooperrider et al., 2008).

Approach

The combined approach was agreed, and the project started towards the year-end. Having studied appreciative inquiry (AI) under David Cooperrider and his colleagues and having applied it successfully before, I felt confident of its utility and relevance. I believed it would help the team find inspiration in the rich history and core strengths of the school, with its alumni and affiliated communities, and grow team collaboration. I believed an AI approach would head-off potential resistance and provide a good springboard into team coaching.

When we shared the approach with the broader team of vice-principals, heads of department, and other key personnel, they were excited. Most were pleased that we would build on their experiences and the legacies of the school. A handful were uncertain but not resistant. As educators, they warmed to the positivity of the AI approach and wanted to learn more about it for themselves. However, they also worried about how much extra work it would entail on top of their normal workload.

Team formation

The 20 team members included the deputy (one level down), heads of departments (two levels down), and three high-potentials, who were being groomed for future leadership roles. As the team coach, I preferred that the team comprised members with clearer roles and responsibilities for the success of the project. However, I failed in this and allowed the team leader and his deputy to make decisions on team member inclusion based on greater diversity and buy-in. Overall, there was good representation for the AI process, but challenging to work with for team coaching. This would have ramifications and will be discussed later.

Methodology deployed

The broad format comprised the following elements:

- Team workshops, including on AI
- Team meetings, including crafting an interview questionnaire

- Small group work, such as analysing data gathered
- Individual work and conducting interviews
- Team reviews and between the leader and team coach
- Coaching the leader and team on the team coaching process.

Early progress

Applying the AI approach, we got off to a good start. Most came on board quickly, except for a few who were initially reticent. The heads of facilities and operations are traditionally not part of the core management team. They felt due to their roles they were obliged to join, but did not feel fully included, or saw the project as an integral part of their responsibility.

After the initial workshops, we moved quickly to developing 'provocative propositions' to design the interview questionnaire, a key part of the AI process (Cooperrider et al., 2008). The intent of the 'provocative propositions' was to craft a narrative enlivened with vivid imagery for a highly desirable and compelling future. As the facilitator and coach, I worked with the leader to ensure everyone's input was actively sought and listened to. The team was split into small groups to craft their version, before engaging in full team discussions and arriving at a final version that the team felt was both an exciting and inspiring future vision.

I trained the team in interview techniques to seek specifics and elicit qualitative data. After this, the team leader and I facilitated discussions on the interview questions, encouraging three simple questions:

1 A high point experience for you in the school?
2 The specific behaviours or actions displayed?
3 Your dream for the school?

We scheduled a meeting where they interviewed each other to experience it for themselves. The result was a palpable shift in the team's energy, abuzz with enthusiasm as they shared inspiring stories. They reconnected with past experiences that made them proud, which renewed and reactivated their deeper purpose.

The analyses gave insight into what was valued and provided input to the 5 Disciplines Model (Hawkins, 2011), which we would next embark upon:

- **Commissioning:** understanding what our stakeholders want from us, what is our collective purpose?
- **Clarifying:** what are we here to achieve that we cannot achieve by working in parallel?
- **Co-creating:** how do we work together in a way that is generative?
- **Connecting:** how do we engage with and create greater value for all our stakeholders?

- **Core learning:** how does the whole team develop and learn, not just the individuals within it?

During the *commissioning* stage, the team was highly motivated, evidenced by their enthusiasm in meetings and active participation in defining the school's purpose. Everyone participated in assimilating the insights from the interview data and through a discursive process, crafted statements of purpose that had broad agreement. The purpose statements covered the values desired, outcomes that balanced the spirit of the school with academic excellence, and the various stakeholders' views.

The commissioning stage was very useful in identifying the school's wider stakeholder groups, some of whom were not initially included. Team members were excited to interview them. Each had to interview between five and eight school staff, parents, and alumni. The team leader, his deputy, and a selected few others were tasked with interviewing HQ staff and other stakeholders.

The interviews took longer than planned because of school holidays. Nevertheless, the results were similar: real life stories that were inspiring, generating much enthusiasm among the interviewees. As interviewees relived their positive experiences associated with the school, they lit up and gave strong support to the project. Interviewees were happy to share their stories and were glad that the school's rich history was being leveraged. The entire process was a validation of the 'broaden-and-build' approach (Fredrickson, 2004) and added extra energy to the team.

So far so good.

Challenges

The challenges latent in the team composition manifested shortly after the interview data was analysed. During the commissioning stage, the team was observably excited and motivated.

As we moved to the *clarifying* stage, contracting with team members' roles and action plans, we observed mild-to-strong resistance on the part of several team members. The refrain of 'lack of resources, time, and priorities' grew. A few turned to the leader to make decisions on work priorities, saying: 'I could do this, but it is going to take time, so I need to drop some of my CCA (co-curricular activities)'.

While acknowledging these challenges, the leader decided to push on. He felt that even if the project was not a complete success, it would provide useful learning. To paraphrase him: 'It's a new thing for us and we have made a good start. I'm happy they are enthusiastic in participating and learning even though it is on top of their normal work. At least we are now aligned on our purpose and vision to co-create a new future'.

We cycled through the other stages of the 5 Disciplines, from commissioning to clarifying team KPIs, goals, and roles; to *co-creating* sub-teams to determine operating principles for how the team would work together; and to *connecting*, setting up processes and tracking mechanisms for more regular engagements with key stakeholders. We only briefly discussed the team's *core learning*.

To be fair, important work was done in some of these stages. The team defined the key goals that needed to be explored further, including more curriculum time on Civics to develop the values and character of students and the training of teachers to do this effectively. They formed sub-teams to look at different parts of the goals – for example, a team to look at better communication processes to engage with students, parents, alumni, and volunteers.

The team leader, however, underestimated the time needed for the project. The delay in the project approval process contributed to a late year-end start that coincided with school holidays. The team leader wanted to complete the project even if it meant cutting some corners, as it would provide useful inputs to the school's work plans for HQ review. He had also contracted me for a period of nine months, and we had by then already expended more than seven of them, and there were real concerns about budget constraints if the project overran.

Results

Despite the challenges faced, the team leader and I felt we had made progress. The team had certainly benefited from the AI process, and there was a noticeable mindset shift in many team members: it gave them a lived experience of the education sector's mantra of encouraging a 'growth mindset' (Dweck, 2006).

- They connected with the purpose and vision they crafted, providing clarity and inspiration into the future.
- They identified core strengths of the school, providing sharper focus on opportunities.
- Goals had been defined to move the school forward.
- Team dynamics had improved. Team members were more open and positive; and the power distance between themselves and the team leader was reduced.

Lessons learned

Despite the benefits gained, from a *team coaching perspective* the project did not quite succeed. These are the lessons learnt.

Team leader readiness

The team leader was keen to promote collective leadership – perhaps too keen, such that at times he failed to take leadership. This was apparent in a number of situations, such as when failing to adequately address the issue of 'lack of resources, or it's not within my remit'.

Also, as much as he was open and keen to empower the team, some were not ready to take the initiative, although they were grateful for the opportunity. This is rooted in the hierarchical structure and culture of the school and the larger system. Most things had to negotiate several layers of approval. Any significant action, even if fully delegated, still needed the obligatory stamp of approval. I often heard team members say, 'Okay, I'll do this *and* come back to you with recommendations' or '*seek* your approval'. This was also reflected in his deputy's reluctance to take decisions.

As a result, I felt it would have been useful to contract to extend and continue the one-to-one coaching of the leader.

Team composition

The composition of the team was not adequately thought through and given enough weight. Looking back, I failed to clearly differentiate the project team from the core team with the leader. While it was useful to involve a larger group of team members for the initial AI process, a clearer separation and definition of the core team members who would be responsible to drive the success of the institution was imperative. A part of this was also the leader's reluctance to make this tough decision, and my unconscious collusion, as a coach, with it.

Access to the full team

I often did not get the time needed with the leader or other key team members. As he was too busy, the leader was quite dependent on his deputy to move the project along. Requests for meetings with members needed to go through the deputy, who was acting more out of compliance than personal leadership and often ended up being more of a go-between. While I was never directly denied access, the protocol created a different dynamic in my interactions with the team members. I felt it created a barrier between me and the team, as if someone needed to 'clear and approve' any meeting. It did not provide good role modelling on how the team should be functioning, with full and unimpeded access to one another. It caused leakage of time and was unproductive. I had failed to contract effectively with the team leader and had underestimated the inherently hierarchical culture. I likely misconstrued their collegiality and respectfulness of each other as openness.

Team time commitment(s)

There were times when not all the team members were available to meet for a scheduled team meeting, which was aggravated by the fact that, to secure a meeting, we had to plan some weeks ahead. Some would come late or not at all. This posed challenges to ensuring clear communications and a common understanding. There were times when absent team members were not able to adequately 'catch up' with the rest of the team. On other occasions, a pre-scheduled four-hour meeting would be reduced to a two- or three-hour meeting at the last minute because of work emergencies, creating delays and constraints.

Team coach expertise

Despite my caution and attempt to ensure I was not seen as the de facto 'expert', there were several occasions when the team leader, the deputy, or team members would defer to me for a decision or a final comment. I was cautious to fend off and reframe, reminding the leader and team members about the need for them to take responsibility. However, the fact that it happened several times and even late in the process, suggested that the team did not fully embrace their responsibility. I recognise this as a limitation on a few fronts. First, because of the budget constraints, I was unable to contract with the team leader for one-to-one coaching with him, enabling him to lead his team more effectively. This consequently blind-sided and limited me. Secondly, the team was quite large. I would have benefited from working with another coach so we could manage different aspects of the team dynamics. Again, this is partly attributable to budget constraints. Thirdly, again given the budget, we should have contracted more clearly on achievable outcomes rather than the entire project. In short, if the budget would only get us to the clarifying stage, we should have contracted as such.

As noted earlier, given the large team size, it would have been very helpful to have re-contracted to bring in another team coach. Together we might have been able to model the teaming process better, look for gaps in our work with the team, as well as with each other. It might have served us well with one focusing on the process and the other on team dynamics.

Culture of the institution

As the school is fundamentally an educational institution, there were occasions when the team members behaved in a manner that suggested they were more keen to learn about the process and the theory behind it than they were about fully participating and living the experience. Part of the solution lies in clearer contracting with the team and with the team leader.

Conclusion

Upon reflection and with more recent team coaching experience, it is clear that team coaching is very challenging when the team we are working with is not yet a real team – in this case study, the team ultimately was more of a work group.

While this does not inevitably lead to a less successful team coaching engagement, it does mean that different interventions need to be taken that are more appropriate. For example, I would set up more structures and processes to work with the group and ensure the team leader has coaching to build a more effective team, even while I hold a systemic team coaching lens to it. This engagement was not as successful because I did not recognise this early enough to apply the relevant interventions and methodologies.

Regardless, this case study is perhaps reflective of how current team coaching delivery may have the intention and use elements of team coaching, but in the final analysis, may have been inappropriately called 'team coaching'.

References

Cooperrider, D.L., Whitney, D., and Starvos, J.M. (2008) *The Appreciative Handbook: For Leaders of Change*, 2nd edition. Brunswick, OH: Crown Custom Publishing.

Dweck, C.S. (2006) *Mindset: The New Psychology of Success*. New York: Random House.

Fredrickson, B. (2004) The broaden-and-build theory of positive emotions, *Philosophical Transaction of the Royal Society of London B*, 359 (1449): 1367–1378.

Hawkins, P. (2011) *Leadership Team Coaching: Developing Collective Transformational Leadership*. London: Kogan Page.

Team coaching for culture change

Jacqueline Peters

Culture change is a complex and long-term venture that requires courageous leadership and perseverance. I was privileged to work with a leadership team of three assistant vice presidents (AVPs) in a post-secondary institution who rose to this challenge. Our two-year journey is outlined in this eclectic and multifaceted case study.

The four of us customised an approach to help the AVPs' three departments in a facilities division better achieve their goals and work together more effectively. We were focused on supporting the division's ongoing transition from a culture of silos to a more collaborative, cross-functional culture. We were guided by a new mission and set of values that we had crafted with all leaders in the division the previous year.

A secondary goal was to enhance the working relationships between the AVPs' staff and the many external contractors who they worked with to complete their complex projects. We were well supported by the AVPs' executive sponsor who was their vice president and one of the executive team members for the institution.

We focused not on the AVPs' individual units, but the connections and collaborations between the units, the division, and its stakeholders. This multifaceted focus for the initiative fit the parameters of what Peter Hawkins (2017) defines as a systemic team coaching initiative. As the coach, I worked with multiple teams when they were together and apart. We worked to improve processes, working agreements, leadership, communication, and collaboration skills within the division and across various stakeholder groups.

A key challenge the AVPs faced in making this culture shift was a build-up of resistance and change fatigue, especially among front-line managers and staff. There had been multiple attempts over the years to improve collaboration and effectiveness. To address this resistance, we created a highly participative approach that required feedback and buy-in from the participants before confirming each next step.

The specific activities in the 'Connect' initiative were informed by the six-phase High Performance Team Coaching model developed by Peters and Carr (2015):

1 **Assessment** of team effectiveness at various points using the *High Performance Relationship and Team Assessment* (Peters, 2015b).

2 **Coaching for team design**, which included identifying the members, structure, and agreements for the teams.
3 **Team launch** activities, such as developing a team charter that defined the collective purpose, goals, working agreements, and success measures for Connect.
4 **Individual coaching** of the AVPs as needed.
5 **Ongoing team coaching sessions** with each team involved in the initiative.
6 **Review of learning and successes** via individual and team reflection and dialogue, and informal feedback from the VP sponsor and other internal stakeholders.

The five teams that participated in Connect included a mix of the AVPs and their directors, managers, and front-line staff. It was a 'team of teams' approach in that there was one large team with all 28 of the Connect participants and an additional four subsets of that large team. The team members were selected because they were all working on a common project. We had relevant, just-in-time conversations to help the team members discuss their challenges, create new working agreements, and implement new ways of interacting as they progressed their common goals.

The three AVPs participated in and provided oversight for all the formal sessions with the five teams. There were four core phases to this team coaching/team development intervention:

1 Listen to understand
2 Create a new model
3 Act
4 Check in and refine

In reality, the phases ended up overlapping in an iterative process of listening, creating, acting, and checking in and refining. The following provides an overview of the core activities in each phase.

Phase 1: Listen to understand. Each team participated in at least one 'Listen to understand' session. The goals for these sessions were to:

- Provide a consistent message about the Connect goals, success measures, and outcomes.
- Gain an understanding of the current state of collaboration – specifically, finding out from each team what was working and what was not.
- Gain an understanding of the patterns of interaction between the teams: How did action in one area affect other areas (system dynamics)? What were the reoccurring themes?
- Ensure that staff felt heard and had a chance to voice their perspective.

We captured the ideas and themes from these conversations and used them to build a shared vision and consensus on the next steps.

Phase 2: Create a new model. Phase 2 focused on defining the behaviours that would create greater collaboration within and between the teams. Each team provided input into a shared Team Charter that provided the map for what they wanted to achieve and how they wanted to work together. There were one to three meetings with each team to develop this collective Charter. We role-modelled a collaborative approach in these sessions so the team members could see and experience how to communicate more effectively among themselves outside of the team coaching sessions.

The key components of the Connect Team Charter were:

Purpose: Connect aims to strengthen and enhance collaboration. Connect is about HOW we work together to strengthen a day-to-day culture that embodies our values.

Key goals:

- Reinforce what it looks like to work as 'one team' in this project
- Reinforce the lessons learned already compiled from previous projects
- Share and apply the lessons learned during this pilot with the rest of the division.

Working agreements:

- Review how we (this group) are working together as a team on a quarterly basis
- Expect/assume good intentions
- Consider taking time to engage in giving and receiving important feedback constructively in person
- Be willing to request feedback
- Pick an appropriate time and place/ask permission to provide feedback
- Be open to alternative ideas
- Be transparent about intentions
- Strive for 5-to-1 positive-to-negative interactions with each other
- Continuously improve and reassess our working agreements periodically.

IMPACT values:

- Inclusive
- Mindful
- People-focused
- Accountable
- Collaborative
- Transparent.

Success measures:

- Strengthen our relationships
- Create even better collaboration and a common understanding of our needs
- Achieve excellence in what we do
- Foster a stronger feeling of what it means to work as 'one team'.

Phase 3: Act. The Act phase was comprised of three to five meetings with each team to achieve the following:

1. Assess the current level of collaboration and team effectiveness behaviours using the research-based *High Performance Relationship and Team Assessment (HPR)* (Peters, 2015b). The HPR assessment asks participants to provide ratings on a scale of 1–10 about the five key building blocks for effective teams and relationships. These five building blocks are Safety, Purpose, Structure, Camaraderie, and Repair. The assessment results fostered rich discussion and action planning among the team members. It also provided a benchmark to track perceptions of team effectiveness over time.
2. Develop a common language and set of collaborative behaviours. The five key building blocks of high-performance relationships and teams (Peters, 2015a) was the core model used. In addition, specific sessions were held to discuss and practise skills that the teams identified they needed to better collaborate together. The topics included: dealing with resistance, providing feedback, and peer coaching. We used the GROW coaching model because it was simple for participants to learn and the four steps of discussing the Goal, Reality, Options, and Will (Action) (Whitmore, 2017) could be scaled to fit a short or long coaching conversation.
3. Identify specific actions to improve shared work processes.
4. Provide ongoing feedback about how the teams were collaborating together.
5. Identify actions, next steps, and agendas for the next sessions together.

We were focused on modelling the collaborative culture change we wanted to see so each team session included elements of coaching, facilitating, and teaching. The team coaching focused on providing opportunities for reflection and the coach offered observations as needed. We supported the team to pause and engage in dialogue about *how* they were working together in the sessions, not just *what* they were working on.

We created an action learning opportunity in these phase 3 sessions by creating sub-groups to address the specific collaboration issues they identified in phase 1. Participants put their collaborative skills and working agreements into action as they tackled these real challenges in their work environment.

One of the important outcomes from the Act phase was that two directors initiated a separate project to address the processes identified as barriers to collaboration and effectiveness. These directors compiled the phase 1 feedback into themes and created an action plan for each group of issues. They then held separate meetings with relevant team members to progress the actions and create meaningful change in the workplace. These improvements were documented in new processes and manuals that were shared with internal and external stakeholders.

Phase 4: Check in and refine. In practice, this was not a distinct phase on its own because we were checking in with participants and refining our goals and plans throughout the Connect initiative. The participants provided feedback at each session and the coach and AVPs designed the next step and session based on this input.

In addition, every team session started with a 'check in' and 'check out' opportunity so participants could reflect on their own learning journey. These activities consisted of a 'trigger question' and then each team member had a minute to write down their response before sharing their thoughts one at a time around the room. The goal was to practise being totally present to each other with focused listening and attention to understand; not listening to respond or react. Some examples of the trigger questions we used are:

- What is one action you implemented since our last session?
- What is one success you have had as a team since our last session?
- What is your key insight and action from today's session?

We reviewed the working agreements at each session to confirm that people were still willing to gently hold themselves and others accountable to these agreements. We also gave people an opportunity to add or refine the agreements based on their work at the last session and/or their interactions with each other between sessions. These agreements were an important part of the culture shift because they represented the behaviours needed from each other to build trust and consistency.

In each session, participants provided an update on the actions from the previous sessions. Our focus was on collaborating within and between sessions, taking real action, reflecting on successes and challenges, and then creating a plan for the next set of actions.

Outcomes

We met with each team at several points over the two years to identify successes, track progress, and celebrate improvements and small wins. A formal conversation to document successes was held near the end of the pilot. The participants indicated the following achievements and outcomes:

- Implemented tangible changes to the project design and delivery operating manuals
- Updated and clarified roles and responsibilities for ongoing projects
- Created an employee engagement plan
- Increased team effectiveness behaviours as measured by the *High Performance Relationship and Team Assessment* (HPR)
- Increased amount of idea sharing between team members and levels
- Enhanced personal connections among all members of these teams
- Improved joint ownership of tasks and projects
- Increased input and buy-in for collaboration from front-line staff.

Months after the last Connect session, one of the AVPs said that it was clear to her that the management staff were demonstrating enhanced communication skills. She also noted that participants were modelling a 'one team' perspective by problem-solving together to get things done. She stated that the amount of blaming of others for errors had reduced. There were clear examples of assuming good intentions and giving others the benefit of the doubt, which was providing a more positive starting point for solving problems. All the AVPs noted that some of their historic critics were 'developing a more self-reflective attitude on their personal role versus pointing to what someone else was not doing, both within and outside of the sessions'. The AVPs also noted that they were hearing more positive feedback from participants, their VP, and other stakeholders.

During the last session, we asked the participants to provide ideas to continue to model, enact, and grow the collaborative culture outside of the teams participating in Connect. We will use this input in the closing sessions for Connect later this year.

Key learnings and insights

What worked well in this pilot was the collaborative and flexible approach, increasing the number of meetings as needed. We engaged managers more frequently than anticipated before we worked with the front-line staff. This resulted in greater engagement, ownership, and role-modelling from the managers to other employees.

Secondly, the coach and three AVPs met frequently. This facilitated ongoing communication and commitment to the culture change we were creating. One AVP team meeting stood out in particular. An AVP stated in an individual coaching session that she was becoming resentful that she had become the default conduit and representative from the AVP team for the Connect follow-up actions and communication. The coaching session helped this leader decide to speak up about her concern in the next AVP team coaching session. The other two AVPs responded positively and agreed to be more accountable for taking action and providing their input in a clear and timely way. The AVPs shared their learning from this feedback conversation with all the Connect participants. They presented a positive role model to the teams about providing and receiving feedback graciously and creating new working agreements to enhance collaboration when needed.

Thirdly, the Connect teams focused on their own internal and cross-functional effectiveness as well as the communication and value they were creating with their many stakeholders, especially their contractors. This systemic view helped create a greater sense of involvement and collective purpose. As noted in phase 3, two Connect directors initiated and took ownership to re-write some processes and standards to ensure greater clarity among all their internal and external colleagues.

Fourthly, we noted early on that the front-line, more operationally focused participants were interested in pragmatic processes and practices and were less comfortable with self-reflection and improving their personal skills. As a result, we made sure that we addressed their need to focus on concrete issues. One AVP stated: 'What was unique in Connect was our "both and" approach; we knew we needed to work on the HOW and to set the stage for this to occur. We also needed to provide the WHAT (content) through tangible evidence of improving the practices, tools, and points of friction in operations'.

The key thing we could have done differently was to identify more tangible measures of the outcomes and value-added when we started the Connect initiative. Specifically, we could have tracked team members' success at meeting project budgets and timelines to see if there were changes pre and post Connect; we had relied on anecdotal evidence of improvements only. We also could have formally tracked the number of major communication breakdowns and conflicts that occurred. This could be a possible follow-up to explore when we do our next check-in meeting.

We also could have solicited formal input and feedback from key external stakeholders (e.g. contractors, executive team) initially and as we progressed. This would have made the external stakeholders a more prominent focus for the initiative, which could have helped the teams be even more accountable about the impact they were having on others outside of Connect. It also might have helped the stakeholders look for changes in the level and quality of collaboration that was happening with their Connect colleagues.

Clutterbuck (2007) and Hawkins (2017) emphasise the role of team coaches to support the learning of the team. While some teams were quite reflective about their learning, there could have been even greater emphasis on co-learning and generalisation of the skills for all of the teams. Specifically, we noticed that session topics became much more concrete and conversations less reflective the closer participants were to working on the front line. As a coach, I could have been more courageous about tackling this reluctance, since I tended to err on the side of keeping discussions practical rather than reflective. This was a difficult balance since the AVPs and I wanted to keep the front-line employees engaged and participating without alienating them by becoming too 'touchy-feely'. As a result, I hesitated at times to challenge participants to go deeper with their reflection, learning, and self-accountability.

We also could have considered having another coach/co-facilitator for the larger team sessions. This might have supported me to be more courageous about intervening in the moment during sessions. However, there was one upside of not having another coach/facilitator: it did require the AVPs to take on greater ownership as co-facilitators and co-leaders of the initiative overall, which was a key success factor.

Summary

Connect was an ambitious culture change initiative that was led by three committed AVPs and a team coach who engaged a team of teams to collaborate more effectively. We were able to draw out historical resistors to collaboration and change and facilitate a positive change in their mindset, skillset, and behaviours in the workplace. This multidisciplinary, multi-team, systemic team coaching initiative ended up impacting hundreds of others as a result of changes to processes and more collaborative interactions between the participants and their stakeholders. One of the AVPs provided a helpful summary of the two-year initiative:

> 'The meetings of the managers and staff in between the formal sessions have been critical to the success of Connect because they demonstrate the tangible commitment to change, to listening to concerns and demonstrating action, and they provide the forum for the leaders to demonstrate what it looks like to work from a one team perspective. That the directors developed the confidence to lead this was key. Key enablers of this were:
>
> 1 the AVPs standing in lock-step, modelling the way both in front of the group and also in one-on-one meetings with our directors, and
>
> 2 the workshops that provided practice and skill-building.
>
> Doing this together created an accountability among the group to walk the talk beyond the practice sessions and it provided a common language to help them/us to better articulate difficult issues. We now all know what high-performance teams look like and what our individual roles are in creating and maintaining this team'.

References

Clutterbuck, D. (2007) *Coaching the Team at Work*. London: Nicholas Brealey.

Hawkins, P. (2017) *Leadership Team Coaching: Developing Collective Transformational Leadership*, 3rd edition. London: Kogan Page.

Peters, J. (2015a) *High Performance Relationships: The Heart and Science Behind Success at Work and Home*. Calgary, Alberta: InnerActive Leadership Associates Inc.

Peters, J. (2015b) *High Performance Relationship and Team Assessment*. Calgary, Alberta: InnerActive Leadership Associates Inc. [http://inneractiveleadership.ca/books/high-performance-relationships/].

Peters, J. and Carr, C. (2015) *High Performance Team Coaching: A Comprehensive System for Leaders and Coaches*. Calgary, Alberta: InnerActive Leadership Associates Inc.

Whitmore, J. (2017) *Coaching for Performance: The Principles and Practice of Coaching and Leadership*. London: Nicholas Brealey.

Into the void: Building leadership through team coaching in the executive team of a government agency

Declan Woods and Georgina Woudstra

Introduction

This case study is based on team coaching over several months with two external team coaches and the executive team of a government agency in the UK. It sets out details about the team, its drive to embark on team coaching, and the differences between the presenting and actual coaching agendas, before turning to the approach taken. The programme included the Middle Circle® team discovery tool and the findings informed the subsequent coaching programme. The team coaches discussed their individual reflections and combined experience of working alongside this team in their ongoing peer supervision. This case is written based on their notes and the diagnostic material gathered. It focuses on the impact of the leadership void left by the CEO and its effect on team coaching. Leadership at the top is critical because senior teams need to take collective responsibility for the whole enterprise.

Context and the presenting team coaching agenda

The government agency had been through significant change over recent years. This was set to continue with a seven-year programme designed to transform the organisation further.

The executive team, comprising a CEO and nine executive directors, faced two challenges: leading the organisation through the transformation and improving performance and delivery to its customers. To this end, the executive team decided to invest in 'self-help' to ensure it was working effectively, to develop a more collaborative approach, and become a truly high-performing team.

Less expressed across the organisation was the degree of stakeholder dissatisfaction with the agency's performance and its slowness to adapt to evolving customer requirements. The agency had responded to this challenge by repeatedly reorganising itself, but this had not brought about the desired changes – or performance improvements. The latest reorganisation had seen the introduction of key strategic partners into the agency's executive team, in effect creating a leadership team comprised of both internal and external leaders with differing priorities and stakeholders to serve. This appeared to be an attempt to meet various stakeholder needs. However, in practice, the voice of the wider organisational system was noticeably absent and had little influence on the executive team or the team coaching, other than through the CEO.

Our approach to team coaching:

Outcomes

- A common and shared understanding of team effectiveness
- A shared view of the success factors for collaborative working
- An understanding of individual styles and preferences
- The impact of leadership style on effective team working
- An agreed framework for managing team working
- An agreement on individual and collective next steps.

We accepted these as an initial contract, acknowledging this would be revisited after gathering more data.

Overall approach to team coaching

Based on these desired outcomes, our overall approach to the team coaching was as follows:

Figure 11 Collab6© team coaching programme design

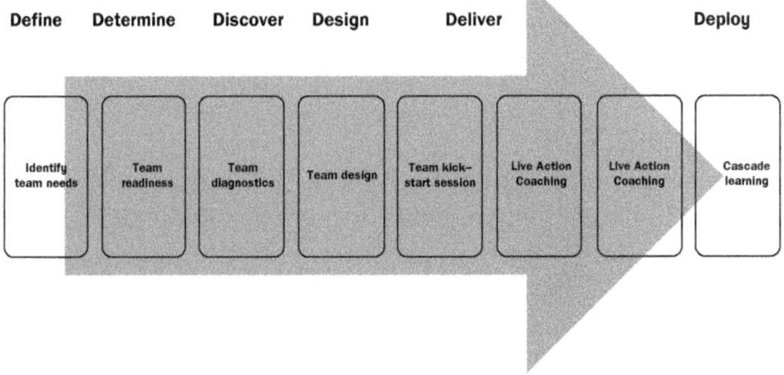

Define	Determine	Discover	Design	Deliver			Deploy
Identify team needs	Team readiness	Team diagnostics	Team design	Team kick-start session	Live Action Coaching	Live Action Coaching	Cascade learning

Stage 1: Define. Dialogue with the CEO and human resources director to understand the team's needs.

Stage 2: Determine. Meet the whole team to build on the team's needs and ascertain engagement and readiness for team coaching.

Stage 3: Discover. Create team development goals using the team-Salient® for Teams effectiveness tool (https://middlecircle.com/for-teams/) and individual member interviews to identify the team's strengths.

Stage 4: Design. Design an overall team coaching programme based on the team's goals.

Stage 5: Deliver. Kick-start the coaching with a team charter session followed by regular team coaching sessions.

Stage 6: Deploy. Review team coaching successes and cascade learning and benefit to the wider organisation.

To build trust and safety in the team, we presented the team coaching as a journey. The neat, linear presentation does not reflect the messy reality of team coaching; nonetheless, it served as a useful overview of our approach.

'Determine' phase of team coaching

The aim of the 'determine' phase was to check whether the conditions were present for successful team coaching outcomes. Up to this point, we had only spoken with the CEO and HR director and wanted to ascertain whether the drive for coaching was shared by the whole team.

We began with an engagement session with the whole team, a 1–2 hour meeting equivalent to a chemistry meeting in individual coaching. During this session we invited the team leader to set the context and sponsor the coaching, stating why it mattered and what he hoped to gain from it. We then asked each team member to say what they hoped the team and they personally would gain from the coaching.

We also invited them to share any concerns they may have about team coaching. We find this useful as any resistance often settles once concerns have been expressed by a team member and heard by the whole team.

After speaking with the CEO, it took three months to arrange the engagement session. The day before the session, the HRD asked us to cancel because half of the team was unavailable. This caused us to wonder how important coaching was to the team. It provided some interesting data about how leadership was exercised in the team, since the CEO had delegated the decision to the HRD who, in turn, had delegated it to us.

Our position was this was a leadership decision and one for the CEO to make and communicate. We reinforced our commitment to the session going ahead and stated that, if cancelled, the session would be chargeable as per agreed terms. They decided to continue with only half of the team. It was a useful session and those present seemed sufficiently engaged and agreed to brief colleagues who were absent.

In our paired reflection post session, we raised a number of questions:

- Was the leader willing and able to lead the team? (This was our biggest concern by far.)
- With ten members, plus others invited into meetings, was the team too big to be effective at strategic decision-making?
- Did they have the right people in terms of skills?
- Was the team now formed and sufficiently stable to grow team capability over time?

We held these as working hypotheses throughout the coaching. Our view was that many of these aspects could benefit from improved team composition, structure, and processes; and that this work could be carried out in parallel with the team coaching. We therefore believed we had enough of a contract to begin the work and agreed to start on that basis.

'Discover' phase of team coaching

The team wanted clarity on where to focus their development to perform at their best. The result of the teamSalient® for Teams profile and individual interviews were debriefed with the team, revealing:

- **Leadership** was identified as a strength. This clarity of leadership proved a relief to the team due to several changes in CEO and two recent appointees to the team. The organisation was hiring 17 new senior managers (direct reports to the executive) to meet capacity and capability gaps – an important part of creating the desired leadership culture.
- **Team structure:** given the personnel changes above, unsurprisingly 'team composition' was highlighted as an area for development, with the team needing to stabilise its membership and improve overall collective leadership. Consistent with our experience of the team in the 'readiness' meeting, it supported our hypothesis about the team's size and organisation.
- **Adaptability:** the team's speed of action (agility) was slower than the pace of externally driven change and insufficient time was being spent on challenges facing the organisation – both worrying findings in light of the transformation agenda.
- **Conflict:** insufficient 'optimal conflict', with most team members being reluctant to challenge one another, which played out with only one member being willing to speak out.

- **Team cohesion:** the lack of executive cohesion mentioned above was mirrored throughout the rest of the organisation, adding to the challenge of leading a complex organisation. This showed up vividly in the 'team glue' driver of team effectiveness in the team's report.

From experience, we know that many newly formed teams lack the psychological safety needed to enable speaking up and risk-taking. This was also reflected in the report, identifying the need for greater team safety and a trust-based relationship between the team and coaches. We therefore chose to speak with team members individually and use their feedback to inform the coaching.

The uncomfortable insights from the teamSalient® report and interview data held up a mirror highlighting opportunities for greater team effectiveness. This informed the agenda for team coaching and pointed to some re-design work on how the team was structured and operated.

'Design' phase of team coaching

The 'discover' phase data identified potential improvements to team structure, composition, and work processes, with the 'design' phase following this. We challenged the CEO around the appropriateness of the team's design offering that re-design work could either be conducted internally or with our support. We knew from experience that the coaching would be hampered if the team didn't first tackle its structure and processes. In a coaching session with the CEO, we explored re-organising the team into a three-person executive (CEO, finance and operations directors) and a separate operational leadership team made up of the remaining members, and some process re-design to improve working procedures. We believed that both of these could make a difference to how the team worked together and improve performance (Siebdrat et al., 2009).

The CEO was reluctant to reorganise the team as it might be misconstrued as excluding people at a time when it needed to come together. While we understood his reasons, the team was reporting that they were too slow at responding to routine matters let alone new, emerging ones. We saw first-hand the team was overloaded with reports, struggling to process them and make decisions quickly. Despite this, there was no agreed mandate from the CEO to make any structural changes to the team.

However, we were able to propose changes that would improve team processes. For instance, we shared our observations that board papers were not read in advance, taking up valuable meeting time and slowing decision-making. We proposed a new team meeting format with one agenda-led meeting to tackle strategic topics and another agenda-free meeting for emergent issues, creating the space to debate key strategic issues without being hijacked by more immediate operational ones. We also introduced and practised increasing the dialogue between team members, with them listening before responding, which led to more of a 'safe zone' to share issues and ask for help.

'Deliver' phase of team coaching

We continued by delivering live action team coaching sessions over consecutive months coinciding with monthly executive team meetings. We observed several dynamics related to the presenting issues. We discussed these openly – and their effect on us – as a co-coaching pair in peer supervision. One dynamic was the question of team leadership. While the CEO was recognised as the leader by the team, we felt that something was missing. When explored in a private conversation, the CEO described his leadership style as 'leading from the back of the boat'. His view was that 'I have hired good people, pay them a lot of money to do a good job, and so I let them get on with it'. During the coaching, we noticed this led to 'zigzag' decision-making – decisions taking different directions and considerable time, and being revisited more than once.

We also felt this leadership void through our counter-transferential reactions to the CEO and team (Maccoby, 2004). We often felt pulled in to provide leadership for the team. We noticed other team members may have experienced this too because they stepped into this leadership gap, often with their own agendas. We witnessed sub-groups developing, with two members of the executive team forming an alliance and holding disruptive side conversations during meetings, splitting the team. The CEO failed to challenge poor behaviours or address 'teaming' problems with any assertiveness. While this was not part of the requested outcomes, it was significant to team functioning.

The deputy CEO's ideas were met by one of his colleagues with a negative response. The CEO then supported the colleague, blocking new initiatives and stifling the deputy. This pattern played out repeatedly and was out of the team's conscious awareness, until named by us.

This leadership void continued and, after a time, we felt as if we were going through the motions. Team members were 'reporting' rather than engaging with each other, using the phrase 'bringing items to your attention' often during meetings. These dynamics appeared connected to the lack of energy, drive, and holding presence on the part of the CEO. We raised this in one-to-one coaching with the CEO, only to be met with denial. He often seemed oblivious to the impact he had on the team.

We tackled this during the live team coaching by asking team members their expectations of the CEO and his of them. This proved a tipping point. Team members said that they wanted the CEO to provide 'clarity of intention', 'clear decisions', 'to hold people to account collectively', and 'to act as the "big gun" and use his authority'. This provided the impetus for the CEO to increase his presence and start to fill the leadership void. We supported him through one-to-one coaching running parallel to the team coaching. We continued to surface the team dynamics in the coaching. Through awareness and encouragement, the CEO found the courage to begin naming the dynamics as they occurred. This curtailed the unhelpful behaviour and brought more focus to meetings.

Outcomes and conclusions

By coaching the whole team, executive team members recognised they were facing similar challenges and united in leading the transformation together. The twin meeting structure and improved processes enabled the team to become more disciplined with time allocated to discuss strategic matters.

Surfacing role expectations proved a fulcrum, with the team reporting clearer leadership roles and stronger team alignment. The CEO reported improved executive mindset and team culture.

Buoyed by a new-found role confidence and ability to name unhelpful dynamics, the CEO eventually restructured the team. He asked a less engaged and under-performing member of the team to 'step down'. This reinforced the authority of the CEO role and increased his ability to exercise more influence and drive through further changes.

Overall, through the team coaching, the executive team made headway in codifying the leadership it could provide. Stakeholders now feel they are listened to. Performance to meet their expectations is improving. There is still work for the team and organisation to do and the change programme continues. Although new to team coaching, the CEO and team concluded that it was 'better and more constructive than expected' and 'time well spent'.

Key learnings of team coaches

What worked well

There were a number of practices that worked well, including:

- Communicating clear conditions for successful team coaching, including our role as team coaches and not being pulled into other roles (e.g. leading).
- Creating enough safety while 'holding up the mirror' at the same time.
- Using metaphor to name particular dynamics (e.g. 'zigzag') to increase the team's ability to recognise them.
- Playing to our individual strengths as team coaches (e.g. our use of felt sense and observational data, respectively).
- Playing to our combined strengths as team coaches (e.g. our willingness to discuss openly and make sense of our experience of the team and ourselves and use this data to inform our work).

Better if …

There were a number of things we might change, including:

- The use of teamSalient® for Teams and interview transcripts from 11 members of the executive team produced a lot of data, which took the team a

long time to assimilate. We now ask teams to complete the survey first and use the results to inform questions for follow-on interviews. This makes the questions much more targeted and the interviews shorter.
- One of the (unspoken) drivers for the coaching was dissatisfaction among key customers and stakeholders. Yet, other than through the filter of the CEO, they were largely out of sight during the coaching. We would prefer to include stakeholder data, but the CEO was unwilling to do so. He hoped to improve performance before seeking feedback.
- The coaching ran its course and reached a logical end-point for the CEO. This meant we didn't get the opportunity to cascade the learning to the wider leadership team.

The coaching achieved the stated outcomes and the CEO was satisfied with it. We felt a sense of disappointment, however, knowing that the team could have gained even more from it and taken their leadership further. It was a reminder that coaching can only go as far as the team is willing to take it. To do so would have taken a much greater commitment to leadership and courage from the CEO. Without us challenging him, we doubt he would have continued to raise his, and the team's, game. We had to be satisfied with doing 'good enough' work in the circumstances.

References

Maccoby, M. (2004) Why people follow the leader: The power of transference, *Harvard Business Review*, 82 (9): 76–85.

Siebdrat, F., Hoegl, M., and Ernst, H. (2009) How to manage virtual teams, *MIT Sloan Management Review*, 50 (4): 63–68.

teamSalient® – see https://www.teamsalient.com (Unpublished).

Philosophies

Foreword: Philosophies section

Paul Lawrence

Though team coaching is still in its infancy, there exist already multiple definitions of team coaching and lots of different models, processes, and frameworks for the prospective team coach to use in practice. The team coaching literature can be quite confusing, in that theoretical perspectives often look quite different, at least in emphasis, and the theoretical foundations of many practice models are not evident. Now may be a time to slow down the rush towards consensus and focus instead on framing, exploring, and seeking to understand all these different approaches.

The reader may find it useful to consider the chapters that follow through the 3Ps framework described by Tatiana Bachkirova and Peter Jackson (Bachkirova, 2016; Jackson and Bachkirova, 2019), building on earlier work by David Lane (2006). With respect to team coaching, the model invites us to consider three questions:

1 What is my philosophy? In other words, what models and theories do I subscribe to?
2 What is my purpose as a team coach?
3 What processes do I use?

As important as answering each question is reviewing the extent to which the answers to these questions are consistent. For example, if I decide that I believe in models that focus on clarifying team goals and objectives, yet the processes I describe are entirely around improving team dynamics, the model *may* not be coherent.

I recently described the 3Ps framework to a group of academics, positioning it at the heart of my teaching practice. Some people in the room were horrified. How can you ask people to come up with their own models, I was asked? Surely published evidence tells us the best way to coach? In the case of team coaching, the evidence certainly does *not* provide us with a definitive approach. Peters and Carr (2019) provide a long list of published approaches to team coaching, whilst at the same time pointing out that most of these models fail to take into account important variables and are not obviously evidence-based. The functioning of teams, within organisations, within society, is complex. To build up an evidence base will take many years. When Clutterbuck et al. (2019) say 'over time, we expect greater clarity to emerge as to what lies in the core of team coaching', we should anticipate that being a *long* time.

Meanwhile, the 3Ps lens enables us to contrast and compare, to enquire and challenge, as we define our own personal approaches to team coaching. In this section of the book, for example, you will discover that some practitioners make full use of psychometric instruments, while another author expresses a dislike of working with such tools. The challenge to all of us in this instance is to explore each practitioner's rationale and seek to understand, not simply whether the use of psychometric tools is a good idea, but also when such approaches may be useful or not.

In considering the first P – Philosophy – we must decide for ourselves the scope of team coaching. The potential scope is vast. The team effectiveness literature encourages us to think about how teams are put together. What is the ideal size for a team? What mix of skills and knowledge should the team leader aspire to? What personality types? The literature encourages the practitioner to take into account leadership styles: transformational, directive, and models of shared leadership. How should the team structure its activities? What skills do team members require to be good team members? How do teams best learn together?

More recent team effectiveness models encourage us to consider 'emergent states', the extent to which there exists trust in a team, the extent to which the team is cohesive, the social identity of the team at any given point in time, and levels of collective emotional intelligence. We are encouraged to consider team mental models, 'transactive memory systems', team efficacy, and goal alignment. To what extent is a particular team collaborating at the moment? What informal roles are team members adopting? What is happening at a deeper level in terms of interpersonal psychodynamics? And how do the answers to all of these questions change if a team is working virtually, or working on particularly complex issues, or working together on tasks where optimal levels of interdependence are particularly high or low?

These are just some of the questions a team coach might ask. Behind each of these questions sits a sizeable body of literature. If we believe we need to be able to help a team address all of these questions at some point, then we team coaches face a never ending journey in terms of continually building our personal 'epistemologies' (Hawkins and Schwenk, 2011).

This is not to say we all aspire to be experts in all these domains. No team coaching models cover all of these areas in depth. Peter Hawkins' Five Disciplines model, for example, is quite explicit on the importance of goal alignment and collaboration. It is not as explicit about different approaches to working with team dynamics or navigating organisational politics, and it makes little reference to team selection (Hawkins, 2017). David Clutterbuck's PERILL model foregrounds purpose, processes, relationships, leadership, and learning (Clutterbuck, 2020). Again, it is less explicit around social identity, the importance of team efficacy, and psychological safety. This is not to criticise either model, rather it is to point out that all models emphasise some aspects of team effectiveness and not others. It us up to us as practitioners to decide for ourselves which models most resonate. If Wageman and Lowe (2019) are correct in asserting that interventions addressing basic team design account for 60% of the variance in influencing team outcomes, that 30% of the variance comes from getting the launch of the team right, and that only 10% of the variance is attributable to hands-on team coaching, then the choices we make about scope are important.

The second P – Purpose – requires us to question ourselves; why do we coach teams? Our Philosophy informs our Purpose. If, for example, I am drawn to models that focus primarily on helping teams agree on their objectives, my Purpose for coaching may be different to someone who believes you cannot help a team become more effective without directly addressing team dynamics. Philosophy informs our Purpose, which in turn informs *how* we coach.

How we coach is addressed by the third P – Process. The coach who is driven to help teams clarify their objectives may draw heavily on facilitation skills. The coach who believes in the importance of working with team dynamics may be more capable in working with process.

Our approach to the 3Ps determines how we define team coaching. Some authors explicitly position facilitation and education as falling under the umbrella of team coaching (e.g. Caillet and Yeager, 2018, Clutterbuck, 2007; Hawkins, 2017). It seems equally valid to me to consider team coaching as distinct from facilitation and education. The path we choose will depend upon our philosophy and purpose and will determine whether we seek to become competent in all these practice domains, or whether we choose to specialise and work as part of a broader team.

If this sounds complex enough in outlining the team coaching landscape, consider some of the questions currently being raised by those questioning the future of team coaching (e.g. Mesmer-Magnus et al., 2016; Tannenbaum et al., 2012; Wageman and Lowe, 2019). Consider the following observations, for example:

- The environment is constantly changing. The purpose of a team therefore shifts and changes. If a team is a group of people all committed to achieving a common purpose, then the composition of the ('real') team may also be constantly shifting and changing and may be different to the espoused team.
- Members of any team are not always focused, at any given point in time, on the achievement of the collective team goals. This implies that a team is a transitory state.
- More people are members of multiple teams these days. Their energies shift and change from team to team. What happens in one team likely impacts on what happens in other teams, these impacts mediated by the constant floating of people from team to team.
- Team boundaries are not real. Team boundaries are imaginary constructs that emerge from conversations between people as they form a collective identity.

What we think about these points depends on our Philosophy as it relates to systems theories, and there are many different systems theories (Lawrence, 2021). It may soon cease to be useful to define ourselves as 'systemic'. Instead, as we become more familiar with the systems literature, we may begin to enquire of each other *what* systemic are we, and how does this impact on the work we do as team coaches?

It is through this lens, then, that I invite you to read the following eight case studies. What do you notice about the underlying philosophies that underpin each approach? How do you relate to the different approaches to team coaching in practice? What will you integrate from each case study into your own personal team coaching approach?

References

Bachkirova, T. (2016) The self of the coach: Conceptualization, issues, and opportunities for practitioner development, *Consulting Psychology Journal: Practice and Research*, 68 (2): 143–156.

Caillet, A. and Yeager, A. (2018) *Introduction to Corentus Team Coaching*. Lexington, MA: Corentus.

Clutterbuck, D. (2007) *Coaching the Team at Work*. London: Nicholas Brealey.

Clutterbuck, D. (2020) *Coaching the Team at Work*, 2nd edition. London: Nicholas Brealey.

Clutterbuck, D., Gannon, J., Hayes, S., Iordanou, I., Lowe, K., and Mackie, D. (2019) Introduction: Defining and differentiating team coaching from other forms of team intervention, in D. Clutterbuck, J. Gannon, S. Hayes, I. Iordanou, K. Lowe, and D. Mackie (eds.) *The Practitioner's Handbook of Team Coaching* (pp. 1–8). Abingdon: Routledge.

Hawkins, P. (2017) *Leadership Team Coaching: Developing Collective Transformational Leadership*, 3rd edition. London: Kogan Page.

Hawkins, P. and Schwenk, G. (2011) The seven-eyed model of supervision, in T. Bachkirova, P. Jackson, and D. Clutterbuck (eds.) *Coaching and Mentoring Supervision: Theory and Practice: The Complete Guide to Best Practice*. Maidenhead: Open University Press.

Jackson, P. and Bachkirova, T. (2019) The 3 Ps of supervision and coaching: Philosophy, purpose and process, in E. Turner and S. Palmer (eds.) *The Heart of Coaching Supervision: Working with Reflection and Self-Care* (pp. 28–40). Abingdon: Routledge.

Lane, D. (2006) The emergence of supervision models. Presentation at the *Annual Conference of the Special Group in Coaching Psychology of the BPS*.

Lawrence, P. (2021) *Coaching Systemically: Five Ways of Thinking About Systems*. Abingdon: Routledge.

Mesmer-Magnus, J.R., Carter, D.R., Asencio, R., and DeChurch, L.A. (2016) Space exploration illuminates the next frontier for teams research, *Group & Organization Management*, 41 (5): 595–628.

Peters, J. and Carr, C. (2019) What does 'good' look like? An overview of the research on the effectiveness of team coaching, in D. Clutterbuck, J. Gannon, S. Hayes, I. Iordanou, K. Lowe, and D. Mackie (eds.) *The Practitioner's Handbook of Team Coaching* (pp. 89–120). Abingdon: Routledge.

Tannenbaum, S.I., Mathieu, J.E., Salas, E., and Cohen, D. (2012) Teams are changing: Are research and practice evolving fast enough?, *Industrial and Organizational Psychology*, 5 (1): 2–24.

Wageman, R. and Lowe, K. (2019) Designing, launching, and coaching teams: The 60-30-10 rule and its implications for team coaching, in D. Clutterbuck, J. Gannon, S. Hayes, I. Iordanou, K. Lowe, and D. MacKie (eds.) *The Practitioner's Handbook of Team Coaching* (pp. 121–137). Abingdon: Routledge.

EthicalCoach Ethiopia Project: A case study of pro bono team coaching through the lens of team coaching competencies

Jane Cooke-Lauder and Sebastian Fox

A pro bono coaching programme designed to support leaders of non-governmental organisations (NGOs) in Ethiopia provides the context for this case study. The lens of a team coaching competency model is used to explore the experience of coaching teams by two and sometimes three coaches, with the coaching being delivered at times completely virtually, sometimes with one coach virtual and, occasionally, with two coaches present in the room.

Overview of the project

The mission of EthicalCoach, incorporated in the USA in 2018 as the charitable arm of the WBECS Group, is to accelerate NGO impact through leadership and team coaching. The journey began in Ethiopia.

Veneration of older individuals, scepticism of the applicability of international experience, and the importance of building relationships are part of the Ethiopian culture and ways of doing business. Initial primary and secondary research suggested these characteristics could reduce the effectiveness of virtual coaching, particularly given limited exposure to leadership coaching and limited local coaching capacity.

A coaching programme was designed to address these factors; initially, 10 coaches located internationally were selected from more than 500 applicants based on their track record, cross-cultural competence, and breadth of coaching expertise. Orienting them to Ethiopia took a number of different forms, including selected readings, customised videos, and panel discussions with Ethiopian leaders. To kick-start local learning as well as provide additional local context, it was decided to build local capacity and pair a local coach with an international coach to deliver team coaching. Thirty local individuals, self-identified as being interested in learning team coaching skills, underwent a pro bono accelerated training programme led by Professor David Clutterbuck and Marita Fridjhon, with supervision support provided by the Global Supervisors' Network and CRR Global.

Four hundred NGO leaders representing 150 NGOs were invited to attend a two-day Summit in Addis Ababa. Following the Summit, 20 teams were selected for coaching: 10 to receive coaching immediately and 10 a year later. A combination of responses to a team coaching readiness questionnaire, based around the '6 Conditions for Team Effectiveness' (Wageman et al., 2008), together with meetings during the Summit, were used for selection purposes and to determine the teams' understanding of 'coaching'. This was of particular importance given the limited exposure of Ethiopian executives, including NGO leaders, to coaching before 2018.

Agreements outlining roles and responsibilities were signed by all parties with EthicalCoach. Local and international coaches were matched and then paired coaches were matched with an NGO, based on available information and expressed preferences. Given the small numbers, there was some degree of randomisation in the final matchups.

Methodology and limitations

From the initial 10 NGOs selected for team coaching, six are included in this study. Four are excluded because little or no coaching took place, primarily due to selection errors such as, in practice, there proving to be no recognisable senior team in place, or misunderstanding on the part of the NGO of the time commitment required for team coaching.

Hypotheses were constructed to guide the data gathering based on the co-authors' insights about the project. These hypotheses were translated into questionnaires for the coaches and NGO leaders. Interviews of between one and two hours were conducted by the co-authors via video- or teleconference, recorded whenever possible, and then summarised using an analytic template. In total, 19 interviews took place over three weeks. Participants were promised anonymity with respect to individual comments but with acknowledgement as contributors.

The limitations of this paper include: no agreed initial measures of effective team coaching; the small sample size; and including in the sample only NGOs where team coaching was delivered successfully.

Framework for the discussion

With no local precedent to follow – and little in the way of documented evidence to guide the design of a virtual team coaching programme in Africa – EthicalCoach adopted a model that included individual coaching for the NGO leader and team coaching of the NGO senior team by a pair of co-coaches (a local coach paired with an international coach). The initial design for the team coaching had the NGO leader being coached by one coach and the NGO team being coached by a pair of different coaches for a total of three coaches (a triad) working with each NGO. Some of the international coaches elected to follow a different approach, with the same international coach coaching the NGO leader individually and working with a local coach to coach the team (dyad model).

In addition, the coaching programme model laid out a few guiding principles – a 'minimum specifications' approach – including: duration of 12 months or 12 coaching sessions; requirement for a co-coach 'contract'; regular guided reflection supervision sessions attended by all coaches; and completion of structured feedback surveys. All other elements of the coaching assignment were developed by the coaches.

A team coaching competency model (Woudstra, 2021) comprising three core elements and 15 competencies divided into five clusters, is used to describe the behaviour and activities of the team coaches.

Core elements and clusters

CORE 1: Coach's philosophy and stance. Notwithstanding diverse backgrounds and practices, it is evident that the coaches shared an understanding of the importance of building relationships as a foundation of team coaching. One coach described her philosophy as: 'To listen and hear more, to love more, to be more and to do less. This establishes trust and connection as if we were dancing together'.

CORE 2: Signature presence and use of self. The coaches paid close attention to being present in the moment to mitigate the impact of the virtual set-up, including frequent interruptions from power outages. An international coach observed: 'I had to be very present, regardless of location, and be the best I could be in the moment. Not being present [in the room] meant I needed to be clear where to interact in any given moment'. Video cameras were used (bandwidth permitting), with the international coach contracting with the co-coach and team as to how they would follow, observe, and reflect on what was happening in the room. One coach explained: 'I extended myself through the space to feel I was in the room. I did this by bringing all my energy together. The impact on the team was to ensure I wasn't just a disembodied voice – that I was really in the room with my co-coach'. In practice, this meant, for example, positioning the screen so that the co-coaches appeared next to each other.

In three instances, it was possible for both coaches to be present in the room for a session. One NGO leader felt this enhanced the coaching experience, commenting: 'It was really special to have the international coach there. The team felt very committed because both coaches were committed'.

Philosophies **149**

CORE 3: Active experimentation. Active experimentation formed an important part of the coaching sessions, particularly in helping team members build connectivity and relationships. Examples include using the empty chair technique to bring the 'system' into the room and playing devil's advocate to make it safe to challenge in a hierarchical culture.

Cluster 1: Setting the foundation. Despite considerable time spent clarifying the offer at the Summit and afterwards, some NGOs believed they were receiving training, consultancy, or even funds to spend on leadership development. As one of the NGO leaders observed: 'Coaching was a first time for me and my team. There were different levels of understanding. Initially, team members were asking "how can we sit for two hours of coaching?" They thought it was going to be training. Over time they saw the relevance and were convinced'. Coaches had to commit additional time at the outset to ensure expectations were set correctly. Initially, this meant having to teach more, rather than coach. The coaches commented on how, ultimately, this extended contracting contributed to the strengthening of their relationship with the team and set the scene for the 'real' work that followed.

Coach team effectiveness was fostered through the deliberate creation of coach team contracts. These covered respective roles, approaches to the coaching, how to work together, and planning. For example:

- Setting boundaries: 'What do we want to learn together and what do we want to learn separately?' and how best to provide feedback, such as helping the international coach understand the local culture.
- Spending time preparing for, and debriefing after, each session. An international coach observed: 'It was important to be supportive of each other. I felt it was my job to hold the local coach up as well as myself, being inclusive of her and modelling effective team behaviours'.
- Agreeing the approach and ongoing communications, particularly when working in a triad: 'Before we started coaching, we had a combined session [with the other two coaches] to agree confidentiality, communication protocols, and boundary management'.

In some instances, the co-coaches found it beneficial to access supervision together.

With a large variance in experience between the international and local coaches, ongoing clarity for both the NGO teams and the coaches over their respective roles was critical. This allowed the roles to evolve over the course of the coaching. While some of the local coaches felt it was a partnership of equals from the outset, others believed it took some time for their role to develop fully. The international coaches describe these relationships as 'dancing in the moment', at times more like a learned foxtrot and at others like 'jazz improvisation'. NGO leaders also commented on this, with observations ranging from 'The local coach was very much the less experienced one and was also being coached by the international coach', to 'It was obvious the coaches were working as a team' and '[The local coach] grew into his own role. In the beginning, he was more tentative and quiet, and had to be pulled into the conversation. By the end, he was functioning as a co-coach'.

Cluster 2: Co-creating the relationship. Mindful of the potential difficulties of virtual coaching, particular emphasis was placed on building psychological safety and trust quickly. This was achieved initially through the coaches working with the NGO team where possible at the Summit and also visiting them on-site. As one NGO leader observed: 'She [the international coach] came to the office and tried to understand us, who we are, and what we want to be'. As a result, 'We were confident to share. It was not like an interview but an opportunity to say what we wanted and to talk freely without fear of making a mistake'. Having the local coach on-site was also helpful: 'It's hard for Ethiopians sometimes to open up … it takes time to build trust. To have the local coach in the room as a "translator", explaining, who "got it" and to pick up on things the virtual coach missed was really good'.

Where the coaches worked as a triad, additional contracting was necessary between the NGO leader, team, and coaches to ensure appropriate boundaries and confidentiality. The emphasis in this contracting was on the client, rather than the coaches, resulting in the clients describing a seamlessness and easy flow of information. Mechanisms, such as establishing a WhatsApp group chat for all four parties, were used.

Cluster 3: Fostering effective communication. Communication was complex with one coach located out of the country, often unreliable technology, and different levels of familiarity with English. Much of this was addressed by having the local coach in the room, which enabled:

- Direct communication, feedback, data and cultural interpretation for the virtual coach. 'It was necessary to have the local coach in the room. The international coach was on the calls, but couldn't always see what was going on, so the local coach was her eyes and used WhatsApp to send a picture of what was going on at any time'.
- Translating or updating the virtual coach if the team discussed something between themselves in the local language. This was important in ensuring accuracy of questions and responses.
- Coaching continuity in the event of technology/power interruptions. An NGO leader commented: 'When the line dropped, sometimes the team didn't even notice because the local coach picked up the conversation'.

The international coaches found the reflective space in their co-coach debriefs particularly useful as a way of understanding nuances that may not have been apparent during a session due to technical constraints. Examples include what was happening off-screen, use of local language, and deferential behaviour towards the NGO leader.

Cluster 4: Working with systems and dynamics. An important consideration in many instances was the impact of the wider system. Some of the coaches found the coaching sessions to be susceptible to last-minute changes due to systemic factors such as changes in funding and macro events in Ethiopia. Interestingly, while there were no formal sponsors for the coaching (and, in some cases, there was resistance from the NGO leader to having a formal sponsor), in many cases the NGO leader stepped into the role and this helped ensure the programme's longevity. 'If the leader wasn't committed, if they hadn't made the time, it wouldn't have happened', and '[The NGO leader] played a great role in bringing the team together for the scheduled sessions'.

Cluster 5: Facilitating learning and growth. It was notable that NGO leaders felt they had increased their capacity to reflect and learn and that they wanted to share what they had learned across the organisation. One leader commented: 'We have learned a coaching culture and how to coach others in the organisation', while another noted: 'Half-way through, we started to look at each other differently. We started to understand the person more, which made them more human and relatable and helped us grow as a team'.

Overall coaching effectiveness and impact

Anecdotal evidence suggests the NGOs found team coaching to be very helpful. Some of the identified benefits include:

- Improved relationships and connectivity within the leadership teams, allowing them to work together in different ways. Typical feedback included: 'They talk more and are a stronger team together', and 'Most of the time they reflected in the sessions by saying, "We never talked like this before!"'
- Increased capacity and capabilities to lead, together with a commitment to scale learning and apply knowledge across the organisation. 'It was great starting to see them using the language in their own meetings and using a coaching style in active experiments with their own teams and stakeholders'.
- An enhanced ability and curiosity to 'core learn' (Hawkins, 2017): 'The team continued to run their own sessions to give themselves time to reflect'.
- A more coaching-based leadership style resulting in increased efficiency and effectiveness, improved fundraising and project management.

There were no identifiable differences in the coaching impact between the dyads and triads. This raises the question of whether the added complexity of a coaching triad is necessary in this context. An NGO leader working with a triad commented that he felt it might have been better if one of the team coaches was also his own coach because it would have provided more coherence between the team coaching and individual coaching sessions. This would seem to be supported, in part, by the experience of the NGO leaders who had the same coach: 'It made a huge difference, as the coach could see what was happening with both [the individual and team coaching], to recognise patterns, and allow me to see what was emerging and what needed working on'. In contrast, another NGO leader working with a triad said that having her coach as the team coach might have reinforced the hierarchy and reduced the effectiveness of the team coaching.

Summary

EthicalCoach's pilot coaching project created the opportunity to test a range of approaches to implementing a coaching programme in challenging environments. Specific challenges faced in Ethiopia included very little knowledge of coaching among NGO leaders, very few qualified local coaches, political instability, and intermittent internet connectivity. The initial programme design intentionally reflected these challenges and was then adapted as more was learned about the specific circumstances of the NGO teams and coaches.

Despite the challenges, it still proved possible to implement a coaching programme that delivered benefit to the NGO leaders and their teams. Key learnings include:

For the coaches:

1.1: Contracting: taking time to contract before, and re-contract during, the coaching to clarify the NGO team's expectations around what coaching is and is not.
1.2: Co-creating the relationships:
   a. Between the co-coaches to enable them to 'dance in the moment' and create sufficient structure for the local coaches who were new to team coaching; and
   b. Between the team and the coaches as individuals, as co-coaches, and as coach triads. Even as the coaches sought to interface seamlessly, connectivity was lost in most sessions at some point, which led to unexpected exits and entrances.
1.3: Presence: the coaches needed to establish their individual presence in being there physically, virtually, or even invisibly when there was a power or internet interruption.

For the NGOs:

2.1: Appreciating their own sense of agency, the NGO leaders and their teams shifted from looking to the 'expert' for answers to becoming more aware of their own power and ability to develop solutions and effect change.

2.2: Embracing the power of reflection and conversation which was visible in at least two ways:
   a. Where sufficient psychological safety and trust were established, the team members became more appreciative of each other, were better connected, and had stronger relationships as a result; and
   b. Team members saw themselves not as individuals in silos but working together as members of the leadership team, strategically guiding the overall organisation.

Acknowledgements

The authors would like to acknowledge the contributions of the following individuals to this case study:

NGO Leaders: Helina Abraham, JeCCDO; Yasmine Abubeker, Farm Africa; Mulugeta Gebru, JeCCDO; Misrak Makonnen, AMREF; Seid Aman Mohammed, Imagine1Day; Andrea Hernandez Tobar, iDE; and Getachew Tesfay Gebru, Operation Rescue Ethiopia.

Coaches outside Ethiopia: Katherine Holt, Chip MacFarlane, Dumi Magadlela, Nobantu Mpotulo, Marilyn O'Hearne, and Veronica Wantenaar.

Coaches within Ethiopia: Yared Abera, Matthew Broderick, Sara Groenendijk, Fouzia Muhsin, Ayinalem Tilahun, and Yonas Tegene.

References

Hawkins, P. (2017) *Leadership Team Coaching: Developing Collective Transformational Leadership*, 3rd edition. London: Kogan Page.

Wageman, R., Nunes, D.A., Burruss, J.A., and Hackman, J.R. (2008) *Senior Leadership Teams: What It Takes to Make Them Great*. Boston: Harvard Business School Press.

Woudstra, G. (2021) *Mastering the Art of Team Coaching: A Comprehensive Guide to Unleashing the Power, Purpose and Potential in Any Team*. Winchester: Team Coaching Studio Press.

What coaching is appropriate for developing leadership within a team context?

Sue Fontannaz

Introduction

Coaching offers a plethora of options, which presents both an opportunity and a challenge for professionals interested in developing team leadership. Is leadership coaching sufficient in the contexts of teams? How can coaching be useful in the context of teams of teams? Are different coaching modalities required as the team develops? This case study seeks to address these questions by navigating the uncharted territory of coaching skippers in a global, amateur sailing race. The focus of the case study is on the role of external coaching in supporting skippers as they transition into team leadership roles. The role of coaching in this transition process is relevant, as there are high failure rates associated with technical experts moving into team leadership roles (Riddle, 2016). This chapter draws on insights from 50 in-depth interviews with multiple stakeholders, including the directors of the client sponsoring organisation, the external coaching team, the 12 skippers, and a selection of the crew from both the higher and lower performing teams. These findings contribute to our understanding of what coaching is appropriate for developing leadership within a team context.

The case study also addresses a gap in the leadership literature, where there appears to be no consensus on what constitutes leadership in the context of teams. The conceptualisation of leadership is becoming more crucial with the shift towards team-based, flatter organisational structures. This shift is recognised as the leading global human resource challenge for both 2016 and 2017 (Malley, 2017). The literature lags behind this shift, as the individualistic, leader-centric perspective still dominates in the literature. Day, Zaccaro, and Halpin (2004) suggested that traditional leadership theory assumes team member roles and linkages are loosely connected, whereas team leadership is characterised by tight interdependencies and subsequent coordination requirements of team members. Day, Harrison, and Halpin proposed that 'leadership exists in the connections between individuals and is a function of the quantity and quality of relationships among a networked group of individuals' (2009: 159).

Leadership, at its most fundamental level, is a 'social influence process' (Day and Dragoni, 2015: 135) or a mutually influencing process (DeRue, 2011; DeRue and Ashford, 2010; McCauley et al., 2010) that enables teams and organisations to navigate both the complexity of their internal and external contexts (Day and Dragoni, 2015). These scholars highlight that leadership extends beyond the formal leader and that team leadership is a collective process. McLaughlin and Cox (2016) recognised that there has been a shift in leadership towards a relational perspective and claimed that there is insufficient emphasis on developing this perspective in the literature. The review of the literature highlights that leadership extends beyond the formal role of the leader.

Some scholars are recognising the shift towards team leadership. Salas, Stagl, and Burke defined team leadership as a form of 'social problem solving that promotes coordinated, adaptive team performance by facilitating goal definition and attainment' (2004: 343). Kartoch (2013: 164) referred to 'the dynamic, enabling-constraining process' that occurs within teams, rather than the individual leader. Ancona, Backman, and Isaacs (2015) described a system of adaptation and coordination, which emerges through harnessing the dynamic tensions within the team to forge broader capacity for direction, alignment, and commitment. Some scholars (Day et al., 2004; Kozlowski et al., 2016) have also recognised the distinctiveness of team leadership from organisational leadership. This distinction is relevant to leadership coaches and organisations who are transitioning towards team-based organisational design.

Although teams are a common structure required in workplaces today, many leaders are unaware of how best to lead their teams to high performance (Wageman et al., 2008). Teams are defined as 'intact social systems that perform one or more tasks within an organisational context' (Clutterbuck, 2007: 38). McGrath, Arrow, and Berdahl (2000) recognised teams as complex, adaptive, dynamic systems, which draws attention to the social dynamics of team leadership. The research on team dynamics has developed, but Tannenbaum et al. (2012: 20) raised the question of whether research and practice are evolving fast enough to address the changes in teams, relating to more fluid, dynamic, and complex environments than in the past. These scholars advocated for rich case studies where teams are examined 'in the wild', under extreme conditions, as this places heightened pressures on their strengths and vulnerabilities. This case study addresses the call to study team leadership 'in the wild', and is a response to Kegan and Lahey's (2009) assertion that leaders are in 'over our heads'. The growing demands placed on leaders are beyond the current understanding of leadership practice (McLaughlin and Cox, 2016; Tourish, 2012; Hawkins, 2014; Kellerman, 2012; Kolb, 2015). It can be argued that the shift towards team leadership has contributed to the conceptual crisis in the field of leadership, which is undermining the practice of leadership, coaching, and leadership development.

The shift towards a broader conceptualisation of leadership has important implications for leadership development and coaching. Day et al. (2014) highlighted this implication by making a valuable distinction between leader and leadership development, with the former focusing on individual leader development and the latter focusing on collective leadership development. This distinction raises the question of what coaching modality is relevant in the context of teams, where the leader is embedded in the team structure. This chapter explores this question and offers a temporal perspective of coaching and leadership development.

The context

Contextualising the case study is important, as leadership does not exist in a vacuum (Holton and Lowe, 2007; Geier, 2016; Athanasopoulou and Dopson, 2018). Johns defined context as the 'situational opportunities and constraints that affect the occurrence and meaning of organisational behaviour as well as the functional relationship between the variables' (2006: 386). Kihl, Leberman, and Schull (2010) suggested that leadership should be considered in context and take into account the socially constructed meanings associated with leadership. Porter and McLaughlin (2006) also found that while there has been greater recognition of the importance of context in leadership research in the past 15 years, context has continued to be neglected as a major factor in empirical leadership research. Context is important for understanding both coaching and leadership development, particularly in team contexts.

A global sailing race offered a novel case study with a clearly bounded context or 'living laboratory' microcosm. The 12 skippers were expected to each lead a dynamic multinational team of between 15 and 20 amateur crews in a circumnavigation of eight different legs. These teams mirror project work teams, which are often dynamic in nature and expected to perform in challenging, uncertain contexts. Approximately 40% of the crews completed the circumnavigation, while 30% of the crews changed after each leg. The diverse crews had different goals for taking part in the race, which contributed to each team's dynamics. The race skippers had professional sailing experience and their key challenge was to lead and manage a dynamic, diverse crew of amateur sailors, who were paying customers of the race organiser.

The coaching programme

The race directors identified that the skippers needed additional support, based on crew feedback from prior races. They appointed an external coaching team to engage with the skippers before and during the race. The coaching team were chosen for their track record in developing high-performance leaders in challenging contexts. The coaching team comprised five coaches, each with extensive team facilitation and leadership coaching experience. The purpose of the coaching programme was to support the skippers in developing their team leadership capabilities and to encourage a coaching style of leadership to contribute to the wellbeing of the crews.

The coaching programme began with an immersive learning group coaching programme held four months before the start of the race. The coaching aims included: equipping the skippers with additional competence and confidence to lead themselves and others consistently, to build and lead their teams effectively, and to manage leadership communications more appropriately. A Strengths Deployment Inventory (SDI) assessment was conducted for each skipper, which provided additional insights into their preferred leadership styles. The key themes coached throughout the programme included developing self-awareness, effective leadership communication, adaptive leadership styles, coaching skills, and building high-performance teams. The external coaching team drew on their experience of coaching the skippers and crew in the previous race, which aligned to the 'world class basics' of coaching, communication, leadership, and teamwork (Anderson, 2011). Coaching was defined by the external coaching team as a non-directive, development technique based mainly on the use of one-to-one discussions to enhance an individual's skills, knowledge, or work performance. The group coaching was followed up with half-day, one-to-one skipper coaching sessions before the start of the race. The coaching organisation also held an introductory, one-day crew coaching workshop attended by 150 crew members in order to develop a common language around a coaching culture. The structure of the coaching programme, including the associated timeline, is detailed in Table 4.

The coaching programme included a combination of individual leadership, group and team coaching sessions with the earlier sessions focusing on group coaching for the skippers, followed by individual coaching sessions. Individual Skype coaching sessions were attempted after the completion of the first leg of the race in September, but there were unexpected issues, which undermined the coaching engagement. The skippers and crews were dealing with the aftermath of a fatality that had occurred during the race and counselling was offered by the race organiser. Technical issues with Skype were also experienced. Some sessions were held with skippers, but the coaching was abandoned as a result of these challenges and unexpected issues. Face-to-face coaching sessions were held in Cape Town (October) with 11 of the 12 skippers. The sessions were limited to one-hour group coaching sessions, with three to four skippers in each session. Crew coaching was also conducted in three sessions with six to eight crew members per session.

Skype coaching was then conducted with 11 skippers and six crew members (evenly spread across three of the teams) in various locations between November and February; and face-to-face individual coaching was conducted in Seattle in April. Team coaching was only introduced towards the later stages of the race to provide additional support to the teams, who were dealing with a second fatality and recovering from challenging racing conditions. The coaching programme was distinctive for the length of time between the different coaching sessions and the variety of modes used by the coaching organisation. The external coaching process was independent from the skipper debriefs that were conducted internally by the race directors.

Table 4 Structure of the coaching programme

Timeline	Coaching mode	Participants	Purpose
March (prior to race start)	Group coaching (4½ days)	12 race skippers, race and deputy race director, and 4 external coaches	To encourage a coaching style of team leadership and develop race expectations
July	½ day of group coaching	2 skippers and race director	Resolve issues of team dynamics
August	Crew coaching workshop (1 day)	150 crew members (Round the World and 'Leggers')	Develop understanding of a coaching culture
September (Rio de Janeiro, Brazil)	Individual Skype coaching sessions	Some skippers (not all completed)	Supporting the skippers in leading their teams
October (Cape Town, South Africa)	Face-to-face coaching with 2–3 skippers in learning group coaching sessions	11 of the 12 skippers and 3–6 crew members from different teams	Supporting skippers in leading their teams and the crew in managing team dynamics
November (Albany, Australia)	Skype coaching sessions	11 skippers and 6 crew members across 3 teams	As above
February (Da Nang, Vietnam)	Skype coaching sessions	11 skippers and some crew members	As above
April (Seattle, USA)	Team coaching and face-to-face individual coaching sessions	Teams and some skippers and crew members	Supporting the teams in managing team dynamics and improving performance
June (New York, USA)	Team coaching and face-to-face individual coaching sessions	Teams and some skippers and crew members	Supporting the teams in managing team dynamics and improving performance
Ongoing during the race	Internal skipper debriefs with race and deputy race director, which some skippers considered as internal coaching	Skippers	Supporting the skippers in dealing with the challenges of leading their teams

Findings

The race organisers and some of the skippers were initially sceptical of the benefits of coaching. Their perceptions shifted during the initial group coaching to recognising that coaching was beneficial in supporting both the skippers and the crews. The initial group coaching was effective in developing confidence in both the coaching process and the use of a coaching leadership style to support others. The relationships between the skippers were strengthened as they practised coaching skills with each other. The race director explained why these peer coaching skills were essential during the race: 'to know that you are one of 12, all in the same situation, and what you've experienced, someone else has probably experienced or is about to; it's important to know that you have someone you can rely on because you are racing against each other, but you are actually all part of one team'.

This finding is relevant to the context of teams of teams, where team leaders can use a coaching style to support each other through shared challenges. The skippers appeared more open to the group coaching prior to the start of the race. Some skippers found the individual coaching sessions more challenging during the race. This finding aligns with coaching in the organisational context where clients find the coaching can become more challenging as they progress with coaching.

The individual leadership coaching was found to be effective in supporting most of the skippers in making sense of their own experience and in managing the social dynamics within their teams. During the race, the high-performing skippers transitioned from using their own technical expertise to focusing on developing the relationships within the team and encouraging the team to take more leadership. The race director confirmed that the skippers had found the individual coaching sessions useful and that the coaching offered 'a slightly different perspective on things perhaps ... and different manner of going about the problem. So, yes it has helped them'.

A ripple effect was experienced from the leadership coaching as the skippers used their experience of being coached to inform the way they led their teams. These findings align with the research, which identified a coaching ripple effect where the positive impact of individual coaching spread throughout the organisational system (O'Connor and Cavanagh, 2013). This finding highlights the role of the leader in supporting the emergence of a coaching culture within the team.

As the race progressed, the coaching modality shifted from individual leadership coaching of the skippers to team coaching. This shift was in response to the leadership evolving from the traditional hierarchical model of 'skipper as leader' to a more shared leadership approach. One of the high-performing skippers highlighted the benefits of the team coaching: 'it was a timed, dedicated period for us to sit down ... the crew to realise what it's all about and different people's views'.

Some team members perceived the team coaching as an opportunity to 'catch the skipper out', which illustrates the social dynamics that can arise in team coaching. The team coaching offered the teams the opportunity to develop collective responsibility in addressing challenges. The lead coach recognised the need for the team coaching: 'classic themes of conflict and crucial conversations – dealing with singular personalities and their effect on the entire crew, personalities not gelling or becoming alienated from their peers and how to deal with that'.

The coach also acknowledged that the team coaching timing was too late in the schedule and, as a result, the sailing team missed out: 'building the rapport and the momentum ... if we had worked with whole crews in Cape Town or Rio earlier. We would have laid down a marker/foundation as they went round the world. Key lesson for us'.

Conversely, a team member highlighted the benefit of having a team coach engaged: 'somebody who could be objective – it wasn't just another opinion. It was a professional who could take a professional view and suggest a solution and that's why we picked that because we had to do something. We wanted to do it in that environment ... which was neutral'.

These findings highlight that team coaching offered additional benefits to the team. While individual leadership coaching of the skippers was beneficial for the skippers and had a ripple effect for the teams, it was not sufficient for leadership development in challenging team contexts, as evidenced by the organic emergence of the team coaching later in the race. These findings are relevant for coaches, leadership development professionals, and organisations adapting to rapidly changing environments, where teams are essential for solving complex challenges.

Implications for team leadership development professionals

A blended coaching approach is effective in team contexts, particularly where technical specialists are transitioning into the team leadership role. The individual leadership coaching offers support to emerging team leaders, whilst the team coaching supports collective leadership development. The case study highlights that coaches and leadership development professionals need to take account of the temporal nature of both individual leader and collective leadership development within the team context. The design of the coaching programme also needs to provide a safe psychological space for both leaders and teams to develop confidence in both the coaching process and exploring collective leadership. Psychological safety is essential for developing fearless organisations (Edmondson, 2018) where team learning can thrive.

Furthermore, group coaching is useful for team leaders to develop a coaching style of leadership and supportive, peer coaching relationships. These relationships support team leaders in facing shared challenges in the context of of teams. Both coaches and commissioners of coaching need to consider l of coaching modalities to optimise team leadership development over time. By focusing on both the collective and temporal nature of leadership development, coaches and organisations will effectively address the challenges associated with the shift to team-based organisational design and the context of teams of teams.

References

Ancona, D., Backman, E., and Isaacs, K. (2015) Two roads to green: A tale of bureaucratic versus distributed leadership models of change, in R. Henderson, R. Gulati, and M. Tushman (eds.) *Leading Sustainable Change: An Organizational Perspective* (pp. 225–249). Oxford: Oxford University Press.

Anderson, N. (2011) *The NLP Coach Companion: What to Do and When to Do It. How to Reveal Potential and Coach Performance*. Kendal: VT Publishing.

Athanasopoulou, A. and Dopson, S. (2018) A systematic review of executive coaching outcomes: Is it the journey or the destination that matters the most?, *The Leadership Quarterly*, 29 (1): 70–88.

Clutterbuck, D. (2007) *Coaching the Team at Work*. London: Nicholas Brealey.

Day, D. and Dragoni, L. (2015) Leadership development: An outcome-oriented review based on time and levels of analyses, *Annual Review of Organizational Psychology and Organizational Behaviour*, 2 (1): 133–156.

Day, D., Fleenor, J., Atwater, L., Sturm, R., and McKee, R. (2014) Advances in leader and leadership development: A review of 25 years of research and theory, *Leadership Quarterly*, 25 (1): 63–82.

Day, D., Harrison, M., and Halpin, S. (2009) *An Integrative Approach to Leader Development: Connecting Adult Development, Identity, and Expertise*. New York: Routledge.

Day, D., Zaccaro, S., and Halpin, S. (2004) *Leader Development for Transforming Organisations: Growing Leaders for Tomorrow*. Hillsdale, NJ: Lawrence Erlbaum Associates.

DeRue, D. (2011) Adaptive leadership theory: Leading and following as a complex adaptive process, *Research in Organizational Behaviour*, 31 (1): 125–150.

DeRue, D. and Ashford, S. (2010) Who will lead and who will follow? A social process of leadership identity construction in organizations, *Academy of Management Review*, 35 (4): 627–647.

Edmondson, A.C. (2018) *The Fearless Organization: Creating Psychological Safety in the Workplace for Learning, Innovation, and Growth*. Hoboken, NJ: Wiley.

Geier, M. (2016) Leadership in extreme contexts: Transformational leadership, performance beyond expectations?, *Journal of Leadership and Organizational Studies*, 23 (3): 234–247.

Hawkins, P. (2014) *Leadership Team Coaching in Practice: Developing High Performance Teams*. London: Kogan Page.

Holton, E. and Lowe, J. (2007) Toward a general research process for using Dubin's theory building model, *Human Resource Development Review*, 6 (3): 297–320.

Johns, G. (2006) The essential impact of context on organizational behaviour, *Academy of Management Review*, 31 (2): 386–408.

Kartoch, D. (2013) Decision-making and the leadership conundrum, *CLAWS Journal*, Summer, 161–173.

Kegan, R. and Lahey, L. (2009) *Immunity to Change*. Boston, MA: Harvard Business Press.

Kellerman, B. (2012) *The End of Leadership*. New York: Harper Collins.

Kihl, L., Leberman, S., and Schull, V. (2010) Stakeholder construction of leadership in intercollegiate athletics, *European Sport Management Quarterly*, 10 (2): 241–275.

Kolb, D. (2015) *Experiential Learning: Experience as the Source of Learning and Development*. Englewood Cliffs, NJ: Prentice-Hall.

Kozlowski, S, Mak, S., and Chao, G. (2016) Team-centric leadership: An integrative review, *Annual Review of Organizational Psychology and Organizational Behavior*, 3 (1): 21–54.

Malley, A. (2017) Global Human Capital Trends 2017 [https://www2.deloitte.com/content/dam/Deloitte/global/Documents/HumanCapital/hc-2017-global-human-capital-trends-gx.pdf].

McCauley, C., Van Velsor, E., and Ruderman, M. (2010) Introduction: Our view of leadership development, in E. Van Velsor, C. McCauley, and M. Ruderman (eds.) *The Center for Creative Leadership Handbook of Leadership Development*, 3rd edition (pp. 1–28). San Francisco, CA: Jossey-Bass.

McGrath, J., Arrow, H., and Berdahl, J. (2000) The study of groups: Past, present, and future, *Personality and Social Psychology Review*, 4 (1): 95–105.

McLaughlin, M. and Cox, E. (2016) *Leadership Coaching: Developing Brave Leaders*. Abingdon: Routledge.

O'Connor, S. and Cavanagh, M. (2013) The coaching ripple effect: The effects of developmental coaching on wellbeing across organizational networks, *Psychology of Well-Being: Theory, Research and Practice*, 3 (2): 1–23.

Porter, L. and McLaughlin, G. (2006) Leadership and the organizational context: Like the weather?, *The Leadership Quarterly*, 17 (6): 559–576.

Riddle, D. (2016) *Executive integration: Equipping transitioning leaders for success*. White paper. Centre for Creative Leadership [http://www.ccl.org/wp-content/uploads/2015/04/ExecutiveIntegration.pdf].

Salas, E., Stagl, K., and Burke, C. (2004) 25 years of team effectiveness in organizations: Research themes and emerging needs, *International Review of Industrial and Organizational Psychology*, 19: 47–92.

Tannenbaum, S., Mathieu, J., Salas, E., and Cohen, D. (2012) Teams are changing: Are research and practice evolving fast enough?, *Industrial and Organizational Psychology*, 5 (1): 2–24.

Tourish, D. (2012) Developing leaders in turbulent times: Five steps towards integrating soft practices with hard measures of organizational performance, *Organizational Dynamics*, 41 (1): 23–31.

Wageman, R., Nunes, D.A., Burruss, J.A., and Hackman, J.R. (2008) *Senior Leadership Teams: What It Takes to Make Them Great*. Boston, MA: Harvard Business Press.

On pairing for team coaching

Lynn Keenaghan and Beatrice Sigrist

Introduction

This case study describes two international coaches pairing to deliver team coaching. The outcome of the pairing process is captured in a 'Pair Readiness Charting Process' to assist other team coaching pairs. Furthermore, we introduce the concept of 'WE-Muscle/WE-Mindset' and identify the potential contribution of team coaching pairs to team coaching effectiveness.

There is a gap in the evidence and literature on pairing and, to the best of our knowledge, we are one of the first coaching pairs to write a case study on the process of pairing in team coaching.

Why we paired

Our pairing evolved from participating in the 'TCS Diploma in Team Coaching' run by Georgina Woudstra and Declan Woods from the Team Coaching Studio (TCS). We both had experience of team coaching and attended a diploma programme to extend our range to include relational team coaching. During the diploma we developed our team coaching practice through triad work. An unplanned absence by our third member adversely affected a compulsory task and our triad entered a storming phase. Our response highlighted our different operating styles: one of us announced 'we are now a pair' and the other 'we are a triad with an absent colleague'. This experience created a learning journey that benefited from having both of us involved.

What we did

We had an opportunity to coach an international team and we considered that working as an international pair would add breadth and depth to match the level of complexity of the team.

One of us held the contract to deliver the team coaching. The contract was to support the on-boarding of a new leader and to increase team effectiveness, taking account of the international nature of the team's roles. We aspired to work as an equal coaching pair. Any new pairing carries risks – in our case, the biggest risk was the established relationship that one of us had with the organisation. We contracted to allow each other to withdraw from the pairing for any reason during this development process.

We drew on executive coaching skills to form our pair by contracting to develop the 4 Cs of team coaching – competence, confidence, coherence, and congruence – as a team coaching pair. We shared autobiographies to explore our drivers, values, and aspirations. We generously shared knowledge, resources, and insights, which created empathy, trust, and respect.

For this international assignment, we considered that the relational TCS model would be most appropriate to focus on how the coach, team leader, and team members all affect and impact on each other. This model promotes 'modes of team coaching' that distinguish between three key stances of the role of team coach (Woudstra, 2021):

- facilitating the team and thereby managing the process, enabling the team to focus on the task at hand;
- observing the 'dance' of the interactional patterns between team members; and
- presence and use of self as a way of intervening for change.

This model enables coaches to 'collect data in the field'; to observe dynamics and patterns; and to feed this back to the team to make what is often implicit more explicit. It is a powerful approach to increase engagement, acknowledge team processes, and remove blocks.

Table 5 describes the preparation we undertook to develop our pair to inhabit the different stances of team coaching.

Table 5 Our pair preparation for the three stances in team coaching

1. *Facilitator*	• Planning the beginning of the team coaching process • Anticipating the teams' emergent needs and reviewing our respective knowledge, skills, and resources
2. *Observer*	• Cultivating team coaching discipline by running our planning sessions as mini team coaching sessions (e.g. check-in, check-out) and practising potential interventions • Journaling between planning sessions (Woods, 2011) to reflect, identify patterns, and share insights • Exploring how to read the room and respond to difficult dynamics
3. *Presence and use of self as instrument*	• Moving beyond offering psychological safety to each other by reassuring nods, smiles, keeping eye contact, and noticing the other • Giving feedback on style and impact. A mini peer coaching session on mindset revealed our edges: one of us assumed the presence of a master coach while the other a humble beginner

Through being disciplined enough to practise this together, we realised the challenge was how to cultivate the appropriate holding space for team coaching. We created the initial holding space with the team leader. Given the agreement was to work emergently with the team, this space could change. Our initial task was to build sufficient psychological safety for ourselves and then to understand how to develop and create a safe and appropriate holding space for team coaching with the team. We did this as a pair by:

- Exploring experientially, with a lot of patience and curiosity.
- Undertaking peer coaching and exploration, which became our cultural practice.
- Working through constellations, explicitly mapping our system, to make our patterns more explicit (Whittington, 2016).
- Pausing when the psychological contract was challenged to understand the triggers and identify how we could notice this earlier. We used somatic experience. We invited each other to relax and think of that trigger in the here and now, check for clues about what is going on in the body, and notice without judgement and curiosity whether images and feelings were arising. We treated these triggers like gold for the pair's development of a safe holding space for our work and to embody the experience of team development. Our aim was to get less hijacked by emotions.
- Acknowledging deeply-held personal indicators of what is safe to help support connecting, establish safety, and renegotiate ground rules which not only supported the development of our pair but built our skills in creating the holding space for teams.
- Re-contracting to allow ourselves to be 'good enough', which helped us gather momentum and more traction on our development.

As expected, our ongoing enquiry brought into sharp focus our divergent approaches to support and challenge. In part, this difference created confidence that we would be able to lean on each other when dealing with emerging dynamics in the team, such as tensions between focus on task and focus on people, potential cultural differences, and different perspectives on leadership. Ultimately, this process enhanced our resilience to 'sit in the fire' and hold heated or delicate moments in team coaching.

The occasional jarring and storming led us to reflect that we were operating as two times 'I'/two individuals seeking the best and mitigating or compensating for individual weaknesses. A critical moment occurred when we completed the compilation of potential resources and one of us announced, 'Great, we are there', to which the other responded, 'We have just started'. Our responses startled each other. What we had achieved was to bring resources as two individuals into a shared space. We had not yet worked out how to deliver as a pair. We began to consciously focus the lens on 'We' to broaden and test our perspectives and help us develop a mindset of exploring and planning from a perspective of 'We'. Once we cultivated 'We', there were critical moments that we experienced psychologically, informed our philosophy, and represented a fundamental shift in our mindset. Negotiating the boundaries of the team coaching holding space became, not what each of us could flex to and tolerate, but what 'We' together could flex to and tolerate. We recognised that, just like developing muscles, we needed to focus on a 'We' perspective to be attuned to, and in resonance with, each other in the service of the team. We gave a name to this state: 'WE-Muscle/WE-Mindset'.

In another critical moment, we unintentionally swapped roles in holding the psychological safety. The person who usually held this, when relieved of the responsibility, became animated and light. The other experienced a more grounded state, increased the creative potential for the other, and cultivating the holding space became more attractive. This realisation, informed by the 'WE-Muscle/WE-Mindset' state led to re-contracting for 'You are OK and I am OK' and this helped us flex roles further.

Outcomes

On the day that we delivered our first team coaching, we arrived with agreement on our drivers, our goals, and critical success factors. We were grounded in our philosophy and mindset. With humility we trusted our ability to work relationally with the issues that would emerge with the team. We were comfortable with our relationship presence and confident in our ability to co-regulate and help dial up and down. We were ready and found time to make the space beautiful and to dance to cultivate lightness and flexibility before the team arrived.

Before delivery of our first team coaching, we sought to articulate our pairing process and we captured this in our first outcome, represented by the Pair Readiness Chart (Figure 12). This provides a model for prospective pairs to follow or focus to realign if presence, intention or connection is lost.

The second key outcome was the development and articulation of the 'WE-Muscle/WE-Mindset'. We propose this is a development phase for team coaching and could be used by developing pairs to assess their relative shift from two individuals to 'WE'.

Drawing on somatic interventions was key. It enabled us to self-regulate with less need to focus on defending against perceived or anticipated threats. More significantly for team coaching was the process of developing co-regulation, which made our work deeper and more effective. As we could offer the team a wider range of resonance between ourselves, we expected that this would transmit to team members, enabling them to feel safer to reveal their key issues earlier and increase the level of openness and willingness to adopt new behaviours, experiment, and let go of past experience. As connectedness enables cooperation, we expected that this would resonate within the team and support the team in enhancing their connectedness; for example, going beyond

Figure 12 Pair Readiness Chart

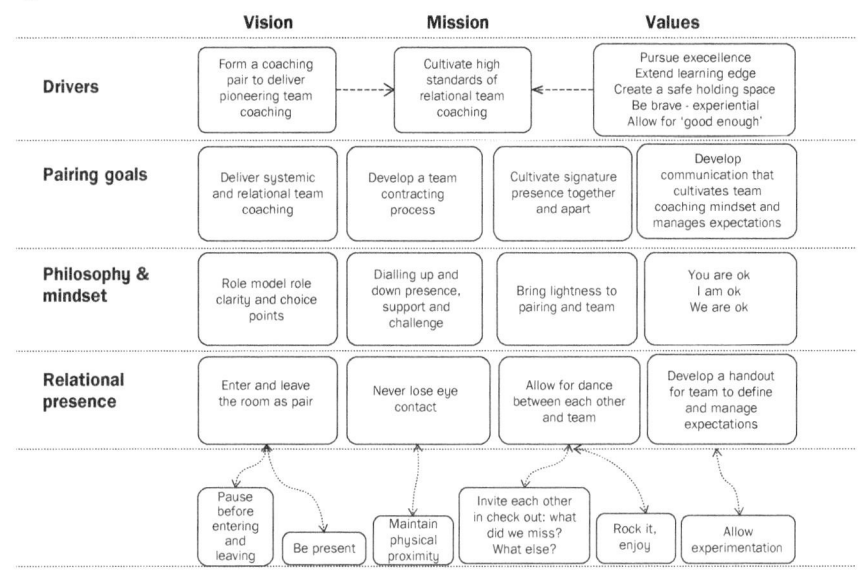

	Vision	Mission	Values	
Drivers	Form a coaching pair to deliver pioneering team coaching	Cultivate high standards of relational team coaching	Pursue excecellence · Extend learning edge · Create a safe holding space · Be brave - experiential · Allow for 'good enough'	
Pairing goals	Deliver systemic and relational team coaching	Develop a team contracting process	Cultivate signature presence together and apart	Develop communication that cultivates team coaching mindset and manages expectations
Philosophy & mindset	Role model role clarity and choice points	Dialling up and down presence, support and challenge	Bring lightness to pairing and team	You are ok · I am ok · We are ok
Relational presence	Enter and leave the room as pair	Never lose eye contact	Allow for dance between each other and team	Develop a handout for team to define and manage expectations
	Pause before entering and leaving / Be present	Maintain physical proximity	Invite each other in check out: what did we miss? What else?	Rock it, enjoy / Allow experimentation

'my bit and your bit' to what the pair/team can do/must do together to increase team effectiveness (Porges, 2011).

We anticipated that embodying our experience of co-creating our pair would help us to role-model effective relating more impactfully. As we moved towards the ability to dance lightly and flex roles, we expected there to be more opportunities to experiment with presence. Significantly, this helped us to develop our signature presence and use, not just of self, but of pair.

The investment in developing co-regulation paid off. We were able to keep our bond moment to moment. The team had contracted for being flexible about time-keeping. Egg timers were used throughout to show how much time was being spent on different elements of the day. One of the pair got triggered and frustrated, as the team spent a lot of time on one issue without making decisions or commitments on how to move forward. The other co-regulated and simply held presence. This in turn released the team to renegotiate their boundaries on time and committing to actions.

We refined our 'Pair Readiness Chart' further after undertaking a meta-reflection on the pairing process. We developed greater clarity of our role, and the resources we needed to generate. These were not just tools but the development of our pair presence as a key instrument. This developed further into an exploration of the potential contribution of a pair to effectiveness in team coaching (Figure 13).

Figure 13 Potential contribution of a pair to team coaching effectiveness

```
                    ┌─────────────────────────────────────────┐
                    │   Enabling teams to fulfil their potential │
                    └─────────────────────────────────────────┘

Key stances         ┌──────────┬──────────┬──────────┬──────────┐
                    │Facilitator│Observer of│Presence  │Presence  │
                    │          │interactional│and use of│and use of│
                    │          │patterns  │self      │pair      │
                    └──────────┴──────────┴──────────┴──────────┘

Resources           ┌──────────┬──────────┬──────────┬──────────┬──────────┐
generated           │Competence│Psychological│'WE-    │Role model│Collective│
by pair             │confidence│safety    │Muscle // │effective │reflective│
                    │coherence │──────────│WE-       │relating  │practice in│
                    │congruence│Co-regulation│mindset'│          │the here  │
                    │          │and holding│          │          │and now   │
                    │          │space     │          │          │          │
                    └──────────┴──────────┴──────────┴──────────┴──────────┘

Input                                  ┌──────────┐
resources                              │  Team    │
for pair                               │  coach   │
                                       └──────────┘
                         ┌──────────┐              ┌──────────┐
                         │Executive │              │  Team    │
                         │coaching  │              │coaching  │
                         │skills    │              │skills    │
                         └──────────┘              └──────────┘

        The grey shaded box identifies the potential unique contribution of a pair
```

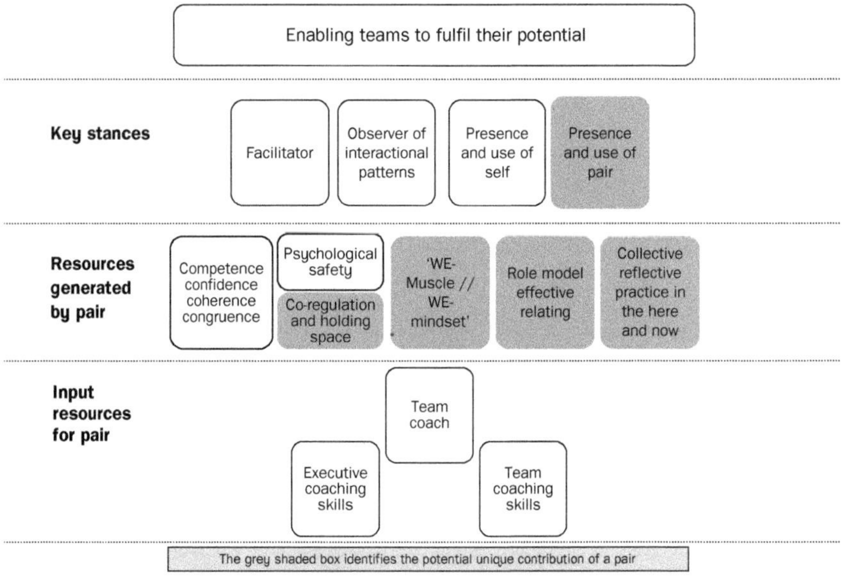

Key learning

Our case study is primarily based on the pairing process, not least because our international team coaching journey came to an abrupt halt because of Covid-19. This meant that we could not demonstrate the potential impact of pairing on team effectiveness. Although this case study focuses on an inward perspective, we consider the system, stakeholder, and future focus perspectives are equally important.

Our early experience of coaching together has led us to develop an hypothesis about the potential contribution of pairing to support team effectiveness. The shaded boxes in Figure 13 identify what we consider to be unique contributions that a pair can offer to team coaching effectiveness.

We experienced the TCS 'modes of team coaching' as fundamental building-blocks in developing our mindset for team coaching. Whilst the three stances could be delivered by an individual coach, we consider all roles are strengthened by working as a pair. Initially, we considered the different roles we could take based on our respective strengths. We concluded that 'WE-Muscle/WE-Mindset' offers dynamic and creative opportunities by changing the interplay between different roles and stances. In addition, we propose that the key stances be extended to four to include 'Presence of and use of pair', and in this regard the pair is a stance in its own right. Furthermore, the pair is being the intervention not doing the intervention.

Our key insight into the pairing process is that two single mindsets are not yet a pair and therefore practice is constrained. We proposed that the 'WE-Muscle/WE-Mindset' enabled us to achieve more than a 'sum greater that the two parts'. The 'WE-Muscle/WE-Mindset' helped inspire our philosophy and pairing contract of 'You are OK and I am OK' and extended our presence and effective relating.

In addition, we propose the unique contribution that a pair can make through the 'WE-Muscle/WE-Mindset': modelling effective relating. We became more confident that our team coaching competencies would continue to evolve and that we would be able to role-model this in team settings.

Usually team coaches draw on supervision for reflection. For pairs there is an additional layer. We appreciated the opportunity to engage in reflective practice together as the pair's capacity was increased by two pairs of eyes and ears, two brains and hearts, that all together enabled greater insight as all were in the here and now.

Our supervisor encouraged us to step up our focus on a process of tracking and describing and responding (TDR). Working as a pair enables this tracking process to be made visible by acknowledging through light touch noticing (oh, hm, keep going) of sharing what each of us witnessed. The opportunity to share insight and felt experience gave us exposure to real-time feedback so that we became more able to encourage teams to also develop team-level reflective practice in the moment. It was evident that it empowered the team to notice and become more engaged and assertive about negotiating choice points (e.g. whether to go faster or deeper or shift the focus to people, stakeholders, task, outcome).

Through our early pairing process, we were focused on what was different in our styles and sought to cultivate a wider range of presence to the team. It was interesting to hear feedback from our supervisor who perceived us as having more similar styles with both having a strong presence, clarity, and the ability to provoke and disrupt. Our learning edge shifted from extending and differentiating the range of our signature presence to a merging of signature presence and to recontract for disrupting interventions to ensure that this important coaching intervention was not stifled.

A critical decision in our pairing process was to aspire to work as an equal coaching pair. This was hindered, as the initial contracting had taken place. The intention was a powerful driver of the pairing process. What is much less clear is the impact on pairing and relationship to the team leader. This would be the key focus of enquiry in future work. Our early perspective is that initial contracting should ideally be undertaken by the pair.

We support our hypothesis that we needed a good understanding of ourselves to develop sufficient psychological safety to develop our pair and holding space for team coaching. Through the beauty of this dance other benefits emerged. Whilst Covid-19 may have halted ongoing delivery for this international team coaching work, it enabled us avoiding becoming emotionally drained and flexing to develop online team coaching skills.

Conclusion

We believe we are pioneers in conceptualising the pairing process in the emerging discipline of team coaching:

- we developed a 'Pair Readiness Chart' that provides a road map for others to follow;
- we propose a model highlighting the potential unique contribution of pairs to team coaching effectiveness;
- we discovered the 'WE-Muscle/WE-Mindset', which we consider is a concept and a developmental stage for pairing.

We consider that the creation of a pair requires:

- commitment to the development of the other;
- commitment to invest in that time with the knowledge that the outcome may be not to pair;
- courage and commitment to support and challenge through feedback.

Challenging ourselves to articulate the contribution of a pair of team coaches to potential team effectiveness clarified that the role of team coaches is to hold the potential and not be the authors of the team story, thereby enabling teams to own their progress (Taylor and Saint-Laurent, 2017).

Working emergently requires confidence of working with soft edges and more preparation compared with pre-determined facilitation or training. Yet, if our experience of developing our pair is replicated in team coaching, it is our view that it will have more lasting impact.

As there was limited evidence, we drew on co-therapy, somatic experience, and group and family therapy to understand pairing. We started distilling the specific implications for other pairs in relation to the discipline of team coaching. We surmise that a developed pair does not guarantee effective team coaching, as this is affected by many variables, but makes it much more possible. Our hypothesis of the impacts for team effectiveness would need to be tested further and we conclude there is a need for more research on the pairing process for team coaching.

References

Porges, S.W. (2011) *The Polyvagal Theory: Neurophysiological Foundations of Emotions, Attachment, Communication, Self-Regulation*. New York: W.W. Norton.

Taylor, P.J. and Saint-Laurent, R. (2017) Group psychotherapy informed by the principles of somatic experiencing: Moving beyond trauma to embodied relationship, *International Journal of Group Psychotherapy*, 67 (suppl. 1): 171–181.

Whittington, J. (2016) *Systemic Coaching and Constellations: The Principles, Practices and Application for Individuals, Teams and Groups*, 2nd edition. London: Kogan Page.

Woods, D. (2011) Coaches' use of reflective journals for learning, in J. Passmore (ed.) *Supervision in Coaching: Supervision, Ethics and Continuous Development* (pp. 265–284). London: Kogan Page.

Woudstra, G. (2021) *Real Team Coaching. Mastering The Art of Team Coaching: A comprehensive guide to unleashing the power, purpose and potential in any team.* Team Coaching Studio Press. England.

Team coaching in Agile software development case study

Stanly Lau

This case study shares how an organisation transforms from managing individuals to empowering the team to decide how to work together and build a product. It also covers the role of Agile Coach and Scrum Master, how it relates to team coaching, and the context of Agile and Scrum that enables this change.

The context of Agile and Scrum

Agile software development started as a reaction to a heavy process-oriented approach involving a lot of planning and documentation that was prevalent in the software industry in the 1990s. In early 2001, a group of programmers met to discuss better ways of developing software. Those people were either the creators or proponents of so-called lightweight frameworks such as Scrum, Extreme Programming, Adaptive Software Development, and several others. The outcome was the Manifesto for Agile Software Development (2001) with a strong focus on people and collaboration.

Agile is an umbrella term and Scrum is one of the frameworks under it (Agile Alliance, 2020). There is a role from the business side (called Product Owner) responsible for delivering value to the customer and business. The Product Owner divides their time between working with stakeholders and the team. The team is cross-functional and consists of people with necessary skills to deliver the product. It is up to the team members to find how to work well together while building a product that satisfies market conditions and stakeholders' expectations. They work in regular short cycles (called Sprints), typically one to two weeks, to plan, deliver, and validate an increment of the product. Most team coaching interventions will happen here.

They are guided by a Scrum Master who has a deep understanding of Scrum and is a servant-leader for the team. They coach the team towards self-management,[1] and helps the Product Owner learn how to maximise value and influence the bigger organisation to improve the overall work environment. A Scrum Master can work with one to three teams.

An Agile Coach is commonly a progression from Scrum Master after working with many teams. They adopt ideas from related disciplines, deals with organisation impediments (Adkins, 2010), and has a breadth of stances (Galen, 2020), including coaching, mentoring, consulting, teaching, and facilitating to name a few.

A common purpose of Agile Coach and Scrum Master is to help people in product development to be Agile. To help effectively in this multidisciplinary and complex domain requires the ability to switch between stances in different situations. In this case study, I will focus only on team coaching.

The case study provides only the gist of how Scrum works. For interested readers, more information can be found in the Scrum Guides (Schwaber and Sutherland, 2020).

Organisation: RealGames

RealGames produces online games and has customers worldwide. It began as a start-up of 10 people and has grown to 300 people over 15 years. They have a young culture with most of the developers in their twenties and senior management in their early forties.

At the time of engaging an external Agile Coach (me) in 2014, they had monthly product releases. There were two departments related to software development: development (software developers) and quality assurance (testers), each led by a manager. There were team leads who broke down the requirements and assigned tasks to team members. Once developers had finished coding, they would handover to testers. Working in this way caused misunderstanding, defects, delays, and a lot of stress and burnout near release dates.

The engagement plan

The management and team leads had joined a Scrum Master course to have a better understanding of the changes and impact it could bring before the engagement. This helped the management to decide early whether the engagement aligned with their goal.

The reasons for the management to adopt Scrum and get external help were:

1 They were interested in the self-management aspect of Scrum because they felt lack of ownership from the staff.
2 They were constantly looking for better ways for product delivery.
3 To resolve high employee turnover.

I proposed an engagement covering three levels of coaching: organisational, team, and technical practices. These could address the above issues (1) and (2), but tackling employee turnover was less certain.

> **Organisational coaching:** helping management to structure their organisation so that it can benefit from Agile development. The focus is on organisation design, human resource practices, managing work, role of management, etc.
>
> **Team coaching:** helping the team to be better at self-managing. It is common for the Agile Coach to take on the role of the Scrum Master as well as the role of a coach/educator of a (future) Scrum Master. The focus is on improving the relationship between the Product Owner and the development team, the team's decision-making, shared responsibility, etc.
>
> **Technical practices coaching:** helping teams to improve skills related to software development for better technical agility. This includes a focus on understanding the codebase, adding feedback mechanisms to detect software defects earlier, collaboration between team members, etc.

The plan was for a three-month pilot starting with one team and me being the Scrum Master. People outside the team, including the management, were to support their needs by providing learning resources and policy changes. Starting small reduced the amount of change in the organisation and also reduced the learning curve in supporting the team. After the pilot, the management decided to expand the adoption to the rest of the organisation. Subsequent engagement focus depended on the needs. It could be helping new teams get started with Scrum, coaching existing teams on self-management and technical practices, or coaching internal Scrum Masters. There were periodic follow-ups with management to discuss how teams were doing, what the management needed to change, and if there was a need to change focus.

Episode: A team decision

I joined a planning event by a relatively new team. They were gauging how much work they could do in the Sprint. David, one of the team members, moved five index cards describing new features and said: 'I think we can do these'. Two soft voices said 'okay' while the other four members were silent, staring at the cards. David exclaimed, 'okay!' and was about to stand up when I intervened.

> *Me:* 'Hi David, are these (the five index cards) the decision?'
> *David:* 'Yes'.

Me: 'I noticed there were two verbal replies to the question of whether those five items could be done right before it is decided. It isn't clear to me that this is a collective decision from the team. Is it for you?' [Most of the people shook their heads.]

Me: 'What could you do differently?'

The team recalled the fist-of-five voting method and went ahead to reach consensus.

> **Reflection**
>
> The team understood why the amount of work they selected should be a team decision. They have learned about the concept of a self-managing team from the Scrum introduction I gave before they volunteered to join the pilot team. From previous experience, I learned that if I had not covered that topic well during the course, or if I had failed to recognise that a new team member was unfamiliar with the concept, it could cause confusion and defensiveness from all team members.
>
> One of the team members shared with me: 'I remember you always observe the whole team and give us "facts" like a mirror, which reflects aspects that we never noticed before. Instead of solving the problem for us, you helped us discover the problems and solutions ourselves. This made the team grow and become more mature'.

Episode: Monitoring and managing progress

It was another new team beginning their first Sprint and I introduced a physical task board to manage their work. It consisted of three columns – Pending, In Progress, and Done – and Post-It notes for the tasks. Midway through the Sprint, Aaron noticed that more than half of the tasks were in the Pending or In Progress columns. He exclaimed, 'Guys, I think we are not progressing well'. Nobody responded to him. I noticed this and decided to wait and see how the team would manage the situation. At the end of the Sprint, they missed their goal and the Product Owner was surprised.

During the retrospective, the team discussed how they were distracted by new requirements and struggled to get dependent systems to work. I asked what they could do differently next time in a similar situation. They figured that they could inform the Product Owner earlier of the risks, reduce the scope of work for the Sprint, and give him a chance to change his plans. In the following Sprint, the team faced a similar situation. Aaron raised the issue of poor progress again. There was a sense of hesitation in the room. 'Who will inform the Product Owner?', one of the team members asked. Eventually, one of the senior members took the lead and a junior member joined him.

> **Reflection**
>
> This team used to work in an environment where a team lead would break down the work, assign tasks to individual members, and manage their progress. These were now part of everyone's responsibility. As the new way of working contains a lot of changes, I decided not to intervene at the beginning in order to provide space for the team to absorb the changes.
>
> Behind the scenes, I asked the Product Owner about his thoughts on the team and helped improve his understanding of what was going on. I also suggested some ways he could communicate to help the team take responsibility in solving problems. I might also find out that person wasn't interested in this new way of working or didn't understand enough, which could jeopardise growing a self-managing team.
>
> Recently, I met with one of the ex-team members and she shared her experience at that time: 'It was really amazing that when we started to practise daily stand up and manage the task board ourselves, everyone volunteered for the tasks and took ownership of it. Furthermore, we helped one another when there was a blocker. I felt we had higher ownership of the product we were delivering'.

Episode: A closure

There is an event at the end of a Sprint called retrospective where the team reflects on what has happened during the Sprint and generates improvements for the next Sprint. Retrospectives often gravitate towards technical issues, such as lack of testing and how to improve handling of production defects, but can evolve into a deeper discussion.

I was facilitating a timeline exercise during the retrospective for a team which had only four members, the others being on vacation. The team had written things on Post-It notes and placed them on the timeline. I was going through each note to help the team mine for insights. One of the Post-Its read, 'I was frustrated from being busy with many things'.

Me (to team):	'Can you tell us more about this?'
Mark:	'Sure, I wrote this. I was so occupied with troubleshooting issues happening in our live systems, I couldn't contribute to work on the product backlog items. I noticed we were behind our goal and yet other members were not picking up new work from the task board, so I was frustrated'.
Me:	'How did you cope with the feeling of frustration?'

Mark:	'I think I didn't. I kept feeling frustrated. I didn't understand why they were not picking up work and were so dependent on me'.
Lyn (raised her hand):	'There's something I'd like to share. I was working on one of the tasks to integrate the analytic monitoring service and I struggled with that for a few days. I knew Mark was swamped with critical live system issues and didn't want to distract him, so I was trying my best to solve it myself. I was also having issues with my family, which greatly affected my focus at work. Sharon supported me emotionally through the tough times'.

At this point Mark's facial expression turned from tense to relaxed:

Mark:	'I didn't know you were going through this. I should have approached you and not kept myself feeling frustrated'.
Me:	'Thanks for sharing your stories, who else could relate to this?'
Sharon:	'Yes. I looked at the service integration issue and could not figure out how to solve it. I was struggling with the task on hand as well while supporting Lyn emotionally, which relates to this Post-It: "Couldn't get service integration to work"'.
Tim:	'I'm sorry, I didn't know these happened while I was away working with the social committee for an upcoming event'.
Me:	'How was it for you (team) to share your story and also listen to the others?'
Mark:	'I feel relieved and see how I got myself into that situation, which isn't helpful. The energy could be better used to check out with the other team members. I also learned that distractions may be necessary to help the team move forward. (To everyone) Please approach me even though I may be occupied, if it is something I'm familiar with I could at least point you in the right direction'.
Lyn:	'I appreciate this conversation. It was a relief for me to share this with the team, thank you so much (looking at other members) and for the safe space'.

Reflection

I followed up with Mark to find out how it went for him. He was grateful for how I facilitated the session, and it came just in time. He was under pressure and wanted to raise it with the team, but he didn't know how to. He feared he might cause it to become a blaming session, although his intention was to see what the team could learn. When he heard that I was available to facilitate, he grabbed the opportunity.

> More than half of the retrospectives I facilitated weren't as fruitful as this one. It was quite common to find teams working and skipping retrospectives because they weren't useful. A few factors that influence skipping:
> - too much focus on following the process resulting in 'follow the motion'
> - topics have low resonance with the team
> - poor past experience with retrospectives reduces motivation and meaning.
>
> In this example, the pressure on the team was high and as Mark said, the retrospective came right in time to talk about it. It was rather accidental for me as I had not been with that team for quite a while and lost their context. What I found useful was listening to their emotions and inviting them to share what went through their minds and surfaced what was connected among them ('who else could relate to this and share your thoughts').

Impact on the organisation

Joni, who was the HR and operations manager, couldn't understand why the pilot team was so special – not required to comply with such HR policies as working hours and individual performance reviews. She had thought Scrum was a software development 'thing' and didn't bother to know more. But after attending a Scrum Master course and a few coaching sessions with me, her mindset began to shift.

> 'I had a better understanding of what Scrum was about and hence, understood the importance of a self-managing team; why it would work in a complex environment and why it is okay to fail (for learning) in an Agile environment. I noticed the gradual change in other managers moving away from a command and control leadership style. I also noticed that during the monthly HR exchange sessions, members who came from the pilot team shared positive things and looked happy, which was different from other teams'.

It also changed how she led her HR and operations department.

> 'I started to delegate and trust my team more, provide boundaries and constraints; and empowered them by telling what needs to be done and not how to complete assigned tasks. My management style changed to less command and control and to seeking for more inputs. My team showed positive outcomes, which helped me to build more confidence in them and to know that I'm doing something right!'

With the increased understanding of self-management and empowerment, the contrast with the dominant management style – command and control – became clearer. RealGames had high staff turnover for many years. Part of the reason was the leadership style did not work effectively with a young workforce. Joni found it was important for Generation Y and millennials to voice their opinions and see the meaning of their work.

After the pilot, RealGames progressively merged the development and the quality assurance departments, extended Scrum to more teams, grew more internal Scrum Masters, eliminated individual performance reviews, and changed the course towards greater team autonomy and self-management. A few factors that drove those decision were:

1. Teams felt safe to ask any questions about issues they didn't understand. This reduced misunderstanding of user requirements and helped to validate assumptions.
2. Focus on customer value to drive development instead of accepting requests from stakeholders without reasons.
3. Increased understanding of the purpose behind a user requirement.
4. Increased frequency and quality of conversation in the teams.
5. Work became more collaborative instead of just working on assigned tasks.

Final thoughts

This case study provides a glimpse of team coaching aspects in Agile/Scrum coaching, beginning with an engagement plan followed by episodes of my interventions with teams and the impact on the organisation. I struggled to omit the details of Agile and Scrum, but I tried to keep them to a minimum because they provide the reason and context for the need of team coaching. For those who are interested to find out more on this topic, Davies and Sedley (2009), Adkins (2010), and Watts (2013) provide further insights.

Note

1. I find the definition of self-managing teams by Richard Hackman (2002) useful. A big part of Scrum adoption is coaching the team from manager-led to self-managing teams.

References

Adkins, L. (2010) *Coaching Agile Teams: A Companion for ScrumMasters, Agile Coaches, and Project Managers in Transition.* Upper Saddle River, NJ: Addison-Wesley.

Agile Alliance (2020) Agile 101 [https://www.agilealliance.org/agile101].

Davies, R. and Sedley, L. (2009) *Agile Coaching*. Raleigh, NC: The Pragmatic Bookshelf.

Galen, B. (2020) Agile Coaches Need More than Coaching Skills, *Agile Moose*, 8 June [https://www.agile-moose.com/blog/2020/6/2/agile-coaches-need-more-than-coaching-skills].

Hackman, J.R. (2002) *Leading Teams: Setting the Stage for Great Performances*. Boston, MA: Harvard Business Press.

International Association of Facilitators (2016) Method of the Month: Fist to Five, 31 July [https://www.iaf-world.org/site/es/articles/2016-07-31/method-month-fist-five].

Manifesto for Agile Software Development (2001) [https://agilemanifesto.org].

Schwaber, K. and Sutherland, J. (2020) Scrum Guides [https://scrumguides.org].

Watts, G. (2013) *Scrum Mastery: From Good to Great Servant-Leadership*. Cheltenham: Inspect & Adapt.

A strength-based approach to developing team leadership and effectiveness

Doug MacKie

Introduction

As a profession, team coaching is in its infancy. Yet there is emerging evidence of its effectiveness in positively enhancing a variety of team outcomes, including team effectiveness (Wageman et al., 2008), skills and knowledge (Liu et al., 2009), innovation and safety (Buljac-Samardžić, 2012), and team member satisfaction and performance (Dimas et al., 2016). The variety of outcome criteria is itself a challenge in that cross-study comparisons become problematic, further inhibiting the collection and comparison of meta-analytic data – one of the hallmarks of theoretical and procedural efficacy. In addition, many of the published studies are methodologically heterogeneous and are too dependent on self-report data (Peters and Carr, 2019), restricting the understanding of the impact of team coaching beyond immediate team members. Recently, however, there has been some convergence on key outcome criteria in team coaching, including task performance, social process, and individual development (Wageman et al., 2008; Overfield, 2016). In addition to identifying the type of indicators that can be reliably measured as consequences of effective team coaching, it is equally important to establish who will be asked to assess these differences over time. The over-reliance of current research on self-report as a means of assessing effectiveness with all the incumbent issues of leniency and confirmatory bias (Dunning et al., 2004) limits the validity of outcome data and requires an extension to other stakeholder groups.

Given the relative recency of team coaching as a professional discipline (Clutterbuck et al., 2019), it is no surprise that there is little consensus as to how team coaching should be conducted. Consequently, team coaching is functionally heterogeneous as potential variables are necessarily explored in the pursuit of effective methodologies. However, there is a developing consensus around the definition of team coaching summarised succinctly as 'helping the team improve performance and the process by which performance is achieved through reflection and dialogue' (Clutterbuck, 2007). This definition covers two of the three outcome criteria outlined above but needs to include individual development within the team context to be fully aligned.

Evidence for the effectiveness of team coaching

A recent review of the evidence base in team coaching identified 17 empirical studies that had been peer reviewed and were sufficiently descriptive in their methodology to enable replication (Peters and Carr, 2019). However, only five of the reported studies employed an external coach and only seven reported data beyond the level of self-report. The review found just four studies that used an external coach, provided feedback from other raters, and reported reliable and valid outcome data (Heimbecker, 2006; Wageman et al., 2008; Carr and Peters, 2012; Gude, 2016). It is noteworthy that after team coaching, none of the reported studies used a leadership measure as the dependent variable to assess the effectiveness of the intervention.

Given that there is now a body of evidence indicating that team coaching can be effective in enhancing team effectiveness utilising a variety outcome measures, it is necessary to further elucidate the individual components of team coaching that may underpin this efficacy. This allows the development of a profile of what methodological factors underpin effective team coaching interventions. Methodologies range from the theoretically coherent (those that centre on a core unifying theoretical construct, such as strength-based approaches) to the theoretically agnostic (those that draw effective techniques from the evidence base of other disciplines, such as after action reviews; Tannenbaum and Cerasoli, 2013) but make no attempt at theoretical consistency. There is, of course, a third category, those interventions that are neither evidence-based nor theoretically coherent, but these approaches are increasingly selected out as a function of the cumulative rigour of the growing evidence base.

Positive psychology and strength-based approaches

Strength-based approaches developed out of the formation of the positive psychology movement that sought to address the overwhelming negativity bias in the study of emotions, capability, and institutions (Seligman and Csikszentmihalyi, 2000). However, like many new paradigms, positive psychology has struggled to replicate many of the initial research findings that supported the project (Biswas-Diener, 2015), and some of the core foundational constructs around the criticality of amplified positivity and its links to performance have been theoretically and empirically challenged (Brown et al., 2013; Wong and Roy, 2017). Furthermore, the concepts implicit in positive psychology, including the heightened emphasis on personal agency and consequential minimisation of environmental impacts, are potentially catalysts for mental ill-health and the placid acceptance of systemic iniquities (Bachkirova and Borrington, 2020).

These empirical findings challenged the prevailing notion that decontextualised positive constructs, including strengths, could be simply identified through various measures of self-assessment, and performance would consequently be enhanced through a linear increase in utilisation (Biswas-Diener et al., 2017). In contrast, multiple empirical studies were suggesting that strengths had an inverted U or non-monotonic relationship with performance. This evidence demanded a radical rethink of how the identification of strengths could enhance performance, including leadership, in both individuals and teams (Grant and Schwartz, 2011; MacKie, 2016). Subsequently, more sophisticated models of strengths development examined the interaction of strengths and how they could be aligned and coordinated at a team level (van Woerkom et al., 2020). These approaches included strengths awareness, alignment, utilisation, and pairing with other complementary strengths and offered a more measured and nuanced approach to strengths development, while still acknowledging that strengths have a greater potential to enhance performance than the historical focus on deficits and weaknesses (Zenger et al., 2011; Linley et al., 2010).

Despite being theoretically coherent, the strength-based approach lacked the empirical substantiation to support the claims of its implicit superior potential to enhance performance. This has been apparent in leadership coaching where strength-based coaching has demonstrated efficacy as a highly effective leadership development process at the individual level (MacKie, 2014). Furthermore, there is compelling evidence to suggest that the specific elements of strength-based leadership coaching that focus on the awareness, alignment, pairing, and utilisation of strengths, predict enhanced transformational leadership effectiveness (MacKie, 2014, 2016). This finding is crucial in the development of both individual and team coaching methodologies, as it confirms the role of specific techniques and factors in increasing coaching effectiveness rather than relying on non-specific process factors like the coaching relationship.

Rationale and aims

The limited number of studies that have examined the impact of team coaching interventions on leadership effectiveness have demonstrated inconsistent results and drawn different inferences, making reliable and valid conclusions about team coaching effectiveness difficult to generalise and disseminate (Peters and Carr, 2019). This study specifically investigates the impact of team coaching on meaningful and valid outcomes, including team effectiveness and satisfaction with team leadership. The dependent variable used to assess outcomes was the full range leadership model (FRLM, Teams) that includes transformational, transactional, and laissez-faire elements of leadership. This leadership outcome provides 360-degree feedback on changes in leadership behaviour throughout the organisation and moves the assessment of team coaching outcomes beyond the reliance on self-report measures. By focusing on a specific strength-based methodology, using a reliable and valid measure of transactional and transformational leadership as the dependent variable; and assessing outcomes by way of a 360-degree feedback methodology, this study aims to bring some clarity and specificity to the question of the impact of team coaching in organisations.

Hypotheses

The following specific research questions will be addressed:

1 Positive changes will be observed in team transformational leadership after strength-based team coaching as measured by all stakeholders using the Multifactor Leadership Questionnaire (MLQ) 360.
2 Positive changes will be observed in team effectiveness, effort, and satisfaction after strength-based team coaching, as measured by all stakeholders using the Multifactor Leadership Questionnaire Team (MLQT).

Method

Participants

The participants in this study were a team of eight wealth managers within a larger professional services small-to-medium enterprise (SME). The team consisted of a team leader, a team manager, and six team members.

Research design

The study utilised an uncontrolled case study design. Measures were taken immediately prior to the initiation of the team coaching protocol and 12 months later once the team coaching had concluded.

Procedure: Strength-based protocol

Each participant received a strength-based interview followed by feedback on their individual MLQ 360 report. The strength-based interview focused on their peak experiences and what energised them about their work. The MLQT provided qualitative and quantitative multi-rater feedback on their scores on the full range leadership model (FRLM) that includes transformational, transactional, and laissez-faire leadership styles.

Measures

Multi-Factor Leadership Questionnaire (MLQ) 360. The MLQ 360 was used for each individual participant to give them some specific feedback on their transformational leadership capabilities prior to completing the team version of the same scale. Cronbach's alpha for the main transformational leadership factor has been reported as 0.85 (Antonakis et al., 2003) and criterion validities vary for satisfaction (0.71), effectiveness (0.64), and performance (0.27) (Judge and Piccolo, 2004).

Multi-Factor Leadership Questionnaire Team (MLQT). The main team diagnostic used in this coaching process was the *MLQT Team*. The MLQ Team (Bass and Avolio, 1997) is a 49-item questionnaire that measures nine elements of the full range leadership model (FRLM), namely: idealised influence attributes (e.g. display a sense of power and confidence), idealised influence behaviour (e.g. talk about my most important values and beliefs), inspirational motivation (e.g. articulate a compelling vision of the future), intellectual stimulation (e.g. seek different perspectives when solving problems), individualised consideration (e.g. help others to develop their strengths), contingent reward (e.g. provide others with assistance in exchange for their efforts), management by exception active (e.g. keep track of all mistakes), management by exception passive (e.g. fail to interfere until things become serious), and laissez-faire (e.g. avoid making decisions). The inventory also contains three measures of leadership outcomes: extra effort (e.g. heighten others' desire to succeed), effectiveness (e.g. lead a group that is effective), and satisfaction (e.g. work with others in a satisfactory way) (Bass and Avolio, 1997). All items are measured on a 5-point Likert scale from 'not at all' to 'frequently, if not always'. The survey also includes a research-validated benchmark which gives an ideal score for the various leadership ratings.

Strength-based team coaching process

The team coaching process involved three discrete stages. First, individual team members were contacted prior to the team workshop to understand their context, assess their readiness for change, and discuss their perceptions of how the team was functioning. Secondly, each team member received an individual debrief on their multi-rater leadership questionnaire (MLQ 360) to help raise awareness of their individual strengths and development areas. This also introduced them to the FRLM and the individual constructs behind it. Finally, all participants attend a one-day team development workshop. The workshop took a strength-based approach to leader and team development (MacKie, 2016), provided input on high-performing teams, assessed the team process, and provided opportunities to generate insights and actions from the team diagnostic. This included a review of the necessary structures for high-performing teams (Hackman and Wageman, 2008) and stage models that articulate the necessary processes for the formation of a high-performing team (Hawkins, 2011). The team was debriefed on the results of their MLQ Team survey. The output was a team charter and a team development plan that identified both strengths and weaknesses from the MLQ Team.

The workshop also debriefed a team diagnostic (the MLQ Team) to gather data related to its leadership and performance from a wide range of stakeholders (Avolio, 2012). It is a major achievement of this process that so many stakeholder groups were included in the survey. The five rater groups consisted of senior partners, partners, managers, the team itself, and an 'other' category for those not included in the previous groupings. These additional stakeholder groups beyond the self-report of the team added significantly to the validity of the results.

Ongoing team coaching

After the initial team coaching workshop, the team had three further team coaching sessions two months apart. During these two-hour sessions, the team co-created the agenda, which included developing and applying the team charter, clarifying team norms, developing a positive team culture, providing each other with peer feedback, and distributing leadership more equally within the team.

Results

Table 6 shows the mean MLQ Team transformational leadership scores for the team pre-coaching (T1) and post-coaching (T2). The results clearly demonstrate that there were significant changes in the team's capacity to build trust

Table 6 Multifactor Leadership Questionnaire Team (MLQT) transformational leadership scores before (T1) and after coaching (T2)

MLQT variable	T1 pre-coaching ($N = 47$)		T2 post-coaching ($N = 47$)		t	df	p
	mean	sd	mean	sd			
Idealised influence attributes	2.8	0.7	3.1*	0.5	2.12	46	0.019
Idealised influence behaviour	2.6	0.7	3.0**	0.5	3.09	46	0.002
Inspirational motivation	3.0	0.7	3.2	0.6	1.43	46	0.079
Intellectual stimulation	2.8	0.7	2.8	0.7	0.47	46	0.320
Individualised consideration	2.7	0.7	3.0**	0.6	2.61	46	0.006

Note: Comparison of means between pre- and post-coaching MNLQT scores using paired *t*-tests. *$p < 0.05$, **$p < 0.01$.

Table 7 Multifactor Leadership Questionnaire Team (MLQT) outcome scores before (T1) and after coaching (T2)

MLQT variable	T1 pre-coaching (N = 47)		T2 post-coaching (N = 47)		t	df	p
	mean	sd	mean	sd			
Extra effort	2.8	0.7	2.9	1.03	1.03	46	0.155
Team effectiveness	2.5	0.8	3.0**	3.39	3.39	46	0.000
Team satisfaction	2.9	0.9	3.4**	4.03	4.03	46	0.000

Note: Comparison of means between pre- and post-coaching MNLQT scores using paired t-tests. *$p < 0.05$, **$p < 0.01$.

(idealised influence attributes), act with integrity (idealised influence behaviour), and, most significantly, coach and develop others (individualised consideration).

Table 7 shows the mean scores for extra effort, effectiveness, and satisfaction both pre- and post-coaching. There were no significant difference in extra effort between T1 and T2. Extra or discretionary effort is a function of increased transformational leadership and is often how raters respond to more motivational leadership behaviours. However, there is a significant difference in the team effectiveness rating from T1 to T2, indicating that all rater groups reported a difference in the overall effectiveness of the team after strength-based team coaching. Finally, the most significant difference in outcomes was the score on satisfaction with the leadership abilities of the team, which showed a large effect size (Cohen's $d = 0.764$).

The small numbers in some of the rater groups precluded any further analysis of group differences in observed changes in the team's leadership and effectiveness over time. However, a trend was observed that the higher level raters (managing partners) were more critical in their ratings than other groups, including the team members themselves.

Team development questions

In addition to the standard questions on leadership and outcomes, seven supplementary questions that aimed to track the development of the team over time were added to the MLQ Team survey. These questions were assessed before and after the team coaching and employed the same 5-point frequency rating scale as the MLQ Team. Of the seven additional questions asked, four showed significant differences over time, including a *'clear and challenging purpose'* ($t = 1.87$; $p = 0.034$), *'engages well with key stakeholders'* ($t = 2.03$; $p = 0.023$), and *'focuses on their own development'* ($t = 2.23$; $p = 0.015$). The most significant change reported in the additional questions was, *'This team makes good use of the collective strength of its members'* ($t = 2.57$; $p = 0.007$), supporting the criticality of strengths deployment and coordination at the team level.

Process variables

The data presented above present a compelling story of meaningful and significant change in team effectiveness perceived across the organisation after strength-based team coaching. However, it does not tell the whole story, which is always the risk in the reductive pursuit of greater rigour and objectivity. Other more subjective data forms the practice-based evidence and professional consensus that can extend and challenge the more quantitative hypotheses about team coaching (MacKie, 2007). These additional perspectives include those of the team, the team leader, the sponsors of the process, and the team coach. There is no doubt this was a challenging process for the team leader.

There were also some structural challenges with the team that mitigated against a more distributed model of team leadership that the strength-based approach is predicated upon. The team was imbalanced with two very experienced leaders and managers and the rest of the team members at a much lower level of skill and capability. This imbalance over time had led to quite a hierarchical and directive style of leadership that was fundamentally challenged by the team coaching process. It took considerable individual coaching to persuade the team leader of the merits of a more egalitarian and distributed leadership style.

By contrast, the team members had been used to a highly directive style of leadership and were equally unsure of the merits of a more participatory approach where their strengths could be more aligned with the formal and informal tasks of the team but where they would also be held more accountable for their actions. The tipping point here was the experiential component of the team development day where the team members got to experience the enhanced engagement that accompanied the identification and utilisation of their individual strengths. This was done by a process of strengths disclosure and subsequent alignment with informal roles within the team.

The context in which the team coaching occurred was also critical. It would be fair to say that the overall organisational climate was equivocal in its support for the team coaching process and this factor potentially mitigated some of the gains of the team coaching. There were several other teams within the business who were not undergoing any form of development and yet whose relationship with the coached team was necessarily changing. This engagement in particular required specific emphasis on supporting the HR director to ensure that the team had strong internal sponsorship from at least one key function. However, the key relationship remained with the directors of the business and coaching them informally around how to support the team, especially in the delivery of balanced and consistent feedback, remained an ongoing challenge.

From the coach's perspective, SMEs present an intriguing blend of challenge and opportunity because they are rarely exposed to the same development opportunities that larger and better resourced organisations are. The potential gains can be greater, but the challenge frequently comes in the absence of a coaching culture to support the gains made in the team coaching process.

Frequently, there is significant scepticism about the value or validity of developmental activities that are seen as remedial and a function of individual incompetence rather than structural or systemic difficulties or opportunities to enhance capability from good to great.

Discussion

This case study adds to the literature on the effectiveness of team coaching in three distinct ways. First, the results show that significant changes in both transformational leadership and team effectiveness occurred after strength-based team coaching. Secondly, these changes were perceived beyond the level of self-report by four additional key stakeholder rater groups as well as the team themselves. Thirdly, the significant change in a rating of the use of strengths by team members lends support to the assertion that the strength-based methodology was at least partially responsible for the significant changes in leadership and effectiveness. This is one of the first case studies in team coaching to demonstrate change over time on a reliable and valid dependent variable that demonstrates change in team leadership and effectiveness beyond the level of self-report.

The pattern of change in transformational leadership contrasts with some of the previous research in team-based transformational leadership (Sosik and Jung, 2011). The sub-scales of transformational leadership reported here suggest the team developed significantly in the domains of idealised influence (a measure of motivation and commitment to the team as well as clarity on mission and purpose) and individualised consideration (a measure of willingness to continually improve and develop). Prior research has suggested that as teams develop, they first enhance their capacity on intellectual stimulation and individualised consideration before going on to develop greater capacity for inspirational motivation and idealised influence. This is clearly an area for future research.

The changes in outcomes that are normally a consequence of enhanced transformational leadership included a significant improvement in team effectiveness and satisfaction with the leadership of the team, but no significant change in reported levels of extra or discretionary effort. One explanation for this is that discretionary effort is usually elicited from followers, who in this case would be embedded in the team, rather than peers or those more senior in the organisation. In addition, there may be a difference in visibility of some of the leadership behaviours that are closely linked to extra effort, including individualised consideration, lacking visibility to those external to the team.

Finally, the additional questions demonstrated significant improvements in a sense of purpose, stakeholder engagement, the team's own development, and the use of strengths in the team. These results demonstrate improvements at the task (effectiveness, purpose), the process (idealised influence, stakeholder engagement), and individual development (focus on own development and individualised consideration) outcome levels. While this study presents compelling evidence for the effectiveness of team coaching as a methodology for enhancing team and leadership effectiveness, it is limited by the case study format that precludes comparison with a control group. Future research requires a greater focus on controlled, quantitative experimental designs with explicit methodologies that use standardised dependent variables to measure impact beyond the level of self-report.

References

Antonakis, J., Avolio, B., and Sivasubramaniam, N. (2003) Context and leadership: An examination of the nine-factor full-range leadership theory using the multifactor leadership questionnaire, *The Leadership Quarterly*, 14 (3): 261–295.

Avolio, B.J. (2012) *Full Range Leadership Development*. London: Sage.

Bachkirova, T. and Borrington, S. (2020) Beautiful ideas that can make us ill: Implications for coaching, *Philosophy of Coaching: An International Journal*, 5 (1): 9–30.

Bass, B.M. and Avolio, B.J. (1997) Concepts of leadership, in R.P. Vecchio (ed.) *Leadership: Understanding the Dynamics of Power and Influence in Organizations* (pp. 3–22). Notre Dame, IN: University of Notre Dame Press.

Biswas-Diener, R. (2015) Should we trust positive psychology?, *Greater Good Magazine*, 7 October [https://greatergood.berkeley.edu/article/item/should_we_trust_positive_psychology/].

Biswas-Diener, R., Kashdan, T.B. and Lyubchik, N. (2017) Psychological strengths at work, in L.G. Oades, M. Steger, A. Delle Fave, and J. Passmore (eds.) *The Wiley Blackwell Handbook of the Psychology of Positivity and Strengths-Based Approaches at Work* (pp. 34–47). Chichester: Wiley.

Brown, N.J.L., Sokal, A.D., and Friedman, H.L. (2013) The complex dynamics of wishful thinking: The critical positivity ratio, *American Psychologist*, 68 (9): 801–813.

Buljac-Samardžić, M. (2012) Health teams: Analyzing and improving team performance in long-term care. Doctoral dissertation, Erasmus University, Rotterdam.

Carr, C. and Peters, J. (2012) The experience and impact of team coaching: A dual case study. Doctoral dissertation, Middlesex University, London.

Clutterbuck, D. (2007) *Coaching the Team at Work*. London: Nicholas Brealey.

Clutterbuck, D., Gannon, J., Hayes, S., Iordanou, I., Lowe, K., and Mackie, D. (eds.) (2019) *The Practitioner's Handbook of Team Coaching*. Abingdon: Routledge.

Dimas, I.D., Rebelo, T., and Lourenço, P.R. (2016) Team coaching: One more clue for fostering team effectiveness, *European Review of Applied Psychology*, 66 (5): 233–242.

Dunning, D., Heath, C., and Suls, J.M. (2004) Flawed self-assessment: Implications for health, education, and the workplace, *Psychological Science in the Public Interest*, 5 (3): 69–106.

Grant, A.M. and Schwartz, B. (2011) Too much of a good thing: The challenge and opportunity of the inverted U, *Perspectives on Psychological Science*, 6 (1): 61–76.

Gude, K. (2016) The role of team coaching in enhancing the effectiveness of a project team. Doctoral dissertation, Stellenbosch University, Stellenbosch.

Hawkins, P. (2011) *Leadership Team Coaching*. London: Kogan Page.

Heimbecker, D.R. (2006) The effects of expert coaching on team productivity at the South Coast Educational Collaborative. Doctoral dissertation, Boston University, Boston, MA.

Judge, T.A. and Piccolo, R.F. (2004) Transformational and transactional leadership: A meta-analytic test of their relative validity, *Journal of Applied Psychology*, 89 (5): 755–768.

Linley, A., Willars, J., Biswas-Diener, R., Garcea, N., and Stairs, M. (2010) *The Strengths Book: Be Confident, Be Successful, and Enjoy Better Relationships by Realising the Best of You*. Coventry: CAPP Press.

Liu, C.-Y., Pirola-Merlo, A., Yang, C.-A., and Huang, C. (2009) Disseminating the functions of team coaching regarding research and development team effectiveness: Evidence from high-tech industries in Taiwan, *Social Behavior and Personality*, 37 (1): 41–57.

MacKie, D.J. (2007) Evaluating the effectiveness of executive coaching: Where are we now and where do we need to be?, *Australian Psychologist*, 42 (4): 310–318.

MacKie, D.J. (2014) The effectiveness of strength-based executive coaching in enhancing full range leadership development: A controlled study, *Consulting Psychology Journal: Practice and Research*, 66: 118–137.

MacKie, D.J. (2016) *Strength-Based Leadership Coaching in Organisations*. London: Kogan Page.

Overfield, D.V. (2016) A comprehensive and integrated framework for developing leadership teams, *Consulting Psychology Journal: Practice and Research*, 68 (1): 1–20.

Peters, J. and Carr, C. (2019) What does 'good' look like? An overview of the research on the effectiveness of team coaching, in D. Clutterbuck, J. Gannon, S. Hayes, I. Iordanou, K. Lowe, and D. Mackie (eds.) *The Practitioner's Handbook of Team Coaching* (pp. 89–120). Abingdon: Routledge.

Seligman, M.E. and Csikszentmihalyi, M. (eds.) (2000) Special issue on happiness, excellence, and optimal human functioning, *American Psychologist*, 55 (1): 5–183.

Sosik, J.J. and Jung, D. (2011) *Full Range Leadership Development: Pathways for People, Profit and Planet*. Hove: Psychology Press.

Tannenbaum, S.I. and Cerasoli, C.P. (2013) Do team and individual debriefs enhance performance? A meta-analysis, *Human Factors*, 55 (1): 231–245.

van Woerkom, M., Meyers, M., and Bakker, A. (2020) Considering strengths use in organizations as a multilevel construct, *Human Resource Management Review* [https://doi.org/10.1016/j.hrmr.2020.100767].

Wageman, R., Nunes, D.A., Burruss, J.A., and Hackman, J.R. (2008) *Senior Leadership Teams: What It Takes to Make Them Great*. Boston, MA: Harvard Business Press.

Wong, P.T.P. and Roy, S. (2017) Critique of positive psychology and positive interventions, in N.J.L. Brown, T. Lomas, and F.J. Eiroa-Orosa (eds.) *The Routledge International Handbook of Critical Positive Psychology* (pp. 142–160). London: Routledge.

Zenger, J.H., Folkman, J.R., and Edinger, S.K. (2011) Making yourself indispensable, *Harvard Business Review*, 89 (10): 84–92.

Towards an Ubuntu team coaching perspective

Dumisani Magadlela

If you want to go fast, go alone. If you want to go far, go together
— African proverb

Introduction

This case study presents and discusses the concept of Ubuntu team coaching. It explores the application of this concept as unique to selected contexts where other coaches use established team coaching practices within organisations. One of the starting points for working with Ubuntu team coaching within organisations is the recognition of the inherent capacity of normal healthy humans to seek to connect with others. An important part of the case study is the unconventional definition of what a team is. The team presented below was selected based on the team's and leaders' descriptions of themselves as a team. The case study presents and explores the application of the concept of Ubuntu using what is called the Lekgotla process as an instrument of team engagement.

An overview of Ubuntu and Ubuntu philosophy

Ubuntu is an isiZulu word meaning, '*I am because you are, you are because we are*'. Humans are inherently interconnected. Ubuntu gives expression to the subordination of individual interests to those of the collective for the greater good. Individual rights are 'fused' with those of the group, team, or collective, and if a choice needs to be made, the interests of the group are sacrosanct.

A critical element of Ubuntu in team coaching is the ability of engagement processes such as *Lekgotla* (traditional meeting place) to galvanise a spirit of inclusion and collective accountability. It lays the foundation for *teaming*. Leaders that lead teams and organisations with Ubuntu values understand the sacredness of every human being. Such leaders value their responsibility as leaders to assist each person they lead towards becoming the best version of themselves in the roles they play.

Ubuntu team coaching as a viable perspective for teams

Ubuntu team coaching is the practical application of Ubuntu principles, values, and practices in team coaching engagements. It involves the ability to hold to account each member of a team in context and the 'presencing' of the collective in team coaching sessions as they unfold. For example, a common question in Ubuntu team coaching engagements is: 'How is this serving the greater good of this team?' Ubuntu coaching often takes the client system into a deeper place of appreciation of the collective value of the team's thinking, actions, and ways of being.

The case study presented below illustrates the use of Ubuntu team coaching as a tool to gain clarity on the emotional pulse and general mood of a team before recommending solutions to identified challenges. Daniel Goleman calls this identifying the 'emotional reality of a team or environment before launching into a solution' (Goleman et al., 2002: 244).

The definition of team and team coaching used in the case study was drawn from the client. The client defined a team as: 'a group of employees working together towards a common goal, you know, like a soccer team' (HR officer from the case study).

Case study: Putting Ubuntu team coaching to work

This case study is about a team of supervisors in a logistics business. They defined themselves as a team by virtue of all of them being supervisors and working together towards building high-performing and efficient work-teams in their areas of operation.

The supervisors generally had the same performance scorecards and managed their teams the same way. They felt neglected, unseen, and unheard by their senior management team. When they eventually met as a team (they described themselves as a team and used the word 'team' repeatedly with reference to each other and to their 'team'), the atmosphere was emotionally charged.

'Sawubona' (I see you): Engaging with others the Ubuntu way

CASE

Netport, not its real name, is a logistics company on the northwest coast of Namibia, a peaceful southern African country that gained independence in 1990. Netport employs just under 200 employees. The chief executive leads six executive directors through an executive committee

(EXCO), who in turn have 12 managers reporting to them (MANCO). The managers lead the 26 supervisors spread around the country supervising distribution depots.

The supervisors did not have any structured ways of meeting. They did not have a platform or structure of their own. The lack of communication among them, and their inability to discuss shared challenges per category or level, let alone meet and engage in person about common business issues, was one of the challenges repeatedly raised by the supervisors, resulting in the HR team inviting the coach to come in and run consultation sessions with them 'to allow them space to vent together'.

THE NEED TO ENGAGE

The multiple calls for this team of supervisors to connect, engage, and discuss their issues were becoming louder, and could not be ignored any longer by either senior management or the HR team. The first two sessions scheduled were with the team of supervisors. They referred to themselves as 'the forgotten Netport team bringing in the juice that keeps the lights on'. HR officials called them 'the team at the heart of the business'.

One of the supervisors had requested a series of (team) coaching sessions to explore how best supervisors can become a stronger and more effective 'team'. There were several engagement and enrolment meetings between the external team coach and the HR manager, together with the lead supervisor. Several engagements had taken place, and individual sessions with the supervisors led to the call for team coaching sessions.

THE LEKGOTLA PROCESS

Lekgotla refers to 'the process' (in a specific place or sacred space designated for engagement). It is what Nancy Kline calls a 'thinking environment' (1999). It enhances the quality of listening to each other, and enhances the ability to focus on issues, not on individuals. There are different types of Lekgotlas. They range from consultative and decision-informing Lekgotlas, through engagement and informing Lekgotlas, to debriefing and consensus-building Lekgotlas.

The Lekgotla process is an important tool for the Ubuntu coaching perspective in team coaching. It helps individuals to be heard in groups, and helps groups build resonance. It also supports teams to raise team awareness as they pursue common goals. During the Lekgotla session, the team leader presents the issues for discussion, and reiterates (reminds everyone of) the rules of engagement. These rules include paying attention to every speaker as they speak, with no interruptions. The leader then proceeds to invite each speaker to share their views before summing up or posing another question (depending on the type of Lekgotla).

The Lekgotla process differs from other formats of running meetings in that it is genuinely regarded as a sacred space for engagement and everyone treats it as such. There is a high level of respect for 'the space' that is not often found in ordinary meetings or other facilitated group sessions. The Lekgotla process values, celebrates, and builds on diversity, while ensuring that leaders learn to listen to, think with, communicate and work with groups differently. A three-day team engagement session was set up for the team of supervisors at Netport. The coach used the Lekgotla process described above as the tool for the team to open up, decompress, and engage on the issues identified and shared in the debrief.

CONTRACTING AND ON-BOARDING THE TEAM COACH

The on-boarding of the team coach included signing the contract for the engagement, which included the three-day sessions and follow-up sessions as agreed with the HR manager and the lead supervisor. Several engagements with the HR executive and the HR manager painted a picture of a team of supervisors needing clarity on the scope of their roles and responsibilities, among other things.

DECOMPRESSION AND TEARS OF CONNECTION

The coach set up the room with chairs (no tables) in a circle with the 22 participants all supervisors from Netport. The HR manager introduced the team coach, and after a few brief remarks from one of the supervisors, handed over the running of the session to the team coach. The team coach introduced the topics of discussion as open team communication, team connection, sharing, debriefing, and 'seeing' each other as part of the same team. The rule was that all participants would have their turn to speak, and when one person was speaking, everyone else in the room would turn their body towards the speaker. The idea was for everyone to pay full attention to the speaker.

This created an emotionally charged atmosphere where almost all participants expressed their gratitude for being listened to, unlike at any other time in their history of working in the organisation. They expressed that they had not been listened to like that before, and had not listened to each other that way either. The process seemed to resonate strongly with most of the supervisors as they took turns to share their stories from the regions.

As the supervisors shared their sense of collective injustice, their shared 'heavy load of work out there', and not being listened to or heard about the need to share tools, solutions, and performance enhancement strategies, many became emotional. Voices shook in emotion, and tears flowed freely as they opened up. Based on previous experiences with the process, the team coach had warned participants that it might get emotional (and fast!). And it did. The coach managed the emotional decompression process carefully and took time with participants that needed time to process. It was clear that the 'team of supervisors' (as they referred to themselves) had a strong bond and shared a common feeling of being an integral part of the business, while at the same time feeling unheard. They were fully aware of who they were as a team, and the team engagement conversations deepened their team awareness.

TESTING THE LIMITS OF PSYCHOLOGICAL SAFETY

One of the key elements of a good team is the establishment of psychological safety within the team, and especially as expressed in team members' interactions and engagements. The supervisors identified themselves as a team as a result of their shared level and purpose in the organisational structure, their similar roles and responsibilities, and their collective accountability in effectively running the regional depots and distribution hubs for the business.

The team of supervisors showed remarkable capacity to bond easily and generate 'instant' rapport when many of them had only interacted virtually through emails and phone calls teaming. The Lekgotla process, and the Ubuntu approach, helped team members with the crucial team coaching process of 'seeing, honouring, and valuing everyone equally with attention'. This was modelled by the team coach as he connected with all supervisors for support as they opened up, connected, and engaged with each other in a safe yet vulnerable way. The process of vulnerability supported the team of supervisors to feel safe to open up and engage with each other.

It could be said that the issues had been bubbling up just under the surface and needed venting, and the Lekgotla framed Ubuntu team coaching sessions enabled that venting by first acknowledging their shared responsibilities, and then 'seeing them' and their collective pain and frustration of not being listened to or heard. Without the intentional creation of safety by individually contracting about the sacred container up front, it would have been a bigger challenge for the team to express themselves in their 'own space'.

CONTRACTING AND ENROLMENT INTO THE TEAM COACHING JOURNEY

The supervisors individually expressed their commitment to create a safe environment and maintain confidentiality, and collectively raised their hands in agreement. As participants in the team coaching sessions that followed the Lekgotla session, they could easily shut down, possibly risking the rest of the remaining two days ahead.

The 'contracting' helped them settle into the team coaching space and engage on the topics for discussion. Admittedly, there were elements of this that were more group facilitation and team-building than team coaching in its pure form. The coach preferred to go with their own description of themselves as a collective, as the 'team of supervisors'. One of the most significant team coaching takeaways from this case study is the team of supervisors' deepening understanding of their shared circumstances and laying foundations for the team to grow their team-ness.

TEAMING KEY TAKEAWAYS AND OUTCOMES

Several follow-up team engagement sessions were held after the initial three-day session, with the Lekgotla, and these led to the supervisors becoming a solid team with a common understanding of the roles they played, and how they could become even more effective as one team. Among the main takeaways or outcomes from the supervisors' team coaching sessions was the establishment of what they called a SupCom (Supervisors' Committee).

Another outcome was the opportunity to consolidate their formation as a team and to be more than just a group of employees sharing their frustrations, stories, workloads, and tools of trade. The team realised an awareness of being part of a team with shared objectives of delivering consistent high performance and great customer service. Every checkout section of every one of the team coaching sessions that followed was filled with similar messages of appreciation of the formation of the team (teaming), and recognition of themselves as a team with shared awareness, responsibilities, and common accountability.

LET'S ALL TEAM UP FROM NOW ON

While most of the first day of the supervisors' team coaching work was carefully designed for decompression and creating psychological safety, along with unearthing and discovering the soul of the team, this did not take away from the teaming process. The HR manager expressed gratitude and said she had not been aware that there were so many issues that needed attention. At the end of the first session, the HR manager called for team coaching sessions for managers at Netport. Team coaching sessions were eventually held with different teams at Netport, and this showed the value of the Ubuntu team coaching approach in building team awareness, especially using the Lekgotla process.

This case study shows that the Lekgotla process, based on Ubuntu values of human connection, is a useful team coaching instrument. The Lekgotla process enables *discovery* in a team, leading to clarity of what needs attention as the team's self-awareness deepens. Each participant in the session is given 'adequate airtime' to express themselves and be listened to without being judged. The process the team coach adopted at Netport – *systemic team self-awareness* – supported the team of supervisors to begin to see themselves in each other. This is an important aspect of team coaching.

Ubuntu team coaching lessons from this case study

Such Ubuntu team coaching – infused with the Lekgotla practice – is comparable to aspects of what Nancy Kline (1999) calls the ten components of a thinking environment. These include: (1) team members giving each other attention, or 'seeing and hearing' each other in safe engagement spaces; (2) embracing equality and treating each other with respect as thinking peers; and (3) giving everyone a turn to speak while showing each other respect. The foundations were laid for teaming into the future at Netport.

Nancy Kline describes the component of expressing feelings as 'allowing sufficient emotional release to restore thinking' (1999: 35). This was experienced in the Netport case above. The team of supervisors illustrated the value of Ubuntu coaching lenses in building ways of teaming that could be continued by the team on its own – after the team coach had disengaged.

Team coaches and people development practitioners are becoming aware of what Hawkins (2011) called an invocation – that in order for us to keep pace with technological and other changes taking place around us, 'we are going to need to adapt and evolve our ways of being in the world with each other, more dramatically than ever before' (2011: 18). This is where Ubuntu team coaching provides the important ingredient of authentic human connection, and growing team awareness of the need to team-up.

Conclusion

Ubuntu team coaching is a potentially powerful way through which organisational cultures can be positively transformed. Ubuntu wisdom suggests that humanity needs to re-embrace the principles of genuine, authentic interconnections. The values and principles of Ubuntu and the process of Lekgotla can be successfully deployed and used in cultures and organisational contexts that are not necessarily familiar with the anthropological nuances of Ubuntu and human connection. This will ensure that we are able to successfully navigate collective challenges impacting all of us across our geographies.

Ubuntu team coaching reminds us that we live and survive in one interconnected global human ecosystem where we need each other, whether we like it or not, or whether we know it or not. We can all benefit from a deeper understanding of the Ubuntu philosophy and practices, Ubuntu coaching, and especially Ubuntu team coaching to impact our shared world. Ubuntu is a global phenomenon. It is about being *humane* and can be found everywhere wherever humans co-exist with each other. It is who we all really are as *interconnected beings*.

References

Goleman, D., Boyatzis, R., and McKee, A. (2002) *The New Leaders: Transforming the Art of Leadership into the Science of Results.* London: Time Warner Paperbacks.

Hawkins, P. (2011) *Leadership Team Coaching: Developing Collective Transformational Leadership.* London. Kogan Page.

Kline, N. (1999) *Time to Think. Listening to Ignite the Human Mind.* London: Cassell.

Recommended reading

Vuyisile Msila (2015) *Ubuntu: Shaping the Current Workplace with (African) Wisdom.* Johannesburg: Knowres Publishing.

Mfuniselwa J. Bhengu (2006) *Ubuntu: The Global Philosophy for Humankind.* Cape Town: Lotcha Publications.

David Clutterbuck and David Megginson (2005) *Making Coaching Work: Creating a Coaching Culture.* London: Chartered Institute of People Development (CIPD).

Dumisani Magadlela (2019) The case for Ubuntu coaching: Working with an African coaching meta-model that strengthens human connection in a fast-changing VUCA world, in Sunny Stout-Rostron (ed.) *Transformational Coaching to Lead Culturally Diverse Teams.* London. Routledge.

Reuel Khoza (2011) *Attuned Leadership: African Humanism as Compass.* Johannesburg: Penguin.

Helena Dolny (2009) Transforming team meetings, in Helena Dolny (ed.) *Team Coaching: Artists at Work. South African Coaches Share Their Theory and Practice.* Johannesburg: Penguin.

A do or die situation

Michel Moral

Background of the team

A large industrial company, let's call it Alpha, had created a new division to market a product in the field of energy saving. Sales were going well but investments were huge and the company was at risk of collapsing if revenues did not increase quickly.

It was hoped a large call for tenders would be opened, which would fix the issue if it were won. Unfortunately, Alpha was too small to handle the case alone and an alliance would be necessary with Beta and Gamma, which had the necessary skills. At the request of Alpha, the three companies joined forces to respond to the call for tenders and a task force of 50 people was assembled, led by a management team of nine members. The leader of the team was from Alpha, an appointment fully supported by Beta and Gamma.

At the same time, the business was declining and Alpha was at greater risk of bankruptcy. Consequently, winning the tender had become a question of life and death. The management team of the task force was under extreme pressure from the executive board of Alpha company. Beta and Gamma were under less pressure and their representatives on the management team of the project were quite serene and behaved professionally.

We will use the following terminology here:

- **Change 1 and Change 2:** Change 1 is an adjustment of the current stable state that can easily be reversed. Change 2 is a major transformation to another stable state.
- **Collective intelligence:** collective performance combined with collective wellbeing and harmony.
- **'Swiss Army knife':** a team member whose mission is to ensure the consistency of the proposal.
- **Individual performance:** how well team members do their job.
- **Individual wellbeing:** the experience of having good mental health, high professional satisfaction, a sense of meaning or purpose, and the ability to manage stress.
- **'We':** the quality of a team over and above the sum of its individual members. It is sometimes called 'team spirit' or 'sense of belonging'. A strong 'We' is key to success.

Reasons for coaching the team

The team already had a very good measured performance: technical and financial elements were delivered in a timely fashion to the sales people, who were very satisfied with the quality of the work to be included in the proposal. But, to win the proposal needed much more than just a good performance – it needed 'the eye of the tiger', that unique selling point that motivates a client to buy this solution rather than any other.

The request for coaching was to help the team to win. What was at stake was that Alpha risked disappearing altogether in the event of failure, with the loss of many jobs, together with fewer, though still negative, effects on Beta and Gamma.

The objectives of the coaching mission were to prepare the team for difficult times ahead as the due date of the bid approached. Indicators of success had to be measurable. Two coaches were selected (most team coaching missions in France are undertaken by a pair of coaches).

Considering the challenge for the client, and consequently for the coaches, the strategy for this coaching mission was to increase the collective intelligence of the team. Collective intelligence has the power to deliver performance, creativity, and wellbeing to teams and organisations. Reliable research studies (Woolley et al., 2010) have shown that while cognitive intelligence, cohesion, and motivation are not determining factors, relational intelligence is, as well as the variance in the number of speaking turns and the proportion of females in the group. The role of technology with respect to collective intelligence has also been studied by David Engel and it appears that collective intelligence exists both in face-to-face and dispersed computer-mediated groups. Value systems also play an essential role in the development of collective intelligence. In particular, values such as trust, autonomy, responsibility, transparency, interdependence, and sharing (of vision, values, and information) are considered favourable assets (Moral and Lamy, 2019). Finally, the existence of clear and explicit rules and processes, as well as the availability of adequate collaborative tools, is essential.

The team

The members of the team came from three different countries and three different organisations (see Figure 14).

- **Alpha:** the team leader, the sales manager, the legal manager, and the 'Swiss Army knife' were all French.
- **Beta:** the engineering manager and the manufacturing manager were both Dutch.
- **Gamma:** the finance manager and the controller were Italian.

Figure 14 The makeup of the team

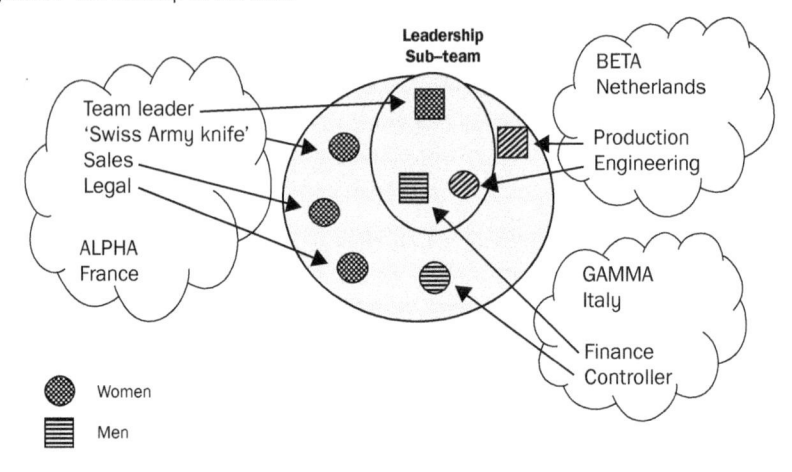

```
                    Leadership
                    Sub-team
                                        BETA
    Team leader                         Netherlands
    'Swiss Army knife'
    Sales                               Production
    Legal                               Engineering

    ALPHA
    France
                                        GAMMA
                                        Italy

                                        Finance
    ● Women                             Controller

    ☰ Men
```

The team leader, the engineering manager, and the finance manager formed a leadership sub-team where decisions were made. With a representative from each of Alpha, Beta, and Gamma, its role was also to liaise with the three companies. This arrangement was approved by the rest of the team.

Of course, differences of national culture, corporate culture, and personality played a role, but this was not a critical issue in day-to-day work. Typical cultural traits emerge from time to time which might create conflicts, but these were solved quickly because all of the team members were positive and very motivated.

Finally, winning a call for tender is not like winning a football match. It's an 18-month process with its daily ups and downs which the team was aware of.

Understanding the team

The following were used in order to understand how the team functioned:

- Observation of a face-to-face meeting
- Interviews with individual team members
- Collective intelligence analysis using the 11 DOTS tool.

Observation of a meeting

The team worked remotely most of the time and a face-to-face meeting was held in Paris once a fortnight. In order to get an idea of how it functioned, the coaches attended one of the meetings as observers. The objective of this observation was to gauge the energy levels, cohesion, complicity, and mutual trust of the team. The focus was not on the 'what' but on the 'how' and 'why'. A systemic sketch was used to represent the team. It is a graphic means of describing a team which shows all of the team members, their interactions (support or disputes), and the components of the 'We' that might appear when someone starts a sentence with 'we'.

Interviews

Each team member was interviewed in person for two hours. The objective was to understand how the members work as a team – a collection of people who have their own needs and wants. For this, a systemic representation of the team was built, both in its current state and in the preferred state as seen by each individual team member.

The interviews had a mix of closed and open-ended questions about interactions between members, interdependence, power, influence, and who were the change agents. A metal board was used with magnetic studs to represent the team members, and their interactions were highlighted using coloured markers. Visual analogue scales were used for the evaluations, such as to assess if 'who does what' was understood by the interviewee. When all the interviews had been completed, the graphic representations were compiled and shared with the team.

A transcript analysis was conducted to extract key words that described the current and desired state of the team. The results were summarised in a few slides that were shared and discussed with the team (see Table 8).

11 DOTS

The 11 DOTS tool was designed by Florence Lamy in 2014 (Lamy and Moral, 2017: 249–251) to provide a systemic representation of a group which seeks to tap into 'collective intelligence'. This online questionnaire is organised around 11 key principles. It diagnoses collective skills, making it possible to target areas of improvement by relying on the strengths of the analysed group. A composite indicator (CI capacity, see Figure 15) provides a measure of the collective intelligence of the team (Moral and Henrichfreise, 2018: 181–191; www.11-dots.com).

Identified strengths and weaknesses of the current state

The data based on observation of the meeting and the interviews showed that the team functioned well. When a disagreement arose, discussions helped to fix the issue and make the right decision. However, the decision process was not clearly defined (see Table 8) and most decisions were the result of a

Table 8 Current state key words

Winning Cards Competences and Expertise 'Nice People' Engagement and Motivation	Handicaps Complex Relationships Lack of Clear Leadership
Explicit Rules Processes Meetings Job Definitions and Roles	Implicit Rules Decision Processes Communications

consensus being reached in a context where complex relationships, unclear leaders' actions, and difficult communications were intertwined. Typical quotes included: 'We are all high-level experts and very motivated but it is difficult to understand how we really function. A lot of what we do is the result of a consensus which emerges magically'.

Desired state

The desired state was defined as more or less the same as the current state, with a strong team consensus but with much more focus on winning. People, relationships, organisational principles, transparency, and engagement had to be maintained by the team. But the team had to accept that there would be more pressure and stress in trying to win the bid. For example, the Alpha legal manager said: 'We don't want to change too much because it is nice as it is. Yes, we are at risk of losing but I fear that I'll have difficulty with my family if I work day and night'.

11 DOTS

Having done more than 150 team coaching missions since 2006, our experience is that a team functions well when the average for the 11 indicators plus CI capacity are within the equilibrium zone (see Figure 15). This was the case in this instance, but it was not enough to win the bid and more indicators needed to fall in the major zone.

The results of 11 DOTS showed that:

- Leadership did not seem to be integrated or even really understood in this team. *Leadership/Followership, Conflict management, Maturity,* and *Values* had an average close to or above the boundary between the equilibrium and major zones but the average of the leadership sub-team was well off that. Consequently, for the other members it was difficult to be a good

Figure 15 Results of 11 DOTS

	Minor	Equilibrium	Major
Leadership/Followership			●——○
Conflict management		●—○	
Maturity		●—●	
Preservation/Transformation		○——●	
Values		●—○	
Creativity		●○	
Interpersonal skills			◉
Governance		◉	
Structuration		◉	
CI capacity		◉	
Meaning			●○
Climate	●		○

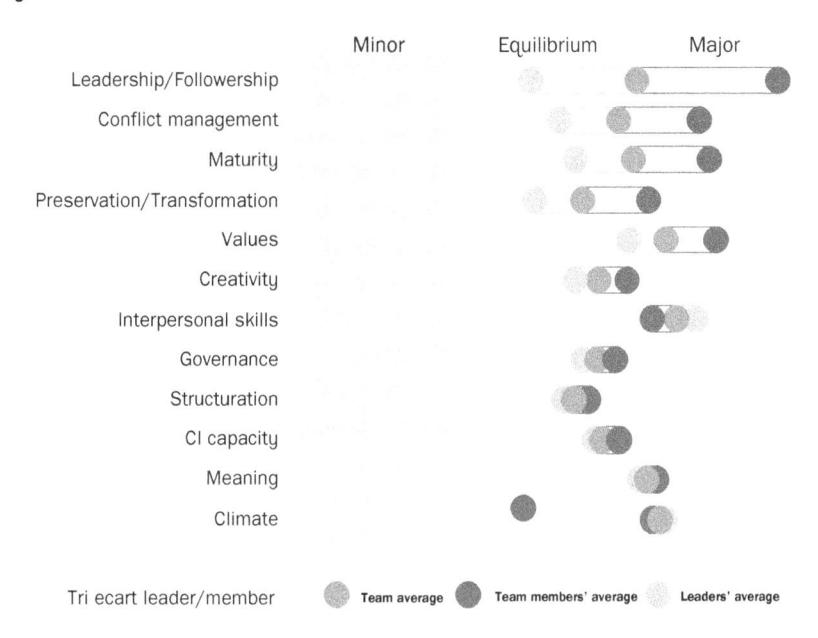

Tri ecart leader/member   ● Team average   ● Team members' average   ○ Leaders' average

follower. The following was shared by the Alpha sales manager: 'We don't always understand the decisions of the leadership sub-team: there is probably some politics going on there'.

- *Meaning, Climate,* and *Interpersonal skills* were already in the major zone. Members of this team already saw strong meaning in what they did. The seeds of a high-quality climate were present, and it was necessary to ensure members acknowledged its multiple advantages. Interpersonal skills such as listening, welcoming differences, appreciating diversity, and equal speaking time were all there. During their interview, the controller said: 'I really like this team, sometimes it's like they read my thoughts and answer before I ask'.

- *Creativity, Governance,* and *Structuration* were in the equilibrium zone but had to improve if this was to become a winning team. In particular, team creativity remained unexploited and the potential for innovation needed to be unleashed. *Governance* was perceived to be weak, vague, and not fully understood. This led to some confusion and a random or inconsistent implementation of directives and regulations which created entropy. This team would greatly benefit from structuring its operations.

Finally, the CI capacity needed to be improved by capitalising on the strong points. The team needed to develop a shared vision and better communication of the team's purpose and how it fit into the strategy of the wider organisation. In Moral and Lamy's (2019) literature review, it appeared that values like trust, shared values, shared vision, information-sharing, risk-taking, etc. are present in organisations that have a high level of collective intelligence. Improving the value systems is an elegant lever of transformation and we suggested the team focus on this. The team could further develop its level of maturity. The team's weak points included governance and structuration, which deserved special attention. Strengthening solidarity and interdependence between team members and leaders would help promote resilience. Making leadership more explicit, recognised, and better understood could increase everyone's involvement and empowerment.

Fulfilling the coaching mission

The team needed to make collective decisions about rules, the quality of relationships, and the components of a cohesive culture. The members of the team should be active participants in this process, each realising how they could contribute to the construction of a collective 'We' that would enable their bid to be successful. One of the questions the coaches asked was: 'How can you fail in becoming a real team?'. The discussion made evident that, in its present state, the members were caught up in a state of affairs whose purpose was to maintain homeostasis. Change would occur if the team were able to recognise that their current functioning was serving something other than success.

Therefore, their strategy would be to:

- disrupt the homeostasis of the system by making the implicit explicit, and
- establish functioning rules that allowed the team to observe its own dysfunctions and address them.

The first action would be to ask all members to read *Team Spirit, Life and Leadership on One of the World's Toughest Yacht Races* by Brendan Hall (2013). This book shows how a leader should behave to create a 'We' and how the crew should engage and follow the leader to become a winning team. Each team member had an idea about what made that race a success and this formed the basis for a charter relating to their own functioning: key commitments were about showing persistence and a positive attitude.

In addition to the interviews and the 11 DOTS questionnaire, the coaching mission consisted of three one-day sessions in start-up mode with the team. Two coaches were involved and they adopted the setting of the Milan therapists, in particular Mara Selvini Palazzoli (Ceccin, 1987): one coach in the role of facilitator, in charge of Change 1; and the other in the role of observer, charged with triggering Change 2. These positions are reversed every hour and a half.

This approach assumes that when acting on a team, the coach in the role of *facilitator* becomes part of the system; the other coach assumes the role of *observer*. Being outside of the system, he is able to trigger Change 2. The observer role is termed 'metaposition' in France, where it has been developed as a fundamental concept in coaching and especially in team coaching since 2000.

The relationship between functioning rules and transformation has been studied by Moral et al. (2011) and a methodology derived. An online tool has since been developed (see https://www.hrs-institute.com/pages/page_out.php) but pen and paper plus a discussion are more effective in a team coaching session.

The following agenda was agreed:

- **Day 1**: create a charter of functioning rules that favours transformation (Moral and Henrichfreise, 2018: 167–188) and implement the 'role delegation in meetings' technique (Cardon, 2003: 184–205).
- **Day 2** (one month later): create a short- and medium-term action plan, deploy the Change4Nine tool (Lamy and Moral, 2019: 224–229), and co-create the set of values (cohesive culture) to drive the team to succeed (Barrett, 2017: 169–191).
- **Day 3** (one month later): reconsider the management style (Barrett, 2017: 123–162), and stress test the team using a simulation and final debriefing.

Implementation of the 'role delegation in meetings' technique created a marked improvement in the team's functioning. This way of running meetings has been widely applied in France since its introduction by Alain Cardon (2003). The idea is that the lead person in a group or team should delegate to group members tasks like 'time management', 'decision pushing', 'facilitation', and 'metaposition'. The lead person, when relieved of these tasks, is fully available for in-depth reflection, inspiration, and second-level 'metaposition'. This, by the way, is also useful in group supervision and is used extensively in France.

Execution of this action plan went as planned and a change of behaviour was observed. It appeared that an increase of collective intelligence can be obtained by building an appropriate charter and showing the team how to observe itself ('metaposition'). This increase can possibly be complemented by improving team cohesion and reducing conflicts but, in the light of theory (Woolley et al., 2010) and practice, this is not essential.

Supervision

The coaches were supervised as a team by the author who is also a very experienced team coach. Designing a common thread for the coaching and mentally preparing are typical tasks. But in this case, the goal of supervision was to understand why expert coaches struggled to distance themselves from the problem experienced by the team. The supervision revealed that a parallel process was fully active between the situation and personal life of the two coaches. Fundamental questions arose such as the meaning of success and failure in one's professional life. For example, one of the coaches was engaged in a one-month sailboat race during the coaching engagement.

We found these supervision sessions particularly confrontational, and a decision was made to ask the members of the client team to read the book written by Brendan Hall (2013) about his victory in the Clipper Around the World yacht race in 2010. In this event, twelve 23-metre yachts race around the world, each with a crew of 18 amateurs led by a seasoned skipper, the only difference being the individual personalities and above all their team spirit. This book perfectly illustrates how team members' attitude and systemic mechanisms prevail on technical skills in a winning team.

Obviously, there was a correlation between the request for coaching and the unusual resistance of the coaches. The bottom line is that, yes, coaching for winning, especially if the mission lasts for several months, affects the coach much more than just coaching for performance. Several inner psychological mechanisms combined to block the coaches in something that is specific to them and which had a strong impact on their mission.

Outcomes and key learnings

The leadership sub-team discovered that it was not easy to be understood by the team members when a complex situation required frequent changes of direction. The leader said, 'We didn't think that it was that bad!' An outcome of team coaching was that the leadership sub-team decided to spend more time on communicating their decisions. Several team members said that 'giving us the "why" of any decision could also allow us to apply it better'.

Before coaching, the team members were a set of experts acting within their areas of expertise and they had to learn how to behave as a crew. They learned how to communicate between themselves more frequently in order to have a better idea of the issues and anticipate when there was a need for a change of direction. The controller said: 'What have I learned? It was a bit of a surprise but I have learned not to waste my time discussing trivia with my colleagues until they talk about their real concerns'.

The team coaches discovered the power of parallel process when it impacts on their beliefs and sometimes their own personal history. They decided to give more attention to their own functioning as a team of coaches and to focus their reflective practice on detecting parallel processes.

Conclusion

The French approach to team coaching is derived from the research headed by Woolley et al. (2010) on collective intelligence, which is correlated with relational intelligence and the taking of turns speaking. In addition, coaching in France focuses on explicit rules and 'metaposition' in the team. Also, a team is more than the sum of its members and includes an entity, the 'We', which has its own life and purposes. Team coaching is a way to wake up this entity and make it work for the team. It can easily be identified when a team member says: 'In our team WE work hard to deliver on time'. It is all the stronger as the interactions between members are numerous, intense, sincere, and tinged with emotion.

References

Barrett, R. (2017) *The Values-Driven Organization: Unleashing Human Potential for Performance and Profit*, 2nd edition. Abingdon: Routledge.
Cardon, A. (2003) *Coaching d'équipe*. Paris: Editions d'Organisation.
Ceccin, G. (1987) Hypothesizing, circularity, and neutrality revisited: An invitation to curiosity, *Family Process*, 26 (4): 405–413.
Hall, B. (2013) *Team Spirit, Life and Leadership on One of the World's Toughest Yacht Races*, London: Adlard Coles Nautical.
Lamy, F. and Moral, M. (2017) *Les outils de la supervision, Bien les choisir, Bien les organiser*, 2nd edition. Paris: InterEditions.
Moral, M. and Henrichfreise, S. (2018) *Le coaching d'organisation*, 3rd edition. Paris: InterEditions.
Moral, M. and Lamy, F. (2019) *Les outils de l'intelligence collective*, 2nd edition. Paris: InterEditions.
Moral, M., Vallée, S., and Lamy, F. (2011) Measuring the capability of a team to fulfil a 'change2', in I. O'Donovan and D. Megginson (eds.) *Developing Mentoring and Coaching Research and Practice* (pp. 42–50). Marlborough: European Mentoring and Coaching Council.
Woolley, A., Chabris, C., Pentland, A., Nada, H., and Malone, T. (2010) Evidence for a collective intelligence factor in the performance of human groups, *Science*, 330 (6004): 686–688.

Sharing the driving seat: A ticket for the game

Asher Rickayzen

Introduction and context

This case study describes the first time I worked as a team coach with a particular executive team and concentrates on the early part of the engagement. I am influenced by the mantra of an experienced consultant, who taught me a huge amount: 'beginnings are fateful, they set the tone for all that follows'.

There were many moments when this project felt doomed to failure, and my journal from that time reflects my concern:

> 'The internal propaganda department, i.e. my thoughts, are saying to me you are heading for failure. You are not paying attention to what is coming up. You are going to fail'.

Anxiety, a familiar companion

My catastrophic visions stem from my own anxiety of working with a new team in a new client organisation. I have learned over the years how it influences my thinking and behaviour, increasing my desire to control. In this case, there were some things that heightened my anxiety:

- The executive team to be coached had been together for an unusually long period and held assumptions about each other that were firmly embedded.
- The CEO (and sponsor) wanted to use psychometric testing, to which I have an aversion.
- The team was limited in the amount of time they could commit to the coaching process.

Alongside the anxiety, I have a belief that if I trust the process the outcome will be good (in nearly all cases). For me the process consists of:

- building trust, relationships and psychological safety;
- helping the team to identify the areas or questions that really matter to them;
- providing enough space, stimulus, and challenge to allow topics to be explored;
- uncovering insights that deepen understanding and awareness;
- encouraging the team to identify actions in service of its development.

In my most anxious state, I will inadvertently sabotage this process; an anxious mindset craves certainty and predictability and is the antithesis of an ideal coaching state in which surprises are welcome and exploration is fun.

Psychometric testing ... oh no!

Early on I had a 'chemistry' meeting with the CEO, which was business-like and formal. He described his dislike of surprises (never a good sign), although he accepted it would be impossible to predict exactly what would happen in this process. I asked him whether he saw himself as an equal in the process with the other members of the team or as separate in some way. To my relief, his reply was the former, although he acknowledged (definitely a very good sign) the difficulty he would have in accepting his own need for change. He requested we use psychometric testing, as it was something he and the team had experienced before. I listened but didn't initiate a discussion about the merits of testing. Early in my consulting career, I was often overly challenging of a client's ideas and suggestions. I continue to work on curbing this instinct.

Psychometric testing is not something I enjoy working with. It increases the risk of casting the coach (me) in the role of 'expert' who has the answers for the team; my preference is to be as equally curious and open to discovery as the clients. Furthermore, I question whether anyone can be reduced to a behavioural caricature given that we behave differently according to context. I fear the way profiling might limit the possibilities of how we see ourselves and others, failing to acknowledge our full human complexity. It can provide an excuse for not changing ourselves or seeing the capability of change in others. At worst, I have seen teams who feel their relationship-building work is complete once they have seen each other's profiles.

In a follow-up email, I expressed my concerns about psychometric testing and we (the CEO, the HR director, and I) exchanged more views. At this stage, winning the argument and not using the tests would have caused more damage to the relationship than agreeing to them. My goal was to ensure we used them as effectively as possible.

I understood from the HR director that the executive team were nervous about the idea of having any form of team coaching. I could see that if the team coaching contained a familiar component, it would enable them to reduce their fears and participate more easily. The tests could be seen as an entry ticket to the game of team coaching and hence a relatively easy way in which to begin a conversation I hoped would develop and deepen.

The HR director was crucial in this engagement, as she had the complete confidence of the CEO and he had delegated much of the organising work to her, with the added advantage that access to her was much easier than to the CEO. I recognised the danger that if her judgement was poor, it would result in a disconnect between myself and the CEO. I 'triangulated' with him whenever possible just in case.

Agreeing the process

I suggested a three-step approach:

1. Team members to complete psychometric questionnaires.
2. 1:1s held with team members to review their profiles and prepare for the workshop.
3. A one-day workshop with the team to share profiles and consider what impact this had on the way they behaved.

The HR director's response by email was:

> 'In terms of timelines and format, we would like to take forward steps 1 and 2 before Christmas and then schedule in two half-day group workshop sessions in January/February. Could you possibly let me know if this approach is workable for you?'

This again raised alarm bells and left me with the dilemma of what to concede and what to contest. Would a half-day session with the team really be sufficient? Given they had never before undertaken this sort of activity together, it felt like a limited amount of time in which to make progress. Without progress they would become disappointed, which of course would reflect on me (something I was fearful of). On the other hand, it felt contradictory to refuse the approach, given my espoused goal stated earlier to be as 'equally curious and open to new discovery as the clients'. I thought about how I could make their preferred approach work to our advantage. My response was as follows:

> 'I'm interested in your suggestion of 2 × half-day workshops, having assumed it would be one full day. I'm happy to go with either approach, both of which have pros and cons. A full day gives the opportunity to create a safer atmosphere (which is helpful). However, the separation into two half days allows for reflection time in between (not a bad thing), although each session might feel a bit rushed. We could have the follow-up 1:1s between the sessions rather than at the end, which might be a helpful catalyst for the second session – I would be interested in your views'.

The HR director replied:

> 'Thank you for your thoughts on the merits of two half days versus one full day. The CEO is quite keen on two half days, in part due to diaries, but I think that the points you have mentioned about allowing some reflection time in between sessions may be a helpful element here. I am keen that the Exec feel that this isn't just a "big bang" one-day event and they all take time to consider their approach both personally and as a group and gain momentum in relation to this.
>
> Having 1:1s in between sessions could be a good idea too – that way you can discuss any reflections on the first session and adapt the second session accordingly. I'll have a chat with [the CEO] about this suggestion when I see him next'.

Excellent! We had co-created a plan for the work! I realise there is nothing better than the client taking ownership, in spite of my inner resistance to relinquish the reins.

The agreed process had a catalysing impact on me. I decided:

- This process *will* be successful – I will not use the fact it differs from my desired approach as an excuse.
- The process can work well for the team, given the opportunity to exploit multiple touch-points.
- There is a need for a significant proportion of the work to be done between sessions without me as well as during sessions with me. Anything I can do to encourage and support this (from afar) will be worthwhile.

After a note from the CEO to the team introducing me and the process, I followed up with an email to begin forming a relationship with each of them before the face-to-face sessions.

The 1:1s to review individual profiles were conducted, allowing an understanding of the way they viewed themselves, the team, and the organisation. At the end of each session, I asked each of them to think of the most important question that had arisen from the conversation – either about themselves or the team. My intention was to ensure there was a firm link between these individual conversations and the two half-day sessions to come.

It was abundantly clear from these 1:1s that the length of time this executive team had been together (in some cases more than 15 years) meant they had lost sight of any possibility for change. Therefore, rather than voice discontent or propose new ideas, they self-censored, having already assumed from previous experience what the response would be. The relationships felt ossified. One of the team described them to me as being 'scratchy and uncooperative'; another said, 'we have a lot of baggage'.

The team all expressed scepticism that the process we were embarking on could make any real difference. They doubted the CEO's ability to relinquish any control; he said himself, 'I recognise I feel such a heavy burden of responsibility for the organisation that I tend to grip the tiller tightly'.

This was new ground for me; I had never worked with an executive team whose membership had endured for such a long time. The question I kept asking myself was, why would any of them want change, given they had put up with the way the team functioned (successfully in many ways) for so long?

The case for change

I think it is essential to have a clear articulation of the case for change. One of the reasons the CEO had decided the time was right for an intervention was his desire to modernise the organisation with a dynamic project structure to break away from functional silos, accountability pushed further down the organisation, open-plan seating (something which caused a great deal of consternation amongst the executive team), and the co-location of the executive team. I decided it was easiest to express the case for change as being that, unless the executive team modelled the collaborative behaviour they sought from the rest of the organisation, the planned change was likely to fail and the significant investment made in new technology, office-space, organisational structure, and process design would all be wasted.

The process itself

I had briefed the CEO and HR director after the 1:1s in advance of the first half-day workshop. During the meeting, I tested their agreement for the business case (which I received) and attempted to set realistic expectations about what could be achieved against the background of over-familiarity. Ideally, I would have liked the whole executive team to be present for this session so they could engage as a collective rather than it being driven by the CEO. I didn't feel confident enough in my relationship with the CEO to press for this. Effectively, I played into the respect for hierarchy that was a dominant feature of the culture. This was a missed opportunity to create a disturbance and provide a small taste of the collaboration they wanted across the organisation. I do not know what the impact would have been if I had pushed for all the team to be part of the briefing.

The briefing meeting went well in that an appropriate balance was found between sharing a flavour of what had emerged from the 1:1s without disclosing any detail and breaking confidence. This provided a sense for the process of the workshop without it being set in concrete, something I try to avoid.

After that meeting, I wrote to each of the participants individually, setting out the objectives of the first workshop, reminding them of the questions they had identified from their 1:1 sessions, requesting they re-familiarise themselves with their profiles so they would be able to describe them at the workshop. I offered them more time with me in case they wanted more information or conversation in advance of the workshop. Some of them took me up on this with further phone calls. All of this helped to establish relationships and build trust. My email concluded with:

> 'Please bring your curiosity, best intentions, and realistic expectations (we can accomplish a lot in 3 hours but we definitely can't do everything!). I anticipate us having a lively, enjoyable, and productive time together'.

The first workshop was successful although it began badly when I arrived to discover we were in a subterranean room with no natural light, tucked away and difficult to find. I felt panicked by this but I propped the door open with the flip-chart, drew a poor cartoon of myself on it with my name and an arrow to indicate the presence of the workshop. To my surprise, as the team arrived they each drew a cartoon of themselves on the chart as well, assuming it was intended as an opening process! It was quite magical and a great way to break the ice.

At the end of the workshop, I sensed the team breathe a collective sigh of relief. They had managed to get through it with relationships enhanced despite the difficulties of some of the conversations they had tackled. This often meant revealing long-held grudges without getting hijacked by their emotions. They had some simple clear actions which they all committed to. These effectively boiled down to spending 1:1 time with each other to share how they felt and see what they could learn about themselves and each other.

They arrived at the second workshop in a buoyant mood, feeling they had made significant progress as a team having been given feedback from many others in the organisation about the behavioural changes witnessed in the executive team. They had received a number of comments that the executive team had exhibited more humour together and a greater sense of ease in their relationships. From my interaction with them, I experienced much less tension in the air. I gave the team plenty of time to talk about the actions they had taken and the things they had learned, prompted by some simple questions.

As an aside, the mechanism I chose to illustrate the difficulties of changing entrenched positions was to put a long piece of paper around the walls of the room. On this I drew a scale which showed the length of time the team had been together to form the opinions they held. And I marked on it (right in the last few centimetres) the length of time they had been working to try to change these entrenched positions. It was a visual symbol referred to again and again whenever there was a sign of frustration that things could not change instantly.

The lessons I took away from this engagement

It is worth noting that these lessons are not necessarily new to me; along with most other people I find the process of change hard!

Understanding and working with anxiety (both my own and that of the client) is a crucial part of the team coaching process. My own anxiety is helpful, as it keeps me on my toes. On the other hand, it is unhelpful in making me 'tight' – that is, wanting to control things and know the answers before the questions have been identified. I would be suspicious of any coach who does not feel at all anxious and I would ask whether that is because anxiety isn't present or because they cannot see it.

When the client changes my suggestions, it is a sure indication they have engaged with them. When I become over-protective of my own ideas, it is a sure sign that I am either anxious or arrogant.

The work in between coaching sessions is as important as the sessions themselves. There is much that can be done by the coach, in terms of nudges, to help the clients make use of these spaces effectively. A 'nudge' can consist of short messages (text, WhatsApp, email) to connect and interact, build relationships, and keep the work in the client's mind. Earlier in my career I concentrated the majority of my efforts on planning the team sessions themselves; more recently, I have realised that provided I have set things up appropriately in advance, the sessions will largely take care of themselves.

The process works. Provide a team with enough space, safety, stimulus, and encouragement, and the conversations they really need to have with each other will emerge naturally and be handled elegantly.

The proof of the pudding

The entry in my journal following this engagement makes me laugh at my angst in advance:

> 'The relatively short 3 hour sessions with 1:1 time in between was very helpful. It allowed the sessions to be very focused and because of the tight boundaries reduced the team's anxiety. It also allowed time for action and reflection in between which was very helpful. Why did I ever doubt that!??'

I have got to know this client very well through a succession of further engagements and they have been kind enough to recommend me to others. Whether or not a client thinks the work has been worthwhile is the ultimate test for me. They describe themselves now as 'chalk and cheese' compared to the way they were before they did the work.

So, what did we learn? Final reflections by the editors

David Clutterbuck, Tammy Turner, and Colm Murphy

One of the key unique aspects of this case book has been the inclusion of the voice of team leaders, team members, and team stakeholders. Here we review in brief what struck us most from reviewing the 23 cases.

A key theme that comes across quite clearly is how difficult it is to ensure we listen to all the voices in the team. We noticed the voices that get heard most often are those of the team leader, the sponsor, then the team, and then the stakeholders. The team coaches often struggled to enable the team to engage with their external stakeholders in a sufficient way to really understand the complexity of the dynamics around them. In some instances, that lack of range of voices may be a benefit, as it gives the team a level of simplicity that enables them to make quick decisions. And yet, team coaching is all about dealing with complexity. This creates a contradiction between how much time is spent listening to various voices in the system, versus what does the team want to actually come out of the coaching conversations? When you've got too many voices, you risk babble.

We suggest, before getting into a team coaching assignment, we ask ourselves: 'How *will we* listen to the voices in the system?' Then, once we're in the assignment, we ask ourselves: 'How *are we* listening to the voices in the system?' And afterwards, 'How *did we* listen?' as part of our own evaluation of our process and approach to the team coaching. This in turn raises the question of what is the team coach actually listening for? Each coach is going to have a bias as to what they're listening for and what they feel comfortable with. One benefit of team coaching in pairs is to expand what is being listened for through the combining of the team coaches' preferences and perspectives.

Another related theme is how do you as a team coach ensure that you realise that you are a part of the system, so you can listen effectively and stay present to what's going on around you? As team coaches, if you're in it, it's often hard to see the system, identify and/or listen to the important elements, or see immediate or potential changes. When the team coach realises that they're part of the system, as well as being an observer of the system, they recognise the difficulty of listening to everything that might be going on.

The case studies also raise the question, 'Who is actually speaking to the stakeholders?' It's easier for the team coach to work with team members, the team leader, or the team sponsor, but what about the connection of the coaches with the internal and external stakeholders and influencers? Various case studies touch on this challenge throughout the book, but it's not always a feature of their analysis. If we accept Hawkins' work on 'future-back/outside-in', engaging those external stakeholders becomes crucial. In our own practice, the intent is always to include team stakeholders, despite the fact that there may be resistance in such engagement, particularly in public sector work, where stakeholders can keep power by not giving feedback to a team. The team coaches also struggled with how does a team coach both work with a team where they are now but keep challenging them to try to do something different, such as engaging stakeholders? They also were impacted, as team coaches, by what the team leader, team, or system felt comfortable with while asking themselves how to stay with the discomfort longer.

In terms of team coaching process, a number of cases involved two or more team coaches in the room during the sessions. What really stands out is the need for constant reflection, both in the room while the team coaching is happening, and outside of the session whether reflecting individually, with a co-coach, with peers, and/or other client stakeholders. When reflection was done often, the depth of quality delivery increased. Constant contracting and re-contracting, not only with each other, but also with the members of the team, the client, the sponsor, and others was important. The ability for the coaches to feel confident with the skill of contracting and the client engaging with it was varied. This highlights the point for us that contracting is a core skill for coaches, especially in the team coaching context.

Also reinforced here is the role of the team coaches as exemplars of good teaming themselves. If they're not demonstrating good teaming, then the intervention is going to be much poorer. A feature of team coaching is what the team learns from the way that the pair of team coaches interact with each other, as well as how they both interact with the team. This is important in enabling the team itself to evolve and learn. Team coaches need to demonstrate the behaviours that they would expect in good teaming – for example, reflection, stepping back, and pausing to just take stock of what's going on, to achieve clarity, and honesty. These delivery components led us to collectively agree the need for supervision as crucial for team coaching.

The role of diagnostics informed most of the cases. Universally, they are diagnostic heavy, and early in the engagement. After reading the cases, we ask, do diagnostics help provide evidence to an emergent intervention like team coaching? Diagnostics are often a linear approach to a systemic problem, perhaps borrowed from the way we've taught and delivered the individual coaching context and are now following suit in team coaching as well. To reflect upon the cases, we ask you to consider, was the decision to introduce the diagnostic by the team coach(es), the client, or HR and what purpose did it serve? We noticed that having the data immediately can introduce bias and/or expectations, whereas when the data was collected in line with client needs after the engagement had started, this seemed to be more impactful. So managing client expectations around diagnostics is important. We wondered if more could be done with the various relationships within a system to build more psychological safety, not only with the team, but also systemically with the client sponsors, stakeholders who interface with the team, and/or other influencers within the system.

Working as a team coaching pair, there's a transition from how we listen for similarity between each other, to listening for differences between each other and embracing these. It's a natural process in teaming to come towards those who we feel are similar to us. But that's not always where the value-add is. An unexpectedly positive sign in the cases is the number of examples where we have external team coaches partnering with a coach within the organisation, which lends both an internal and external lens on the team in its system and perhaps of the system itself.

The future of team coaching does not just sit with external people. One of the most useful examples in the book explores the challenges of being an internal team coach, where the coach is not just part of the organisational culture, but also a member of the team. This required the coach to recognise multiple different hats and be constantly contracting and re-contracting. This internal role is a key area for future development within the field of team coaching. We wonder how this scenario may have been different for this coach if an external co-coach had worked alongside them.

How to hold structure during a session was also interesting to note. In some cases, the sessions were quite structured and had almost a workshop or facilitation style, while others were led by purpose or agreed goals and became emergent quite quickly. This seemed to be multifactorial around team readiness, coach readiness, relationships, client sponsor expectations, and early interventions such as data collection. As team coach educators, we ask what kind of foundational work is required to allow team coaching to be more emergent earlier on? As team coaches we are curious about how to become a bit more flexible with structure so that it's more in tune with where the team is and where their experience of development is.

Finally, the importance of supervision also comes across from the cases. To deliver the best quality, team coaches need to be thinking about how they are working as a team and with the team. Supervision is a means for them to look at the complexity of their practice and the complexity of the context for the team they are coaching. If we did an unofficial poll of all of our authors, most, if not all of them, would say that supervision was critical in their work with the teams.

In conclusion, the 23 cases demonstrate the diversity of team types, team contexts, and team coaching approaches while also highlighting the commonality in importance of contracting, working systemically, and actively seeking a range of voices to be part of the team coaching conversation in service of co-created sustainable awareness and change. Our hope for future team coaches is that this book is a resource to learn from and share with others to make their coaching engagements fulfilling and gratifying for both the coach and clients alike.

Index

Page numbers in *italics* are figures; with 't' are tables.

3Ps framework 141–2
3 Factor RAA model 18, *18*, 21
4 Cs of team coaching 164
4-Quadrant model 34
5 Conditions/Disciplines (5Cs) Model xvii, 17, 18, 66, 115, 116–18, 142
6 Conditions for Team Effectiveness 75, *76*, 147
11 dots tool 203, 204–6, *205*, 206

accountability 18, *18*, 19, 21, 22
addiction institution case study 45–54
Agile software development case study 172–9
alert mode 70, 71, 75–6, 77, 78
'Alpha' industrial company case study 200–9, *202*, 204t, *205*
anxiety 210–11, 215–16
appreciative inquiry 41, 66, 80, 84
　and the educational institution case study 114–21
approaches, definition 65
assumptions, challenging 67–8
attractors 40, 43, 44
Australia
　bias case study 15–22, *18*
　public sector organisation case study 97–106, *100*, 101t

Bachkirova, Tatiana 141
Bateson, Gregory 4
beginner's mind 32–3
bias case study 15–22, *18*
Big Hairy Audacious Goals (BHAG) 24–7, 28
blind spots 3, 58, 59, 60
Burke, C. 155
buy-in 67, 95

Canada, bias case study 15–22, *18*
Carr, Catherine 112, 141
Change4Nine tool 207
climate, positive 40–1

cognitive diversity 19–20
Collab6© team coaching programme design 132–3, *132*
collective intelligence 200, 201, 202, 203, 204–6, *205*, 207, 209
collective leadership, Australian public sector organisation 97–106, *100*, 101t
Collective Leadership Assessment™ (CLA) 98, 99, *100*
command and control leadership *see* heroic leadership approach
communications team case study 79–86, *82*
complex adaptive systems (CAS) xvii–xviii, 37–44
conflict 31, 35, 81, 88, 134, 160
　avoidance of 99, *100*, 101t
　management 204, *205*
Connect initiative 122–4, 126–9
constellations 80–1, 165
construction company case study 23–9
containers 33
context 3–6, 35–6, 156
contracting 43, 104–5, 149, 152, 195, 196–7
critical moments 24, 28–9
critical performance-enhancing behaviours (CPEBs) 71, 74
culture change case study 122–9

Day, D. 155–6
De Haan, E. 24, 26
debriefing 76, 84
diagnostics 24–5, 66, 67–8, 218–19
　team diagnostic assessments™ (TDAs) 80, 108, 109
　team diagnostic surveys (TDSs) 27, 75–6, *76*, 77
dialogue 41
distributed leadership 32, 188
diversity 19–20, 34, 219
dualistic thinking 4

educational institutions case study
  114–21
effectiveness, team coaching case study
  181–90, 186t, 187t
effortless effort 32, 33, 36
  11 dots tool 203, 204–6, *205*, 206
emergence 32, 40
EthicalCoach, Ethiopia project
  146–53
Ethiopian NGO case study 146–53
experiential methods 104

facilitators 58, 164t, *168*, 206
feedback loops xvii, 40, 43
  5 Conditions/Disciplines (5Cs) Model
    xvii, 17, 18, 66, 115, 116–18, 142
flow states 33
  4 Cs of team coaching 164
  4-Quadrant model 34
frameworks, definition 66
full range leadership model (FRLM,
  Teams) 183–4, 185
future-back/outside-in 39, 218

gender, and bias 19–20
ghost roles 34–5
global issues 4–5
Global Leadership Community (GLC)
  case study 30–6
  7 principles 32
  11 essential qualities of high-value
    teams 32
government agency case study 131–8,
  132
GROW coaching model 125

Hall, Brendan, *Team Spirit* 206, 208
Halpin, S. 155
hanging out 11–12
Heffernan, Margaret 67
Helium-stick exercise 108
heroic leadership approach 15, 16, 19, 22,
  178
*High Performance Relationship and
  Team Assessment* (HPR) 125, 127
High Performance Team Coaching
  model 122–3
high-performing teams (HPTs), and
  internal coaches 53–61, 55t
HR Partner team case study, Swedish
  Migration Agency 107–13, 112t

Immunity to Change 103–4
IMPACT 124
'inclusion coach' 48, 49, 51
inclusive leadership 15, 16, 19, 22
individual development 102, 181, 182,
  189
input–process–output (IPO) framework
  75
integrative systemic team coaching
  (ISTC) 69–78, *72–3*, *76*
internal coaches xv, 7, 14, 219
  HPT case study 53–61, *55*
  law firm case study 37, 42, 43, 44
International Mining Company (IMC)
  16–22

Jackson, Peter 141

Kline, Nancy 194, 198

Lamy, Florence 203, 205
Lane, David 141
law firms, internal and external team
  coaching 37–44
Leadership Circle, Australian public
  sector organisation case study 97–8,
  102, 104, 106
leadership development 154–61,
  158t
  strength-based approach 181–90, 186t,
    187t
leadership teams 23–9
leadership theory 154–5
leadership void case study 131–8, *132*
Lekgotla process 192, 194–5, 196, 197–8
Level Two/Three learning 4
linear approaches xvii
listening 5, 41, 217
logistics business case study 193–8

mapping 66, 67, 68, 165
  network 40
  sociomapping 70–4, *72–3*
Middle Circle® 131
models 66, 68, 141–2
  3 Factor RAA model 18, *18*, 21
  5 Conditions/Disciplines (5Cs) Model
    xvii, 17, 18, 66, 115, 116–18, 142
  full range leadership model (FRLM,
    Teams) 183–4, 185
  GROW coaching model 125

High Performance Team Coaching model 122–3
Playbook model 107, 108, 109–10, 111
Rocket Model 23, 24–5
SCORE model 49, 50
team coaching competency model 146, 148–51
see also PERILL model
Multi-Factor Leadership Questionnaire Team (MLQT) 184, 185, 186, 186t, 187t
multidimensional systems 30, 32
Multifactor Leadership Questionnaire (MLQ) 360 184–5
multinational resources organization case study 15–22, *18*

nested approach 66
nested systems 4, 34
nested teams 3

observers 84, 164t, *168*, 202–3, 206–7, 217
organisational coaching 174

Pair Readiness Chart 166–7, *167–8*, 170
paired coaching 163–70, 164t, *167–8*, 218, 219
parallel process 207, 208
PERILL model xviii, 54, 56, 60, 66, 142
and the Australian public sector organisation case study 97–8, 99, 100, 101t
pharmaceutical division case study 87–95, *91–2*
philosophies 141–4
pillars, strategic 25, 26–7, 28, 29
Playbook model 107, 108, 109–10, 111
polar diagrams *82*
positive psychology movement 182–3
privilege 35
process (3Ps framework) 143
professional services firm case study 38–44
psychological safety 45–54, 165, 166, 196, 219
psychometric tools 142
  case study using 210–16
public sector case study 97–106, *100*, 101t
purpose (3Ps framework) 141, 142–3

reactive-creative scale/shift 99, *100*, 103
RealGames case study 173–9
reflective practice 4, 33, 42, 44, *168*, 169, 218
ripple effect 57, 60, 159–60
Rocket Model 23, 24–5
'role delegation in meetings' technique 207

safety, psychological 45–54, 165, 166, 196, 219
sailing race case study 156–60, 158t
Salas, E. 155
Scharmer, Otto 5
SCORE model 49, 50
Scrum Masters 172–3, 178–9
self-awareness 34, 56, 59, *100*, 157, 197–8
self-management 172, 173, 174, 175, 176, 178–9
senior leadership team case study 7–14, *8*
sensing 33–4
service level agreements (SLAs) 113
simple (closed) systems xvii
  6 Conditions for Team Effectiveness 75, *76*, 147
Skype 157
small-to-medium enterprises (SMEs) 188
SMEs *see* small-to-medium enterprises
sociomapping 70–4, *72–3*
Stagl, K. 155
stakeholders 27–8, 67, 217, 218
strength-based approach to leadership development 181–90, 186t, 187t
Strengths Deployment Inventory (SDI) assessment 157
stuckness 36
supervision 3, 21, 68, 85–6, 207–8, 219
  Ethiopia case study 148, 149
  and government agency case study 131, 136
  HPT development case study 57, 59, 60
  and law firm case study 42, 43, 44
  Swedish migration agency case study 107–13, 112t
systematic team coaching initiative 122–9
systemic approaches xvii–xviii
  integrative systemic team coaching 69–78, *72–3*, *76*

taboo subjects 50
talent dynamics (TD) 16, 17
   and gender and cognitive diversity bias 20
team agreeableness (TA) 90, 91, 93
team coaching competency model 146, 148–51
team coaching (defined) xvi, 181
Team Coaching International (TCI) 66
   Measurement Team Diagnostic Assessment™ 107
   Team Diagnostic Assessment™ (TDA) 80, 81, 108, 109, 112
   team diagnostic surveys (TDS) 75–6, *76*, 77
Team Coaching Studio (TCS) 163
   modes of team coaching 164, 164t, 168
TEAM Connect 360 assessments 17, 20, 21
team diagnostic surveys (TDS) 75–6, *76*, 77
team dynamic quality (TDQ) 90
team effectiveness (TE) 90, 92, *92*, 93
team performance indicators (TPIs) 109, 110
team of teams approach 123, 129

teams, defined 155
teamSalient® for Teams profile 133, 134, 137
Theory U 5
   3Ps framework 141–2
   3 Factor RAA model 18, *18*, 21
tool and techniques method 66
TQ™ assessment, pharmaceutical division case study 87–95, *91–2*
tracking/describing/responding (TDR) 169

Ubuntu team coaching perspective 192–8
United Kingdom, government agency case study 131–8, *132*

'Walls of Pride' 66, 84
We 200, 209
   and systemic bias 20–1
   WE-Muscle/WE-Mindset 163, 166, 168–9, *168*, 170
World Café 30, 31

'You are OK and I am OK' 166, *167*, 169

Zaccaro, S. 155